Picture - Perfect

Lessons, K–2

Using Children's Books
to Inspire STEM Learning

Picture - Perfect

STEM

Lessons, K–2

Using Children's Books
to Inspire STEM Learning

by Emily Morgan and Karen Ansberry

NSTApress

National Science Teachers Association

Arlington, Virginia

National Science Teachers Association

Claire Reinburg, Director
Wendy Rubin, Managing Editor
Rachel Ledbetter, Associate Editor
Amanda Van Beuren, Associate Editor
Donna Yudkin, Book Acquisitions Coordinator

ART AND DESIGN
Will Thomas Jr., Director
Linda Olliver, Cover, Interior Design, Illustrations

PRINTING AND PRODUCTION
Catherine Lorrain, Director

NATIONAL SCIENCE TEACHERS ASSOCIATION
David L. Evans, Executive Director
David Beacom, Publisher

1840 Wilson Blvd., Arlington, VA 22201
www.nsta.org/store
For customer service inquiries, please call 800-277-5300.

NSTA is committed to publishing material that promotes the best in inquiry-based science education. However, conditions of actual use may vary, and the safety procedures and practices described in this book are intended to serve only as a guide. Additional precautionary measures may be required. NSTA and the authors do not warrant or represent that the procedures and practices in this book meet any safety code or standard of federal, state, or local regulations. NSTA and the authors disclaim any liability for personal injury or damage to property arising out of or relating to the use of this book, including any of the recommendations, instructions, or materials contained therein.

Library of Congress Cataloging-in-Publication Data
Names: Morgan, Emily R. (Emily Rachel), 1973- author. | Ansberry, Karen Rohrich, 1966- author.
Title: Picture-perfect STEM lessons, K-2 : using children's books to inspire stem learning / Emily Morgan, Karen Ansberry.
Description: Arlington, VA : National Science Teachers Association, [2017]
Identifiers: LCCN 2016054312 (print) | LCCN 2017008547 (ebook) | ISBN 9781681403281 (print) | ISBN 9781681403304 (e-book) | ISBN 9781681403298 (pdf)
Subjects: LCSH: Science--Study and teaching (Primary) | Picture books for children--Educational aspects.
Classification: LCC LB1532 .M59 2017 (print) | LCC LB1532 (ebook) | DDC 372.35/044--dc23
LC record available at *https://lccn.loc.gov/2016054312*

Contents

Preface

First-grade students listen as their teacher reads *The Day the Crayons Came Home,* the clever story of a group of wayward crayons left in various places by a boy named Duncan. The crayons are sending postcards to Duncan, each with a woeful tale and a plea to return to the crayon box. One postcard (p. 10) reads as follows:

Duncan!

It's us … Yellow and Orange. We know we used to argue over which of us was the color of the Sun … but guess what? NEITHER of us wants to be the color of the Sun anymore. Not since we were left outside and the Sun melted us … TOGETHER! You know the real color of the Sun?? HOT. That's what. We're sorry for arguing. You can make GREEN the Sun for all we care, just BRING US HOME!

Your not-so-sunny friends,

Yellow & Orange

The first-grade students giggle at the silly postcards sent by the desperate crayons. After the read-aloud, they recount some of the ways the crayons were changed in the book—broken, melted by the Sun, chewed by a dog, sharpened, melted in the dryer, and so on. This discussion leads them to an exploration of crayon properties (including measurements), an investigation of ways crayons' physical properties can be changed, and a read-aloud and video about how crayons are manufactured. Students discover that there is a surprising amount of engineering and technology behind the design and production of this classroom staple, and they apply the steps of the engineering design process to come up with a way to recycle crayons into new and interesting shapes and colors. This activity addresses the engineering core idea that a situation people want to change or create can be solved through engineering. Finally, students incorporate English Language Arts standards by writing their own postcard from an adventurous crayon who has been through a number of changes. Thus, students demonstrate their understanding of the physical science core idea that heating or cooling a substance may cause changes that can be observed, and sometimes these changes are reversible. Through this engaging lesson found in Chapter 14, students learn about the interdependence of science, technology, engineering, and mathematics in the crayon-manufacturing industry—all within the context of an amusing fictional story.

What Is Picture-Perfect STEM?

The Picture-Perfect Science program was developed to help elementary teachers integrate science and reading in an engaging, kid-friendly way. Since the debut of the first book in the *Picture-Perfect Science Lesson* series in 2005, teachers across the country have been using the lessons to integrate science and literacy. This new series of Picture-Perfect books, *Picture-Perfect STEM Lessons: Using Children's Books to Inspire STEM Learning,* follows the same philosophy and lesson format as the original books but adds an emphasis on the intersection of science, technology, engineering, and mathematics in the real world. *Picture-Perfect STEM Lessons, K–2* contains 15 lessons for students in kindergarten through grade 2, with embedded reading-comprehension strategies to help them learn to read and read to learn while engaged in STEM activities. To help you set up a learning environment consistent with the principles of *A Framework for K–12 Science Education* (*Framework;* NRC 2012), the lessons are written in an easy-to-follow format of constructivist learning—the Biological Sciences Curriculum Study (BSCS) 5E Instructional Model (Bybee 1997, used with permission from BSCS; see Chapter 3 for more information). This learning cycle model allows students to construct their own understanding of scientific concepts as they cycle through the following phases: engage, explore, explain, elaborate, and evaluate. Although *Picture-Perfect STEM Lessons* is primarily a book for teaching STEM concepts, reading-comprehension strategies and the *Common Core State Standards for English Language Arts* (NGAC and CCSSO 2010) are embedded in each lesson. These essential strategies can be modeled while keeping the focus of the lessons on STEM.

Use This Book Within Your Curriculum

We wrote *Picture-Perfect STEM Lessons* to supplement, not replace, your school's existing science or STEM program. Although each lesson stands alone as a carefully planned learning cycle based on clearly defined objectives, the lessons are intended to be integrated into a complete curriculum in which concepts can be more fully developed. The lessons are not designed to be taught sequentially. We want you to use *Picture-Perfect STEM Lessons* where appropriate within your school's current STEM program to support, enrich, and extend it. We also want you to adapt the lessons to fit your school's curriculum, your students' needs, and your own teaching style.

Special Features of This Book

Ready-to-Use Lessons With Assessments

Each lesson contains engagement activities, hands-on explorations, student pages, suggestions for student and teacher explanations, elaboration activities,

assessment suggestions, opportunities for STEM education at home, and annotated bibliographies of more books to read on the topic. Assessments include poster sessions, writing assignments, design challenges, demonstrations, presentations, and multiple-choice and extended-response questions.

Background for Teachers

This section provides easy-to-understand background information for teachers to review before facilitating the lesson. Some information in the background section goes beyond the assessment boundary for students, but it is provided to give teachers a deeper understanding of the content presented in the lesson.

Time Needed

The information in this section helps you pace each lesson. We estimate a primary class period to be about 30–45 min.

Reading-Comprehension Strategies

Reading-comprehension strategies based on the book *Strategies That Work* (Harvey and Goudvis 2007) and specific activities to enhance comprehension are embedded throughout the lessons and clearly marked with an icon. Chapter 2 describes how to model these strategies while reading aloud to students.

Standards-Based Objectives

All lesson objectives are aligned to the *Framework* (NRC 2012) and are clearly identified at the beginning of each lesson. An alignment with the *Next Generation Science Standards* (NGSS Lead States 2013) is included in the appendix (p. 309). The lessons also incorporate the *Common Core State Standards for English Language Arts and Mathematics* (NGAC and CCSSO 2010). In a box titled "Connecting to the Common Core," you will find the Common Core subject the activity addresses as well as the grade level and standard number. You will see that writing assignments are specifically labeled with an icon:

STEM at Home

Each lesson also provides an extension activity that is intended to be done with a parent or other adult helper at home. Students write about what they learned about each topic and share their favorite part of the lesson. Then, together with their adult helper, they complete an activity to apply and extend the learning. If students are unable to complete the extension at home, the activities in this section also work well as in-class extensions.

Ideas for Further Exploration

A "For Further Exploration" box is provided at the end of each lesson to help you encourage your students to use the science and engineering practices in a more student-directed format. This box lists questions and challenges related to the lesson that students may select to research, investigate, or innovate. Students may also use the questions as examples to help them generate their own questions. After selecting one of the questions in the box or formulating their own questions, students can make predictions, design investigations to test their predictions, collect evidence, devise explanations, design solutions, examine related resources, and communicate their findings.

References

Bybee, R. W. 1997. *Achieving scientific literacy: From purposes to practices*. Portsmouth, NH: Heinemann.

Harvey, S., and A. Goudvis. 2007. *Strategies that work: Teaching comprehension for understanding and engagement*. 2nd ed. Portland, ME: Stenhouse Publishers.

National Governors Association Center for Best Practices and Council of Chief State School Officers (NGAC and CCSSO). 2010. *Common core state standards*. Washington, DC: NGAC and CCSSO.

National Research Council (NRC). 2012. *A framework for K–12 science education: Practices, crosscutting concepts, and core ideas*. Washington, DC: National Academies Press.

NGSS Lead States. 2013. *Next Generation Science Standards: For states, by states*. Washington, DC: National Academies Press. *www.nextgenscience.org/next-generation-science-standards*.

Children's Book Cited

Daywalt, D. 2015. *The day the crayons came home*. New York: Philomel Books.

Editor's Note

Picture-Perfect STEM Lessons, K–2 builds on the texts of 29 children's picture books to teach STEM. Some of these books feature objects that have been anthropomorphized, such as crayons that pack their bags and travel the world. Although we recognize that many scientists and educators believe that personification, teleology, animism, and anthropomorphism promote misconceptions among young children, others believe that removing these elements would leave children's literature severely underpopulated. Furthermore, backers of these techniques not only see little harm in their use but also argue that they facilitate learning. Because *Picture-Perfect STEM Lessons, K–2* specifically and carefully supports science and engineering practices, we, as do our authors, feel the question remains open.

Acknowledgments

We would like to dedicate this book to the memory of Dr. Robert Yearout, who gave us the opportunity to present our first teacher workshop at the "Sharing What Works" Conference in Columbus, Ohio, in 2000. Dr. Yearout's leadership of the High Achievement in Math and Science Consortium, which we were both fortunate to be a part of for many years, provided us with opportunities and encouragement to grow as educators and advocates of science and math education. Dr. Yearout's selfless leadership style and utmost respect for the teaching profession continue to inspire us today.

We appreciate the care and attention to detail given to this project by Rachel Ledbetter, Wendy Rubin, and Claire Reinburg at NSTA Press.

And these thank-yous as well:

- To Linda Olliver for her "Picture-Perfect" illustrations
- To Tom Uhlman for his photography
- To Kim Stilwell for facilitating workshops to give us time to write and for sharing *Picture-Perfect Science* with teachers across the country
- To the staff and students of Ann Arbor Open School, Blue Springs School District, Heritage Elementary, Indian Hill Elementary, Lebanon United Methodist Preschool and Kindergarten, Mason City Schools, and Sand Hill–Venable Elementary for field-testing lessons and providing "photo ops"
- To Amie Austin, Alyson Coffman, Mary Beth Hatterschide, Amy Kleinfeldt, and their second graders for field-testing Chapter 7, "Build It!"
- To Libby Beck and Nancy Smith for contributing photographs
- To Ken Roy for his thorough safety review
- To Ted Willard for answering all of our *Next Generation Science Standards* (*NGSS*) questions and creating his helpful *NGSS* guides
- To Bill Robertson, Debbie Rupp, Christina Sherman, and Rand Harrington for sharing their content knowledge
- To Christine Anne Royce for her help with research on using children's books to teach STEM
- To Andrea Beaty for giving us a sneak peek of *Ada Twist, Scientist;* promoting STEM education; and encouraging innovation, curiosity, and creativity in kids everywhere

The contributions of the following reviewers are also gratefully acknowledged:

- Kevin Anderson
- Mark McDermott
- Ruth McDonald
- Bill Robertson
- Kristina Tank

About the Authors

Emily Morgan is a former elementary science lab teacher for Mason City Schools in Mason, Ohio, and seventh-grade science teacher at Northridge Local Schools in Dayton, Ohio. She served as a science consultant for the Hamilton County Educational Service Center and science leader for the High AIMS Consortium. She has a bachelor of science in elementary education from Wright State University and a master of science in education from the University of Dayton. She is also the author of the *Next Time You See* picture book series from NSTA Press. Emily lives in West Chester, Ohio, with her husband, son, and an assortment of animals.

Karen Ansberry is a former elementary science curriculum leader and fifth- and sixth-grade teacher at Mason City Schools in Mason, Ohio. She has a bachelor of science in biology from Xavier University and a master of arts in teaching from Miami University. Karen lives in historic Lebanon, Ohio, with her husband, two sons, two daughters, and two dogs.

Emily and Karen enjoy facilitating teacher workshops at elementary schools, universities, and professional conferences across the country. This is Emily and Karen's fourth book in the *Picture-Perfect Science Lessons* series. For more information on this series and teacher workshops, visit *www.pictureperfectscience.com.*

Safety Practices for Science Activities

With hands-on, process- and inquiry-based science activities, the teaching and learning of science today can be both effective and exciting. The challenge to securing this success needs to be met by addressing potential safety issues relative to engineering controls (ventilation, eye wash station, etc.), administrative procedures and safety operating procedures, and use of appropriate personal protective equipment (indirectly vented chemicals splash goggles meeting ANSI Z87.1 standard, chemical resistant aprons and gloves, etc.). Teachers can make it safer for students and themselves by adopting, implementing, and enforcing legal safety standards and better professional safety practices in the science classroom and laboratory. Throughout this book, safety notes are provided for science activities and need to be adopted and enforced in efforts to provide for a safer learning and teaching experience. Teachers should also review and follow local policies and protocols used in their school district and/or school (e.g., employer OSHA Hazard Communication Safety Plan and Board of Education safety policies).

Additional applicable standard operating procedures can be found in the National Science Teacher Association's "Safety in the Science Classroom, Laboratory, or Field Sites" (*www.nsta.org/docs/SafetyInTheScienceClassroomLabAndField.pdf*). Students should be required to review the document or one similar to it for elementary-level students under the direction of the teacher. It is important to also include safety information about working at home for the "STEM at Home" activities. Both the student and the parent or guardian should then sign the document acknowledging procedures that must be followed for a safer working and learning experience in the classroom, laboratory, or field. The Council of State Science Supervisors also has a safety resource for elementary science activities titled "Science and Safety: It's Elementary!" Teachers can consult this document at *www.csss-science.org/downloads/scisaf_cal.pdf*.

Please note that the safety precautions of each activity are based, in part, on use of the recommended materials and instructions, legal safety standards, and better professional practices. Selection of alternative materials or procedures for these activities may jeopardize the level of safety and therefore is at the user's own risk.

Why Use Picture Books to Teach STEM?

Think about a book you loved as a child. Maybe you remember the zany characters and rhyming text of Dr. Seuss classics such as *Green Eggs and Ham* or the delightful poems in Robert Louis Stevenson's *A Child's Garden of Verses*. Perhaps you enjoyed the page-turning suspense of Jon Stone's *The Monster at the End of This Book* or the powerful lessons in Shel Silverstein's *The Giving Tree*. Maybe your curiosity was piqued by the technical illustrations and fascinating explanations in *The Way Things Work* by David Macauley or the illustrated anthology *Childcraft: The How and Why Library*. Perhaps you dreamed of space travel after reading the classic adventure *You Will Go to the Moon* by Mae and Ira Freeman. You may have seen a little of yourself in *Madeline* by Ludwig Bemelmans, *Where the Wild Things Are* by Maurice Sendak, *Ramona the Pest* by Beverly Cleary, or *Curious George* by H. A. Rey. Perhaps your imagination was stirred by *Cloudy with a Chance of Meatballs* by Judi and Ronald Barrett or *A Wrinkle in Time* by Madeleine L'Engle. You most likely remember the warm, cozy feeling of having a treasured book such as Don Freeman's *Corduroy*, Margery Williams's *The Velveteen Rabbit*, or Robert Munsch's *Love You Forever* being read to you by a parent or grandparent. But chances are your favorite book as a child was not your second-grade science textbook. The format of picture books offers certain unique advantages over textbooks and chapter books for engaging students in a STEM lesson. More often than other books, fiction and nonfiction picture books stimulate students on both the emotional and intellectual levels. They

TEACHERS LOVE USING PICTURE BOOKS!

are appealing and memorable because children readily connect with the imaginative illustrations, vivid photographs, exciting experiences and adventures of characters, engaging storylines, fascinating information that supports them in their quest for knowledge, and warm emotions that surround the reading experience.

What characterizes a picture book? We like what *Beginning Reading and Writing* says: "Picture books are unique to children's literature as they are defined by format rather than content. That is, they are books in which the illustrations are of equal importance as or more important than the text in the creation of meaning" (Strickland and Morrow 2000, p. 137). Because picture books are more likely to hold children's attention, they lend themselves to reading-comprehension strategy instruction and to engaging students within an inquiry-based cycle of science instruction. "Picture books, both fiction and nonfiction, are more likely to hold our attention and engage us than reading dry, formulaic text. … Engagement leads to remembering what is read, acquiring knowledge and enhancing understanding" (Harvey and Goudvis 2000, p. 46). We wrote the *Picture-Perfect STEM Lessons* series so teachers can take advantage of the positive features of children's picture books by supplementing the traditional textbook or kit program with a wide variety of high-quality fiction and nonfiction STEM-related picture books.

Why STEM?

Turn on the television news, open a newspaper, or browse an internet news source, and you'll likely find a story about a new STEM initiative or program at a school, library, or museum—STEM is everywhere these days! Historically, these four disciplines (science, technology, engineering, and mathematics) have been taught independently (see the box on the next page for more details about each discipline), with engineering often overlooked in the elementary classroom. But over the past several years, STEM education has gained momentum as an interdisciplinary way of teaching that goes beyond what is being learned in these disciplines to include the *application* of what is being learned.

The U.S. Department of Education states in the STEM section of its website,

The current emphasis on STEM education is due to an ever-increasing demand for highly skilled workers, including women and minorities who are underrepresented in STEM-related fields. As our world becomes more technologically advanced and as problems become more complex and multidisciplinary, this demand will continue to grow. The STEM-capable workforce and STEM-literate society of America's future will meet challenges as varied as improving human health and well-being, harnessing clean energy, protecting national security, and succeeding in the global economy. In remarks on the "Educate to Innovate" initiative to improve STEM achievement, President Barack Obama said, "The key to meeting these challenges … will be reaffirming and strengthening America's role as the world's engine of scientific discovery and technological innovation. And that leadership tomorrow depends on how we educate our students today." (The White House, Office of the Secretary 2009)

As educators, we must be equipped to prepare our students for meeting the challenges of our rapidly changing world. Mariel Milano, a member of the *Next Generation Science Standards* writing team, explains it this way:

Students entering kindergarten this year will likely enter job fields upon graduation that have not yet been developed, using knowledge that has not been discovered and tools that have not yet been engineered. It will be the responsibility of elementary teachers to prepare their students for a changing world by arming them with the science and engineering background necessary to one day make informed choices and decisions. (Milano 2013, p. 10)

The Four STEM Disciplines

Science is the study of the natural world, including the laws of nature associated with physics, chemistry, and biology and the treatment or application of facts, principles, concepts, or conventions associated with these disciplines. Science is both a body of knowledge that has been accumulated over time and a process—scientific inquiry—that generates new knowledge. Knowledge from science informs the engineering design process.

Technology comprises the entire system of people and organizations, knowledge, processes, and devices that go into creating and operating technological artifacts, as well as the artifacts themselves. Throughout history, humans have created technology to satisfy their wants and needs. Much of modern technology is a product of science and engineering, and technological tools are used in both fields.

Engineering is both a body of knowledge—about the design and creation of human-made products—and a process for solving problems. This process is design under constraint. One constraint in engineering design is the laws of nature, or science. Other constraints include time, cost, available materials, ergonomics, environmental regulations, manufacturability, and repairability. Engineering uses concepts in science and mathematics as well as technological tools.

Mathematics is the study of patterns and relationships among quantities, numbers, and shapes. Specific branches of mathematics include arithmetic, geometry, algebra, trigonometry, and calculus. Mathematics is used in science and in engineering.

Source: National Academy of Engineering and National Research Council 2009.

So what exactly is meant by "STEM education"? A quick web search yields a long list of definitions, interpretations, and philosophies. But our approach to STEM education is simple: It involves making natural connections among the four STEM disciplines as students investigate and problem-solve within a meaningful context. In *Picture-Perfect STEM Lessons,* picture books provide this meaningful context. The books help engage and motivate students, introduce topics and establish themes, set up investigations and real-world problem-solving opportunities, spark creativity and innovation, and explain science and engineering concepts. Science and engineering standards provide the learning framework, while reading strategies, technology, and mathematics are used as tools within this framework to support and extend student learning. The lessons are written so that the connections among the four disciplines are natural, not forced. For example, mathematics is applied where it fits within the overall goal of the lesson (not simply to meet a mathematics objective). So you will not see all four STEM disciplines given equal emphasis in every lesson.

Our previous *Picture-Perfect Science Lessons* books are based on research that shows that integrating science with literacy makes science more meaningful to students and can lead to increases in achievement in both subjects. We believe that these benefits apply to STEM and literacy integration, because students are provided meaningful context in which to investigate, innovate, and communicate.

The Research

Context for Concepts

The wide array of high-quality STEM-related children's literature currently available can help you model reading-comprehension strategies while teaching STEM content in a meaningful context.

Children's picture books, a branch of literature, have interesting storylines that can help students understand and remember concepts better than they would by using only textbooks, which tend to present science as lists of facts to be memorized (Butzow and Butzow 2000). In addition, the colorful pictures and graphics in picture books are superior to many texts for explaining abstract ideas (Kralina 1993). Many studies, including one by Van den Heuvel-Panhuizen, Elia, and Robitzsch (2014), show that reading picture books can have a positive influence on children's mathematical performance as well. As more and more content is packed into the school day and higher expectations are placed on student performance, teachers must make more efficient use of their time. Zemelman, Daniels, and Hyde (2012) suggest that connecting various content areas can lead to deep engagement as students read, write, talk, view, watch, explore, create, and interact around a topic. Although research is limited on the impact of picture books on integrated STEM learning, we feel that teaching STEM in conjunction with literacy may enhance learning in all areas.

More Depth of Coverage

Science textbooks can be overwhelming for many children, especially those who have reading problems. Textbooks often contain unfamiliar vocabulary and tend to cover a broad range of topics (Casteel and Isom 1994; Short and Armstrong 1993; Tyson and Woodward 1989). However, fiction and nonfiction picture books tend to focus on fewer topics and give more in-depth coverage of the concepts. It can be useful to pair an engaging fiction book with a nonfiction book to round out the science content being presented.

For example, "The Handiest Things" lesson in Chapter 6 features *The Handiest Things in the World*, an engaging book about some commonplace inventions that make our everyday lives easier. It is paired with *Engineering in Our Everyday Lives*, which explains how engineers design technologies to solve everyday problems. The engaging verse and illustrations in *The Handiest Things in the World* hook the reader, while the information in *Engineering in Our Everyday Lives* helps students

understand how the engineering design process is used in the real world. Together, those books offer a balanced, in-depth look at what engineers do and how engineering affects our everyday lives.

Improved Reading and Science Skills

Research by Morrow et al. (1997) on using children's literature and literacy instruction in the science program indicated gains in science as well as literacy. Romance and Vitale (1992) found significant improvement in the science and reading scores of fourth graders when the regular basal reading program was replaced with reading in science that correlated with the science curriculum. They also found an improvement in students' attitudes toward the study of science.

Opportunities to Correct Science Misconceptions

Students often have strongly held misconceptions about science that can interfere with their learning. "Misconceptions, in the field of science education, are preconceived ideas that differ from those currently accepted by the scientific community" (Colburn 2003, p. 59). Children's picture books, reinforced with hands-on inquiries, can help students correct their misconceptions. Repetition of the correct concept by reading several books, doing a number of experiments, and inviting scientists to the classroom can facilitate a conceptual change in children (Miller, Steiner, and Larson 1996).

But teachers must be aware that scientific misconceptions can be inherent in the picture books. Although many errors are explicit, some of the misinformation is more implicit or may be inferred from text and illustrations (Rice 2002). This problem is more likely to occur in fictionalized material. Mayer's (1995) study demonstrated that when both inaccuracies and science facts are presented in the same book, children do not necessarily remember the correct information.

Selection of Books

Each lesson in *Picture-Perfect STEM Lessons* focuses on *A Framework for K–12 Science Education*

(*Framework;* NRC 2012). We selected fiction and nonfiction children's picture books that closely relate to the *Framework.* An annotated "More Books to Read" section is provided at the end of each lesson. If you would like to select more children's literature to use in your science classroom, try the Outstanding Science Trade Books for Students K–12 listing, which is a cooperative project between the National Science Teachers Association (NSTA) and the Children's Book Council (CBC). The books are selected by a book-review panel appointed by NSTA and assembled in cooperation with CBC. Each year, a new list is featured in the March issue of NSTA's elementary school teacher journal *Science and Children.* See *www.nsta.org/ostbc* for archived lists.

When you select children's picture books for science instruction, you might consult with a knowledgeable colleague who can help you check them for errors or misinformation. Young and Moss (2006) describe five essential things to consider when selecting nonfiction trade books for science:

1. The authority of the author (i.e., the author's credibility and qualifications for writing the book)
2. The accuracy of the text, illustrations, and graphics
3. The appropriateness of the book for its intended audience (e.g., the book makes complex concepts understandable for young readers)
4. The literary artistry and quality of writing
5. The appearance or visual impact of the book

Using a rubric may also be valuable to help you make informed decisions about the science trade books you use in your classroom. One such tool that provides a systematic framework to simplify the trade book evaluation process is the Science Trade Book Evaluation Rubric, found in the article "Making Science Trade Book Choices for Elementary Classrooms" (Atkison, Matusevich, and Huber 2009).

Finding the Picture-Perfect Books

Each lesson includes a "Featured Picture Books" section with titles, author and illustrator names, publication details, and summaries of each book. The years and publisher names listed are for the most recent editions available—paperback whenever possible—as of the printing of *Picture-Perfect STEM Lessons, K–2.*

All of the trade books featured in the lessons in this book are currently in print and can be found at your local bookstore or from an online retailer or library. NSTA Press has made available a tote bag full of all of the *Picture-Perfect STEM Lessons* books in one handy collection at a reduced cost, in addition to ClassPacks that contain the materials you need to do each lesson. You can purchase these items at the NSTA Science Store (*www.nsta.org/store*).

Considering Genre

Considering genre when you determine how to use a particular picture book within a STEM lesson is important. Donovan and Smolkin (2002) identify four different genres frequently recommended for teachers to use in their science instruction: story, non-narrative information, narrative information, and dual purpose. *Even More Picture-Perfect Science Lessons, K–5* (Morgan and Ansberry 2013) identifies the genre of each featured book at the beginning of each lesson. Summaries of the four genres, a representative picture book for each genre, and suggestions for using each genre within the Biological Sciences Curriculum Study (BSCS) 5E learning cycle follow. (Chapter 3 describes in detail the science learning cycle, known as the BSCS 5E Instructional Model, which we follow.)

Storybooks

Storybooks center on specific characters who work to resolve a conflict or problem. The major purpose of stories is to entertain, not to present factual information. The vocabulary is typically commonsense, everyday language. An engaging storybook can spark interest in a science topic and move students toward informational texts to answer questions

inspired by the story. For example, the "Build It!" lesson in Chapter 7 begins with a read-aloud of *Iggy Peck, Architect,* an amusing book about a boy who is obsessed with building. The charming story hooks the learners and engages them in explorations of architecture.

Non-Narrative Information Books

Non-narrative information books are nonfiction texts that introduce a topic, describe the attributes of the topic, or describe typical events that occur. The focus of these texts is on the subject matter, not specific characters. The vocabulary is typically technical. Readers can enter the text at any point in the book. Many non-narrative information books contain features found in nonfiction, such as a table of contents, bold-print vocabulary words, a glossary, and an index. Some research suggests that these types of books are "the best resources for fostering children's scientific concepts as well as their appropriation of science discourse" (Pappas 2006). Young children tend to be less familiar with this genre and need many opportunities to experience this type of text. Using non-narrative information books will help students become familiar with the structure of textbooks, as well as "real-world" reading, which is primarily nonfiction. Teachers may want to read only those sections that provide the concepts and facts needed to meet particular science objectives.

One example of non-narrative information writing is the book *National Geographic Kids: Robots,* which contains nonfiction text features such as a table of contents, diagrams, insets, a glossary, and an index. This book is featured in Chapter 8, "Robots Everywhere," and Chapter 17, "Pillbots." The appropriate placement of non-narrative information text in a science learning cycle is typically after students have had the opportunity to explore concepts through hands-on activities. At that point, students are engaged in the topic and are motivated to read the non-narrative informational text to learn more.

Narrative Information Books

Narrative information books, another subset of nonfiction text, are sometimes called hybrid books.

They provide an engaging format for factual information. They communicate a sequence of factual events over time and sometimes recount the events of a specific case to generalize to all cases. When using these books within science instruction, establish a purpose for reading so that students focus on the science content rather than the storyline can be useful. In some cases, teachers may want to read the book one time through for the aesthetic components of the book and a second time to look for specific science content or engineering practices. *Wangari's Trees of Peace: A True Story From Africa* is an example of a narrative information text and is used in Chapter 16, "Plant a Tree." This narrative tells the true story of Wangari Maathai, who started the Green Belt Movement in Africa. The narrative information genre can be used at any point in a science learning cycle. This genre can be both engaging and informative.

Dual-Purpose Books

Dual-purpose books are intended to serve two purposes: present a story and provide facts. They employ a format that allows readers to use the book like a storybook or to use it like a non-narrative information book. Sometimes, information can be found in the running text, but more frequently information appears in insets and diagrams. Readers can enter on any page to access specific facts, or they can read the book through as a story. You can use the story component of a dual-purpose book to engage the reader at the beginning of the science learning cycle.

Dual-purpose books typically have little science content within the story. If the insets and diagrams are read, discussed, explained, and related to the story, these books can be very useful in helping students refine concepts and acquire scientific vocabulary after they have had opportunities for hands-on exploration.

Using Fiction and Nonfiction Texts

It can be useful to pair fiction and nonfiction books in read-alouds to round out the science or

engineering content being presented. Because fiction books tend to be very engaging for students, they can be used to hook students at the beginning of a science lesson. But most of the reading people do in everyday life is nonfiction. We are immersed in informational text every day, and we must be able to comprehend it to be successful in school, at work, and in society. Nonfiction books and other informational text such as articles should be used frequently in the elementary classroom. They often include text structures that differ from stories, and the opportunity to experience these structures in read-alouds can strengthen students' abilities to read and understand informational text. Duke (2004) recommends four strategies to help teachers improve students' comprehension of informational text:

1. Increase students' access to informational text.
2. Increase the time students spend working with informational text.
3. Teach comprehension strategies through direct instruction.
4. Create opportunities for students to use informational text for authentic purposes.

Picture-Perfect STEM Lessons addresses these recommendations in several ways. The lessons expose students to a variety of nonfiction picture books, articles, and websites on science topics, thereby increasing access to informational text. Various tools (e.g., card sorts, anticipation guides, "Stop and Try It"; see Chapter 2 for a complete list of these tools) help enhance students' comprehension of the informational text by increasing the time they spend working with it. Each lesson includes instructions for explicitly teaching comprehension strategies within the learning cycle. The inquiry-based lessons provide an authentic purpose for reading informational text, as students are motivated to read or listen to find the answers to questions generated in the inquiry activities.

References

Atkison, T., M. N. Matusevich, and L. Huber. 2009. Making science trade book choices for elementary classrooms. *The Reading Teacher* 62 (6): 484–497.

Butzow, J., and C. Butzow. 2000. *Science through children's literature: An integrated approach.* Portsmouth, NH: Teacher Ideas Press.

Casteel, C. P., and B. A. Isom. 1994. Reciprocal processes in science and literacy learning. *The Reading Teacher* 47 (7): 538–544.

Colburn, A. 2003. *The lingo of learning: 88 education terms every science teacher should know.* Arlington, VA: NSTA Press.

Donovan, C., and L. Smolkin. 2002. Considering genre, content, and visual features in the selection of trade books for science instruction. *The Reading Teacher* 55 (6): 502–520.

Duke, N. K. 2004. The case for informational text. *Educational Leadership* 61 (6): 40–44.

Harvey, S., and A. Goudvis. 2000. *Strategies that work: Teaching comprehension to enhance understanding.* York, ME: Stenhouse Publishers.

Kralina, L. 1993. Tricks of the trades: Supplementing your science texts. *The Science Teacher* 60 (9): 33–37.

Martin, D. J. 1997. *Elementary science methods: A constructivist approach.* Albany, NY: Delmar.

Mayer, D. A. 1995. How can we best use children's literature in teaching science concepts? *Science and Children* 32 (6): 16–19, 43.

Milano, M. 2013. The *Next Generation Science Standards* and engineering for young learners: Beyond bridges and egg drops. *Science and Children* 51 (2): 10–16.

Miller, K. W., S. F. Steiner, and C. D. Larson. 1996. Strategies for science learning. *Science and Children* 33 (6): 24–27.

Morgan, E., and K. Ansberry. 2013. *Even more picture-perfect science lessons, K–5: Using children's books to guide inquiry.* Arlington, VA: NSTA Press.

Morrow, L. M., M. Pressley, J. K. Smith, and M. Smith. 1997. The effect of a literature-based program integrated into literacy and science instruction with children from diverse backgrounds. *Reading Research Quarterly* 32 (1): 54–76.

National Academy of Engineering and National Research Council. 2009. *Engineering in K–12 education: Understanding the status and improving the prospects.* Washington, DC: National Academies Press.

National Research Council (NRC). 2012. *A framework for K–12 science education: Practices, crosscutting* concepts, and core ideas. Washington, DC: National Academies Press.

Pappas, C. 2006. The information book genre: Its role in integrated science literacy research and practice. *Reading Research Quarterly* 41 (2): 226–250.

Rice, D. C. 2002. Using trade books in teaching elementary science: Facts and fallacies. *The Reading Teacher* 55 (6): 552–565.

Romance, N. R., and M. R. Vitale. 1992. A curriculum strategy that expands time for in-depth elementary science instruction by using science-based reading strategies: Effects of a year-long study in grade four. *Journal of Research in Science Teaching* 29 (6): 545–554.

Short, K. G., and J. Armstrong. 1993. Moving toward inquiry: Integrating literature into the science curriculum. *New Advocate* 6 (3): 183–200.

Strickland, D. S., and L. M. Morrow, eds. 2000. *Beginning reading and writing*. New York: Teachers College Press.

Tyson, H., and A. Woodward. 1989. Why aren't students learning very much from textbooks? *Educational Leadership* 47 (3): 14–17.

U.S. Department of Education. 2009. Science, technology, engineering and math: Education for global leadership. *www.ed.gov/stem*.

Van den Heuvel-Panhuizen, M., I. Elia, and A. Robitzsch. 2014. Effects of reading picture books on kindergartners' mathematics performance. *Educational Psychology* 36 (2): 323–346.

Young, T. A., and B. Moss. 2006. Nonfiction in the classroom library: A literary necessity. *Childhood Education* 82 (4): 207–212.

Zemelman, S., H. Daniels, and A. Hyde. 2012. *Best practice: Bringing standards to life in America's classrooms*. 4th ed. Portsmouth, NH: Heinemann.

Children's Books Cited

Barrett, J., and R. Barrett. 1978. *Cloudy with a chance of meatballs*. New York: Atheneum Books for Young Readers.

Beaty, A. 2007. *Iggy Peck, architect*. New York: Abrams Books for Young Readers.

Bemelmans, L. 1958. *Madeline*. New York: Penguin Young Readers Group.

Childcraft Editors. 1973. *Childcraft: The how and why library*. New York: World Book.

Cleary, B. 1968. *Ramona the pest*. New York: HarperCollins.

Clements, A. 2010. *The handiest things in the world*. New York: Atheneum Books for Young Readers.

Freeman, D. 1968. *Corduroy*. New York: Viking Press.

Freeman, M., and I. Freeman. 1959. *You will go to the moon*. New York: Random House Children's Books.

L'Engle, M. 1963. *A wrinkle in time*. New York: Farrar, Straus & Giroux.

Macauley, D. 1988. *The way things work*. New York: Houghton Mifflin/Walter Lorraine Books.

Miller, R. 2014. *Engineering in our everyday lives*. New York: Crabtree.

Munsch, R. 1986. *Love you forever*. Scarborough, Ontario: Firefly Books.

Rey, H. A. 1973. *Curious George*. Boston: Houghton Mifflin.

Sendak, M. 1988. *Where the wild things are*. New York: HarperCollins.

Seuss, Dr. 1960. *Green eggs and ham*. New York: Random House Books for Young Readers.

Silverstein, S. 1964. *The giving tree*. New York: HarperCollins.

Stevenson, R. L. 1957. *A child's garden of verses*. New York: Grosset & Dunlap.

Stewart, M. 2014. *National Geographic Kids: Robots*. New York: National Geographic Children's Books.

Stone, J. 2003. *The monster at the end of this book*. New York: Golden Books.

Williams, M. 1922. *The velveteen rabbit*. New York: Doubleday & Company.

Winter, J. 2008. *Wangari's trees of peace: A true story from Africa*. New York: Harcourt.

Reading Aloud

This chapter addresses some of the research supporting the importance of reading aloud, tips to make your read-aloud time more valuable, descriptions of Harvey and Goudvis's six key reading strategies (2007), and tools you can use to enhance students' comprehension during read-aloud time.

Why Read Aloud?

Being read to is the most influential element in building the knowledge required for eventual success in reading (Anderson et al. 1985). It improves reading skills, increases interest in reading and literature, and can even improve overall academic achievement. A good reader demonstrates fluent, expressive reading and models the thinking strategies of proficient readers, helping build background knowledge and fine-tune students' listening skills. When a teacher does the reading, children's minds are free to anticipate, infer, connect, question, and comprehend (Calkins 2000). In addition, being read to is risk free. In *Yellow Brick Roads: Shared and Guided Paths to Independent Reading, 4–12,* Allen (2000) says, "For students who struggle with word-by-word reading, experiencing the whole story can finally give them a sense of the wonder and magic of a book" (p. 45).

Reading aloud is appropriate in all grade levels and for all subjects. Appendix A of the *Common Core State Standards for English Language Arts (CCSS ELA;* NGAC and CCSSO 2010) states that "children in the early grades—particularly kindergarten through grade 3—benefit from participating in rich, structured conversations with an adult in response to written texts that are read aloud, orally comparing and contrasting as well as analyzing and synthesizing" (p. 27). Reading aloud is important not only when children can't read well on their own but also after they have become proficient readers (Anderson et al. 1985). Allen (2000) supports this

READ-ALOUD TIME

view: "Given the body of research supporting the importance of read-aloud for modeling fluency, building background knowledge, and developing language acquisition, we should remind ourselves that those same benefits occur when we extend read-aloud beyond the early years" (p. 44). Likewise, the *CCSS ELA* advocate the use of read-alouds in upper elementary:

Because children's listening comprehension likely outpaces reading comprehension until the middle school years, it is particularly important that students in the earliest grades build knowledge through being read to as well as through reading, with the balance gradually shifting to reading independently. By reading a story or nonfiction selection aloud, teachers allow children to experience written language without the burden of decoding, granting them access to content that they may not be able to read and understand by themselves. Children are then free to focus their mental energy on the words and ideas presented in the text, and they will eventually be better prepared to tackle rich written content on their own. (NGAC and CCSSO 2010, Appendix A, p. 27)

Ten Tips for Reading Aloud

We have provided a list of tips to help you get the most from your read-aloud time. Using these suggestions can help set the stage for learning, improve comprehension of science material, and make the read-aloud experience richer and more meaningful for both you and your students.

1. Preview the Book

Select a book that meets your science objectives and lends itself to reading aloud. Preview it carefully before sharing it with your students. Are there any errors in scientific concepts or misinformation that could be inferred from the text or illustrations? If the book is not in story form, is there any non-essential information you could omit to make the read-aloud experience better? If you are not going to read the whole book, choose appropriate starting and stopping points before reading. Consider generating questions and inferences about the book in advance and placing them on sticky notes inside the book to help you model your thought processes as you read aloud.

2. Set the Stage

Because reading aloud is a performance, you should pay attention to the atmosphere and physical setting of the session. Gather the students in a special reading area, such as on a carpet or in a semicircle of chairs. Seat yourself slightly above them. Do not sit in front of a bright window where the glare will keep students from seeing you well or in an area where students can be easily distracted. You may want to turn off the overhead lights and read by the light of a lamp or use soft music as a way to draw students into the mood of the text. Establish expectations for appropriate behavior during read-aloud time, and, before reading, give the students an opportunity to settle down and focus their attention on the book.

3. Celebrate the Author and Illustrator

Tell students the names of the author and the illustrator before reading. Build connections by asking students if they have read other books by the author or illustrator. Increase interest by sharing facts about the author or illustrator from the book's cover or from library or internet research.

4. Read With Expression

Practice reading aloud to improve your performance. Can you read with more expression to more fully engage your audience? Try louder or softer speech, funny voices, facial expressions, or gestures. Make eye contact with your students every now and then as you read. This strengthens the bond between reader and listener, helps you gauge your audience's response, and cuts down on off-task behaviors. Read slowly enough that your students have time to build mental images of what you are reading, but not so slowly that they lose interest. When reading a nonfiction book aloud, you may want to pause after reading about a key concept to let it sink in and then reread that part. At suspenseful parts in a storybook, use dramatic pauses or slow down and read softly. This can move the audience to the edges of their seats!

5. Share the Pictures

Don't forget the power of visual images to help students connect with and comprehend what you are reading. Make sure that you hold the book in such a way that students can see the pictures on each page. Read captions if appropriate. In some cases, you may want to hide certain pictures so students can visualize what is happening in the text before you reveal the illustrator's interpretation.

6. Encourage Interaction

Keep chart paper and markers nearby in case you want to record questions or new information. Try providing students with "think pads" in the form of sticky notes to write on as you read aloud. Not only does this help extremely active children keep their hands busy while listening, but it also encourages students to interact with the text as they jot down questions or comments. After the read-aloud, have students share their questions and comments. You may want students to place their sticky notes on a class chart whose subject is the topic being studied. Another way to encourage interaction without taking the time for each student to ask questions or comment is to do an occasional "turn and talk" during the read-aloud. Stop reading, ask a question, allow thinking time, and then have each student share ideas with a partner.

7. Keep the Flow

Although you want to encourage interaction during a read-aloud, avoid excessive interruptions that may disrupt fluent, expressive reading. Aim for a balance between allowing students to hear the language of the book uninterrupted and providing them with opportunities to make comments, ask questions, and share connections to the reading. You may want to read the book all the way through one time so students can enjoy the aesthetic components of the story, and then go back and read the book for the purpose of meeting the science objectives.

8. Model Reading Strategies

As you read aloud, it is important that you help children access what they already know and build bridges to new understandings. Think out loud, model your questions for the author, and make connections to yourself, other books, and the world. Show students how to determine the important parts of the text or story, and demonstrate how you synthesize meaning from the text. Modeling these reading-comprehension strategies when appropriate before, during, or after reading helps students internalize the strategies and begin to use them in their own reading. Six key strategies are described in detail in the next section.

9. Don't Put It Away

Keep the read-aloud book accessible to students after you read it. They will want to get a close-up look at the pictures and will enjoy reading the book independently. Don't be afraid of reading the same book more than once—children benefit from the repetition.

10. Have Fun

Let your passion for books show. It is contagious! Read nonfiction books with interest and wonder. Share your thoughts, question the author's intent, synthesize meaning out loud, and voice your own connections to the text. When reading a story, let your emotions show—laugh at the funny parts and cry at the sad parts. Seeing an authentic response from the reader is important for students. If you read with enthusiasm, read-aloud time will become special and enjoyable for everyone involved.

We hope these tips will help you and your students reap the many benefits of read-alouds. As Miller (2002) writes in *Reading With Meaning: Teaching Comprehension in the Primary Grades,* "Learning to read should be a joyful experience. Give children the luxury of listening to well-written stories with interesting plots, singing songs and playing with their words, and exploring a wide range of fiction, nonfiction, poetry and rhymes. … Be genuine. Laugh. Love. Be patient. You're creating a community of readers and thinkers" (p. 26).

Reading-Comprehension Strategies

Children's author Madeleine L'Engle (1995) says, "Readers usually grossly underestimate their own importance. If a reader cannot create a book along with the writer, the book will never come to life. The author and the reader … meet on the bridge of words" (p. 34). It is our responsibility as teachers, no matter what subjects we are assigned to teach, to help children realize the importance of their own thoughts and ideas as they read. Modeling our own thinking as we read aloud is the first step. Becoming a proficient reader is an ongoing, complex process, and children need to be explicitly taught the strategies that good readers use. In *Strategies That Work,* Harvey and Goudvis (2007) identify six key reading strategies essential to achieving full understanding when we read. These strategies are used where appropriate in each lesson and are seamlessly embedded into the 5E Model. The strategies should be modeled as you read aloud to students from both fiction and nonfiction texts.

Research shows that explicit teaching of reading-comprehension strategies can foster comprehension development (Duke and Pearson 2002). Explicit teaching of the strategies is the initial step in the gradual-release-of-responsibility approach to delivering reading instruction (Fielding and Pearson 1994). During this first phase of the gradual-release method, the teacher *explains* the strategy, demonstrates *how* and *when* to use the strategy, explains *why* it is worth using, and *thinks aloud* to model the mental processes used by good readers. Duke (2004, p. 42) describes the process in this way:

> *I often discuss the strategies in terms of good readers, as in "Good readers think about what might be coming next." I also model the uses of comprehension strategies by thinking aloud as I read. For example, to model the importance of monitoring understanding, I make comments such as, "That doesn't make sense to me because …" or "I didn't understand that last part—I'd better go back."*

Using the teacher-modeling phase within a science learning cycle will reinforce what students do during reading instruction, when the gradual-release-of-responsibility model can be continued. When students have truly mastered a strategy, they are able to apply it to a variety of texts and curricular areas and can explain how the strategy helps them construct meaning.

Descriptions of the six key reading-comprehension strategies featured in *Strategies That Work* (Harvey and Goudvis 2007) follow. The following icon highlights these strategies here and within the lessons: .

Making Connections

Making meaningful connections during reading can improve learners' comprehension and engagement by helping them better relate to what they read. Comprehension breakdown that occurs when reading or listening to expository text can come from a lack of prior information. These three techniques can help readers build background knowledge where little exists:

- *Text-to-self connections* occur when readers and listeners link the text to their past experiences or background knowledge.
- *Text-to-text connections* occur when readers and listeners recognize connections from one book to another.
- *Text-to-world connections* occur when readers and listeners connect the text to events or issues in the real world.

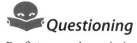 Questioning

Proficient readers ask themselves questions before, during, and after reading. Questioning allows readers to construct meaning, find answers, solve problems, and eliminate confusion as they read. Harvey and Goudvis (2007) write, "Questioning is the strategy that propels readers forward. When readers have questions, they are less likely to abandon the text" (p. 18). Asking questions not only is a critical reading skill but also is at the heart of scientific inquiry and can lead students into meaningful investigations. Questioning as a scientific practice is clearly articulated in *A Framework for K–12 Science Education,* which suggests that students ask questions based on observations to find more information or to design an investigation (NRC 2012).

Visualizing

Visualizing is the creation of mental images while reading or listening to text. Mental images are created from the learner's emotions and senses, making the text more concrete and memorable. Imagining the sensory qualities of things described in a text can help engage learners and stimulate their interest in the reading. When readers form pictures in their minds, they are also more likely to stick with a challenging text. During a reading, you can stop and ask students to visualize the scene. What sights, sounds, smells, and colors are they imagining?

 Inferring

Reading between the lines, or inferring, involves a learner's merging clues from the reading with prior knowledge to draw conclusions and interpret the text. Good readers make inferences before, during, and after reading. Inferential thinking is also an important science skill and can be reinforced during reading instruction.

Determining Importance

Reading to learn requires readers to identify essential information by distinguishing it from non-essential details. Deciding what is important in the text depends on the purpose for reading. In *Picture-Perfect STEM Lessons,* each lesson's objectives determine importance. Learners read or listen to the text to find answers to specific questions, to gain understanding of concepts, and to identify misconceptions.

 Synthesizing

In synthesizing, readers combine information gained through reading with prior knowledge and experience to form new ideas. To synthesize, readers must stop, think about what they have read, and contemplate its meaning before continuing on through the text. The highest level of synthesis involves those "aha!" moments when readers achieve new insight and, as a result, change their thinking.

Tools to Enhance Comprehension

We have identified several activities and organizers that can enhance students' science understanding and reading-comprehension in the lessons. These tools, which support the reading comprehension strategies from *Strategies That Work* listed in the previous section, are briefly described on the following pages and in more detail within the lessons.

Anticipation Guides

Anticipation guides (Herber 1978) are sets of questions that serve as a pre- and postreading activity for a text. They can be used to activate and assess prior knowledge, determine misconceptions, focus thinking on the reading, and motivate reluctant readers by stimulating interest in the topic. An anticipation guide should revolve around four to six key concepts from the reading that learners respond to before reading. They will be motivated to read or listen carefully to find the evidence that supports their predictions. After reading, learners revisit their anticipation guide to check their responses. In a revised extended anticipation guide (Duffelmeyer and Baum 1992), learners are required to justify their responses and explain why their choices were correct or incorrect.

CARD SEQUENCING

Card Sorts and Sequencing

Card sorts help learners understand the relationships among key concepts and help teach classification. They can also reveal misconceptions and increase motivation to read when used as a pre-reading activity. Learners are asked to sort words or phrases written on cards into different categories or sequence the events described on the cards. In an "open sort," learners sort the cards into categories of their own making or sequence events any way they wish. They can re-sort and re-sequence to help refine their understanding of concepts or events. In a "closed sort," the teacher gives them the categories for sorting or provides more information for correctly sequencing their cards.

Chunking

Chunking is dividing the text into manageable sections and reading only a section at any one time. This gives learners time to digest the information in a section before moving on. Chunking is also a useful technique for weeding out nonessential information when reading nonfiction books. Reading only those parts of the text that meet your learning objectives focuses the learning on what is important. Remember: Nowhere is it written that you must read nonfiction books cover to cover when doing a read-aloud. Feel free to omit parts that are inaccurate, out of date, or don't contribute in a meaningful way to the lesson.

Visual Representations

Organizers such as T-charts, semantic maps, or word webs (Billmeyer and Barton 1998) and personal vocabulary lists (Beers and Howell 2004) can help learners activate prior knowledge, organize their thinking, understand the essential characteristics of concepts, or see relationships among concepts. They can be used for prereading, assessment, summarizing, or reviewing material. Visual representations are effective because they help learners perceive abstract ideas in a more concrete form. Examples of these visual representations, with instructions for using them within the lesson, can be found throughout the book.

Cloze Strategy

Cloze refers to an activity that helps readers infer the meanings of unfamiliar words. In the cloze strategy, key words are deleted in a passage. Students then fill in the blanks with words that make sense and sound right. Words can be printed on cards for the students to place in the blanks before reading a passage in order for students to predict where they go. Then, after reading the passage, students can move them if necessary.

Rereading

Nonfiction text is often full of unfamiliar ideas and difficult vocabulary. *Rereading* content for clarification is an essential skill of proficient readers, and you should model this frequently. Rereading content for a different purpose can aid comprehension.

STOP AND TRY IT

For example, you might read aloud a text for enjoyment and then revisit the text to focus on specific science content.

Picture Walk

A picture walk consists of showing students the cover of a book and browsing through the pages in order, without reading the text. The purpose of this tool is to establish interest in the story and expectations about what is to come. It also reinforces the importance of using visual cues while reading. Students look at the pictures and talk about what they see, what may be happening in each illustration, and how the pictures come together to make a story. Some useful questions to ask during a picture walk are as follows:

- From looking at the cover, what do you think this book is about?
- What do you see?
- What do you think is happening?
- What do you think will happen next?
- What are you curious to know more about in the book?

Stop and Try It

Stop and Try It is a read-aloud format in which the teacher stops reading the text periodically to allow students to observe a demonstration or take part in a hands-on activity to better understand the content being presented. For example, in Chapter 10, "Move It!," we recommend that the teacher stop reading the book *Move It! Motion, Forces and You* at key points to allow students to perform some of the activities described in the book. This way, students have an experience that connects to the information they are learning from the book.

Turn and Talk

Learners each pair up with a partner to share their ideas, explain concepts in their own words, or talk about a connection they have to the book. This method allows each child to respond so that everyone in the group is involved as either a talker or a listener. Saying, "Take a few minutes to share your thoughts with someone" gives students an opportunity to satisfy their needs to express their own thoughts about the reading. "Walk and talk" and "stretch and share" are variations of this strategy that incorporate movement.

Using Features of Nonfiction

Many nonfiction books include a table of contents, index, glossary, bold-print words, picture captions, diagrams, and charts that provide valuable information. Because children are generally more used to narrative text, they often skip over these text structures. It is important to model how to interpret the information these features provide the reader. To begin, show the cover of a nonfiction book and read the title and table of contents. Ask students to predict what they'll find in the book. Show students how to use the index in the back of the book to find specific information. Point out other nonfiction text structures as you read, and note that these features are unique to nonfiction. Model how nonfiction books can be entered at any point in the text, because they generally don't follow a storyline.

USING THE TABLE OF CONTENTS

How Do Picture Books Enhance Comprehension?

Students should be encouraged to read a wide range of print materials, but picture books offer many advantages when teaching reading-comprehension strategies. Harvey and Goudvis (2007) not only believe that interest is essential to comprehension but also maintain that, because picture books are extremely effective for building background knowledge and teaching content, instruction in reading-comprehension strategies during picture book read-alouds allows students to better access that content. In summary, picture books are invaluable for teaching reading-comprehension strategies because they are extraordinarily effective at keeping readers engaged and thinking.

References

Allen, J. 2000. *Yellow brick roads: Shared and guided paths to independent reading, 4–12.* Portland, ME: Stenhouse Publishers.

Anderson, R. C., E. H. Heibert, J. Scott, and I. A. G. Wilkinson. 1985. *Becoming a nation of readers: The report of the Commission on Reading.* Washington, DC: National Institute of Education, U.S. Department of Education.

Beers, S., and L. Howell. 2004. *Reading strategies for the content areas: An action toolkit, volume 2.* Alexandria, VA: Association for Supervision and Curriculum Development.

Billmeyer, R., and M. L. Barton. 1998. *Teaching reading in the content areas: If not me, then who?* Aurora, CO: Mid-continent Regional Education Leadership Laboratory.

Calkins, L. M. 2000. *The art of teaching reading.* Boston: Pearson Allyn & Bacon.

Duffelmeyer, F. A., and D. D. Baum. 1992. The extended anticipation guide revisited. *Journal of Reading* 35 (8): 654–656.

Duke, N. K. 2004. The case for informational text. *Educational Leadership* 61 (6): 40–44.

Duke, N. K., and P. D. Pearson. 2002. Effective practices for developing reading comprehension. In *What research has to say about reading instruction,* ed. A. E. Farstrup and S. J. Samuels, 205–242. Newark, DE: International Reading Association.

Fielding, L., and P. D. Pearson. 1994. Reading comprehension: What works? *Educational Leadership* 51 (5): 62–67.

Harvey, S., and A. Goudvis. 2007. *Strategies that work: Teaching comprehension for understanding and engagement.* 2nd ed. Portland, ME: Stenhouse Publishers.

Herber, H. 1978. *Teaching reading in the content areas.* Englewood Cliffs, NJ: Prentice Hall.

L'Engle, M. 1995. *Walking on water: Reflections on faith and art.* New York: North Point Press.

Miller, D. 2002. *Reading with meaning: Teaching comprehension in the primary grades.* Portland, ME: Stenhouse Publishers.

National Governors Association Center for Best Practices and Council of Chief State School Officers (NGAC and CCSSO). 2010. *Common core state standards.* Washington, DC: NGAC and CCSSO.

National Research Council (NRC). 2012. *A framework for K–12 science education: Practices, crosscutting concepts, and core ideas.* Washington, DC: National Academies Press.

Children's Book Cited

Mason, A. 2005. *Move it! Motion, forces and you.* Toronto: Kids Can Press.

BSCS 5E Instructional Model

The guided inquiries in this book are designed using the BSCS 5E Instructional Model, commonly referred to as the 5E Model (or the 5Es). Developed by the Biological Sciences Curriculum Study (BSCS), the 5E Model is a learning cycle based on a constructivist view of learning. Constructivism embraces the idea that learners bring with them preconceived ideas about how the world works. According to the constructivist view, "learners test new ideas against that which they already believe to be true. If the new ideas seem to fit in with their pictures of the world, they have little difficulty learning the ideas … if the new ideas don't seem to fit the learners' picture of reality then they won't seem to make sense. Learners may dismiss them … or eventually accommodate the new ideas and change the way they understand the world" (Colburn 2003, p. 59). The objective of a constructivist model, therefore, is to provide students with experiences that make them reconsider their conceptions. Then, students "redefine, reorganize, elaborate, and change their initial concepts through self-reflection and interaction with their peers and their environment" (Bybee 1997, p. 176). The 5E Model (Figure 3.1) provides a planned sequence of instruction that places students at the center of their learning experiences, encouraging them to explore, construct their own understanding of science and engineering concepts, and relate those understandings to other concepts. The phases of the 5E Model—engage, explore, explain, elaborate, and evaluate—are described here.

Figure 3.1. The BSCS 5Es as a Cycle of Learning

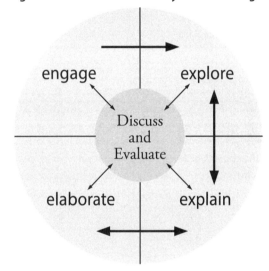

Source: Adapted from Barman, C. R. 1997. *The learning cycle revised: A modification of an effective teaching model.* Arlington, VA: Council for Elementary Science International.

Phases of the 5E Model

engage

The purpose of this introductory phase, *engage,* is to capture students' interest and draw them into a STEM lesson. Here, you can uncover what students know and think about a topic as well as determine their misconceptions. The engage phase can also serve to establish a theme for the lesson or set up opportunities for investigating or innovating in the explore phase. Engagement activities might include a reading, a demonstration, or other activity that piques students' curiosity.

ENGAGING WITH A READ-ALOUD

EXPLAINING WITH A GRAPH

explore

In the *explore* phase, you provide students with cooperative exploration activities, giving them common, concrete experiences that help them begin constructing concepts and developing skills. Students can build models, collect data, make and test predictions, or design and test technological solutions. The purpose is to provide hands-on experiences you can use later to formally introduce a concept, process, or skill.

EXPLORING WITH MATTER OBSERVATIONS

explain

In the *explain* phase, learners articulate their ideas in their own words and listen critically to one another. You clarify their concepts, support learners as they develop scientifically accurate conceptions, and introduce scientific or engineering terminology. It

is important that you clearly connect the students' explanations to experiences they had in the engage and explore phases.

elaborate

At the beginning of the *elaborate* phase, some students may still have misconceptions or may understand the concepts only in the context of the previous exploration. Elaboration activities can help students correct their remaining misconceptions and generalize the concepts in a broader context. These activities also challenge students to apply, extend, or elaborate on concepts and skills in a new situation, resulting in deeper understanding. Often, the elaborate phase is where students can apply what they have learned to meet a design challenge.

ELABORATING WITH A DESIGN CHALLENGE

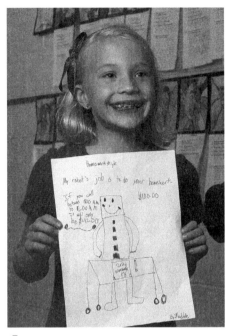

EVALUATING WITH A POSTER PROJECT

evaluate

In the *evaluate* phase, you evaluate students' understanding of concepts and their proficiency with various skills. You can use a variety of formal and informal procedures to assess conceptual understanding and progress toward learning outcomes. The evaluation phase also provides an opportunity for students to test their own understanding and skills.

Although the fifth phase is devoted to evaluation, a skillful teacher evaluates throughout the 5E Model, continually checking to see if students need more time or instruction to learn the key points in a lesson. Some ways to do this include informal questioning, teacher checkpoints, and class discussions. Each lesson in *Picture-Perfect STEM Lessons* also includes a formal evaluation such as extended-response questions or a poster session. These formal evaluations take place at the end of the lesson. A good resource for more information and practical suggestions for evaluating student understanding throughout the 5Es is *Seamless Assessment in Science:*

A Guide for Elementary and Middle School Teachers by Abell and Volkmann (2006).

Roles of the Teacher and Student

The traditional roles of the teacher and student are virtually reversed in the 5E Model. Students take on much of the responsibility for learning as they construct knowledge through discovery, whereas in traditional models the teacher is responsible for dispensing information to be learned by the students. Table 3.1 (p. 20) shows actions of the teacher that are consistent with the 5E Model and actions that are inconsistent with the model.

In the 5E Model, the teacher acts as a guide: raising questions, providing opportunities for exploration or problem solving, asking for evidence to support student explanations, referring students to existing explanations, correcting misconceptions, and coaching students as they apply new concepts. This model differs greatly from the traditional format of lecturing, leading students step by step to a solution, providing definite answers, and testing isolated facts. The 5E Model requires the students to take on much of the responsibility for their own learning. Table 3.2 (p. 21) shows the actions of the student that are consistent with the 5E Model and those that are inconsistent with the model.

The *Next Generation Science Standards* and the 5Es

In his book *Translating the* NGSS *for Classroom Instruction,* Rodger Bybee (2013) suggests that when planning learning experiences with the *Next Generation Science Standards* (*NGSS;* NGSS Lead States 2013), teachers use an integrated instructional sequence such as the 5E Model. In his book *The BSCS 5E Instructional Model: Creating Teachable Moments,* Bybee (2015) recommends working backward from the performance expectations outlined in the *NGSS* to plan the learning experiences:

> *Begin by identifying your desired learning outcomes—for example, the performance expectations from* NGSS. *Then determine what would*

Table 3.1. The BSCS 5Es Teacher

Stage of the Instructional Model	What the Teacher Does That Is …	
	Consistent With This Model	**Inconsistent With This Model**
Engage	• Creates interest • Generates curiosity • Raises questions • Elicits responses that uncover what the students know or think about the concept or topic	• Explains concepts • Provides definitions and answers • States conclusions • Provides closure • Involves lectures
Explore	• Encourages the students to work together without direct instruction from the teacher • Observes and listens to the students as they interact • Asks probing questions to redirect the students' investigations when necessary • Provides time for the students to puzzle through problems • Acts as a consultant for students	• Provides answers • Tells or explains how to work through the problem • Provides closure • Tells the students that they are wrong • Gives information or facts that solve the problem • Leads the students step by step to a solution
Explain	• Encourages the students to explain concepts and definitions in their own words • Asks for justification (evidence) and clarification from students • Formally provides definitions, explanations, and new labels • Uses students' previous experiences as the basis for explaining concepts	• Accepts explanations that have no justification • Neglects to solicit the students' explanations • Introduces unrelated concepts or skills
Elaborate	• Expects the students to use formal labels, definitions, and explanations provided previously • Encourages the students to apply or extend the concepts and skills in new situations • Reminds the students of alternate explanations • Refers the students to existing data and evidence and asks, "What do you already know?" "Why do you think *x*?" (Strategies from Explore also apply here.)	• Provides definitive answers • Tells the students that they are wrong • Involves lectures • Leads students step by step to a solution • Explains how to work through the problem
Evaluate	• Observes the students as they apply new concepts and skills • Assesses students' knowledge and/or skills • Looks for evidence that the students have changed their thinking or behaviors • Allows students to assess their own learning and group-process skills • Asks open-ended questions such as "Why do you think … ?" "What evidence do you have?" "What do you know about *x*?" "How would you explain *x*?"	• Tests vocabulary words, terms, and isolated facts • Introduces new ideas or concepts • Creates ambiguity • Promotes open-ended discussion unrelated to the concept or skill

Table 3.2. The BSCS 5Es Student

Stage of the Instructional Model	What the Student Does That Is ...	
	Consistent With This Model	**Inconsistent With This Model**
Engage	• Asks questions such as "Why did this happen?" "What do I already know about this?" "What can I find out about this?" • Shows interest in the topic	• Asks for the "right" answer • Offers the "right" answer • Insists on answers or explanations • Seeks one solution
Explore	• Thinks freely, within the limits of the activity • Tests predictions and hypotheses • Forms new predictions and hypotheses • Tries alternatives and discusses them with others • Records observations and ideas • Suspends judgment	• Lets others do the thinking and exploring (passive involvement) • Works quietly with little or no interaction with others (only appropriate when exploring ideas or feelings) • "Plays around" indiscriminately with no goal in mind • Stops with one solution
Explain	• Explains possible solutions or answers to others • Listens critically to others' explanations • Questions others' explanations • Listens to and tries to comprehend explanations that the teacher offers • Refers to previous activities • Uses recorded observations in explanations	• Proposes explanations from "thin air" with no relationship to previous experiences • Brings up irrelevant experiences and examples • Accepts explanations without justification • Does not attend to other plausible explanations
Elaborate	• Applies new labels, definitions, explanations, and skills in new but similar situations • Uses previous information to ask questions, propose solutions, make decisions, and design experiments • Draws reasonable conclusions from evidence • Records observations and explanations • Checks for understanding among peers	• "Plays around" with no goal in mind • Ignores previous information or evidence • Draws conclusions from "thin air" • Uses only those labels that the teacher provided in discussions
Evaluate	• Answers open-ended questions by using observations, evidence, and previously accepted explanations • Demonstrates an understanding or knowledge of the concept or skill • Evaluates his or her own progress and knowledge • Asks related questions that would encourage future investigations	• Draws conclusions without using evidence or previously accepted explanations • Offers only yes or no and memorized definitions or explanations as answers • Fails to express satisfactory explanations in his or her own words • Introduces new, irrelevant topics

count as acceptable evidence of student learning. You should formulate strategies that set forth what counts as evidence of learning for the instructional sequence. This should be followed by actually designing assessments that will provide the evidence that students have learned the competencies described in the performance expectations. Then, and only then, begin developing the activities that will provide students opportunities to learn the concepts and practices described in the three dimensions of the performance expectations. (p. 68)

Picture-Perfect STEM Lessons are designed using this model. Although we recognize that some districts have not fully adopted the NGSS as standards for their science teaching, the NGSS performance expectations are written in a way that integrates all three dimensions of *A Framework for K–12 Science Education* (NRC 2012; see Chapter 4 in this book for more on the three dimensions). These expectations serve to guide the learning outcomes for our lessons. From these outcomes, we work backward to formulate the activities that compose each stage of the 5E Model. We select quality STEM-related picture books for the engage and explain phases, and develop student-centered explorations and design challenges for the explore and elaborate phases. A wide range of assessments are used in the evaluate phase, including writing tasks, poster and multimedia projects, and quizzes, with the goal that these lessons are a step toward preparing students for the *NGSS* performance expectations outlined for each grade.

Using Picture Books in the 5Es

Both fiction and nonfiction picture books can be valuable components of the 5E Model when placed strategically within the cycle. We often begin lessons with a fiction book to pique students' curiosity or motivate them to want to learn more about a science concept. For example, Chapter 8, "Robots Everywhere," begins with a read-aloud of *Beep! Beep! Go to Sleep!,* a humorous story about a boy whose robots keep him from going to sleep at night.

This read-aloud during the engage phase inspires the question "What is a robot?" and is followed by activities and a nonfiction read-aloud to find out. A storybook, however, might not be appropriate to use during the explore phase of the 5Es, in which students are participating in concrete, hands-on experiences. Likewise, a storybook might not be appropriate to use during the explain phase to clarify scientific concepts and introduce vocabulary. Sometimes, a narrative nonfiction text can be used to engage students. For example, in Chapter 16, "Plant a Tree," we use *Wangari's Trees of Peace,* the true story of a Kenyan environmentalist, to draw students into the STEM lesson. The inspirational message of how one person's vision and determination can inspire great change serves as a powerful invitation to inquiry.

You should avoid using too early in the learning cycle books that contain a lot of scientific terminology or "give away" information students could discover on their own. It is important for students to have opportunities to construct meaning and articulate ideas in their own words before being introduced to scientific vocabulary. Nonfiction books, therefore, are most appropriate to use in the explain phase only after students have had these opportunities. For example, in the explain phase of Chapter 10, "Move It!," students compare the results of their force and motion investigations with the information presented in the nonfiction book *Move It! Motion, Forces and You.*

The 5Es provide an ideal format for a constructivist sequence of activities, allowing students to form their own ideas, collect evidence to confirm or discount their ideas, design solutions to real-world problems, apply what they have learned to new situations, and demonstrate what they have learned. Thoughtful placement of fiction and nonfiction picture books within the 5E Model can help you engage, motivate, and explain while immersing your students in meaningful, integrated STEM learning experiences.

References

Abell, S. K., and M. J. Volkmann. 2006. *Seamless assessment in science: A guide for elementary and middle school teachers.* Chicago: Heinemann; Arlington, VA: NSTA Press.

Bybee, R. W. 1997. *Achieving scientific literacy: From purposes to practices.* Portsmouth, NH: Heinemann.

Bybee, R. W. 2013. *Translating the* NGSS *for classroom instruction.* Arlington, VA: NSTA Press.

Bybee, R. W. 2015. *The BSCS 5E Instructional Model: Creating teachable moments.* Arlington, VA: NSTA Press.

Colburn, A. 2003. *The lingo of learning: 88 education terms every science teacher should know.* Arlington, VA: NSTA Press.

National Research Council (NRC). 2012. *A framework for K–12 science education: Practices, crosscutting concepts, and core ideas.* Washington, DC: National Academies Press.

NGSS Lead States. 2013. *Next Generation Science Standards: For states, by states.* Washington, DC: National Academies Press. *www.nextgenscience. org/next-generation-science-standards.*

Children's Books Cited

Mason, A. 2005. *Move it! Motion, forces and you.* Toronto: Kids Can Press.

Tarpley, T. 2015. *Beep! Beep! Go to sleep!* New York: Little, Brown, and Company.

Winter, J. 2008. *Wangari's trees of peace: A true story from Africa.* New York: Harcourt.

Connecting to the Standards

A Framework for K–12 Science Education and the *Common Core State Standards for English Language Arts and Mathematics*

In this book, the science, language arts, and mathematics standards that are addressed in the activities for each lesson are clearly identified. On the first page of each chapter, you will find a box titled "Lesson Objectives Connecting to the *Framework,*" which lists the science and engineering practices, disciplinary core ideas, and crosscutting concepts that the lesson addresses. Throughout the lessons, you will find boxes noting the *Common Core State Standards, English Language Arts* (*CCSS ELA*) that are used during read-alouds and writing assignments and the *Common Core State Standards, Mathematics* (*CCSS Mathematics*) that are addressed in various activities. This chapter provides some background information about *A Framework for K–12 Science Education* (*Framework;* NRC 2012) and the *CCSS* and how our lessons connect to them.

A Framework for K–12 Science Education

The *Framework* was developed by the National Research Council, whose overarching goal was "to ensure that by the end of 12th grade, all students have some appreciation of the beauty and wonder of science; possess sufficient knowledge of science and engineering to engage in public discussions on related issues; are careful consumers of scientific and technological information related to their everyday lives; are able to continue to learn about science outside school; and have the skills to enter

careers of their choice, including (but not limited to) careers in science, engineering, and technology" (NRC 2012, p. 1).

The *Framework* was developed around three major dimensions: (1) scientific and engineering practices, (2) crosscutting concepts, and (3) disciplinary core ideas. These three dimensions are the key components of the *Next Generation Science Standards* (*NGSS;* NGSS Lead States 2013) and many other state standards.

Dimension 1: Scientific and Engineering Practices

This dimension describes eight fundamental practices that scientists use as they investigate and build models and theories about the world, as well as the engineering practices that engineers use as they design and build systems (NRC 2012, p. 42). These practices are as follows:

1. Asking questions (for science) and defining problems (for engineering)
2. Developing and using models
3. Planning and carrying out investigations
4. Analyzing and interpreting data
5. Using mathematics and computational thinking
6. Constructing explanations (for science) and designing solutions (for engineering)
7. Engaging in argument from evidence
8. Obtaining, evaluating, and communicating information

For detailed information on the integration of science and engineering practices into the lessons in this book, see Chapter 5.

Dimension 2: Crosscutting Concepts

The seven crosscutting concepts outlined in the *Framework* appear throughout the lessons in this book. Table 4.1 shows an outline of the crosscutting concepts as they pertain to grades K–2.

As you implement the lessons in this book, you can incorporate these important themes, which appear over and over again throughout the disciplines of science, technology, engineering, and mathematics. Recognizing these themes helps students make connections between disciplines and understand that the same concept is relevant across different contexts. For example, the crosscutting concept of structure and function is in several lessons. In Chapter 8, "Robots Everywhere," students learn that the structures on a robot are related to their functions. In Chapter 15, "Design a Habitat," students design a habitat for a "pet" that has structures that serve the function of meeting the needs of the animal. In Chapter 17, "Pillbots," students learn how engineers mimic the structures of living things to design objects to serve a specific function.

And in Chapter 18, "Flight of the Pollinators," students learn how the structures and functions of flowers and pollinators make pollination possible. Recognizing the relationship between structure and function in both the natural and designed world is a key concept that relates to science and engineering.

Because students often do not make the connections on their own, teachers must make these seven crosscutting concepts explicit for students to help them connect knowledge from different science fields into a coherent and scientifically based view of the world.

Dimension 3: Disciplinary Core Ideas

Disciplinary core ideas are grouped in four domains: (1) physical science; (2) life science; (3) Earth and space science; and (4) engineering, technology, and applications of science. The *Framework* committee has identified these core ideas of science and engineering as meeting at least two of the following criteria (NRC 2012):

1. Have broad importance across multiple sciences or engineering disciplines or be a key organizing principle of a single discipline.

2. Provide a key tool for understanding or investigating more complex ideas and solving problems.

Table 4.1. The Framework's *Crosscutting Concepts for Grades K–2*

Crosscutting Concepts for Grades K–2	
Patterns	• Patterns in the natural and human designed world can be observed, used to describe phenomena, and used as evidence.
Cause and Effect: Mechanism and Explanation	• Events have causes that generate observable patterns. • Simple tests can be designed to gather evidence to support or refute student ideas about causes.
Scale, Proportion, and Quantity	• Relative scales allow objects and events to be compared and described (e.g., bigger and smaller, hotter and colder, faster and slower). • Standard units are used to measure length.
Systems and System Models	• Objects and organisms can be described in terms of their parts. • Systems in the natural and designed world have parts that work together.
Energy and Matter: Flows, Cycles, and Conservation	• Objects may break into smaller pieces, be put together into larger pieces, or change shapes.
Structure and Function	• The shape and stability of structures of natural and designed objects are related to their function(s).
Stability and Change	• Some things stay the same while other things change. • Things may change slowly or rapidly.

Source: Willard 2015, p. 90.

3. Relate to the interests and life experiences of students or be connected to societal or personal concerns that require scientific or technological knowledge.

4. Be teachable and learnable over multiple grades at increasing levels of depth and sophistication. That is, the idea can be made accessible to younger students but is broad enough to sustain continued investigation over years.

The disciplinary core ideas are listed in a quick-reference chart in Table 4.2 (p. 28).

The lesson objectives in this book are closely aligned to a variety of the disciplinary core ideas outlined in dimension three. At the beginning of each lesson, we provide the disciplinary core ideas that are targeted within the lesson.

Next Generation Science Standards

For districts that have adopted the *NGSS,* the appendix (p. 309) provides a detailed correlation among the lessons presented in *Picture-Perfect STEM Lessons,* the three dimensions of the *NGSS,* and the corresponding performance expectations. Even if your district has not adopted the *NGSS* as the standard for science teaching, we encourage you to read through the charts in the appendix. Understanding how these lessons align to specific *NGSS* disciplinary core ideas, crosscutting concepts, science and engineering practices, and performance expectations will be helpful as you select and implement *Picture-Perfect STEM Lessons* in your classroom.

A note about *NGSS* performance expectations: The *NGSS* provide performance expectations that depict what students must do to show proficiency at each grade level. Performance expectations integrate all three dimensions of the *NGSS* into one task and are to be offered after students have had multiple experiences with the topic. The lessons in this book are intended to help students move toward specific performance expectations, which are identified at the beginning of each lesson. *However, the lesson will not by itself be sufficient to reach the performance expectations; rather, the lesson is meant to be one in a series of lessons that work toward the performance expectations.*

Common Core State Standards

The Common Core State Standards Initiative (*www.corestandards.org*) is a state-led effort to define the knowledge and skills students should acquire in their K–12 mathematics and ELA courses. It is a result of an extended, broad-based effort to fulfill the charge issued by the states to craft the next generation of K–12 standards to ensure that all students are college and career ready by the end of high school. The standards are research and evidence based, aligned with college and work expectations, rigorous, and internationally benchmarked. The lessons in this book were not designed to teach the *CCSS ELA* and *CCSS Mathematics* standards, but to provide opportunities for students to apply the standards appropriate to their grade level in an authentic way and in a meaningful context.

Common Core State Standards, English Language Arts

The *Common Core* suggests that the ELA standards be taught in the context of history/social studies, science, and technical subjects (NGAC and CCSO 2010). Grade-specific K–12 standards in reading, writing, speaking, listening, and language are included. Many of these grade-specific standards are used in *Picture-Perfect STEM Lessons* through the use of high-quality children's fiction and nonfiction picture books, research-based reading strategies, poster presentations, vocabulary development activities, and various writing assignments. In the boxes titled "Connecting to the *Common Core*," you will find the *CCSS ELA* strand(s) and topic the activity addresses, the grade level(s), and the standard number(s) (see Figure 4.1, p. 29).

Because the codes for the *CCSS ELA* Standards are listed in the lessons instead of the actual standards statements, we have included the *CCSS ELA* grade-level statements in Table 4.3 (pp. 30–35). This table is not a complete version of the *CCSS ELA.* Rather, it includes only the standards we

Table 4.2. The Framework's Disciplinary Core Ideas

Disciplinary Core Ideas in Physical Science	Disciplinary Core Ideas in Life Science	Disciplinary Core Ideas in Earth and Space Science	Disciplinary Core Ideas in Engineering, Technology, and Applications of Science
PS1: Matter and Its Interactions PS1.A: Structure and Properties of Matter PS1.B: Chemical Reactions PS1.C: Nuclear Processes **PS2: Motion and Stability: Forces and Interactions** PS2.A: Forces and Motion PS2.B: Types of Interactions PS2.C: Stability and Instability in Physical Systems **PS3: Energy** PS3.A: Definitions of Energy PS3.B: Conservation of Energy and Energy Transfer PS3.C: Relationship Between Energy and Forces PS3.D: Energy in Chemical Processes and Everyday Life **PS4: Waves and Their Applications in Technologies for Information Transfer** PS4.A: Wave Properties PS4.B: Electromagnetic Radiation PS4.C: Information Technologies and Instrumentation	**LS1: From Molecules to Organisms: Structures and Processes** LS1.A: Structure and Function LS1.B: Growth and Development of Organisms LS1.C: Organization for Matter and Energy Flow in Organisms LS1.D: Information Processing **LS2: Ecosystems: Interactions, Energy, and Dynamics** LS2.A: Interdependent Relationships in Ecosystems LS2.B: Cycles of Matter and Energy Transfer in Ecosystems LS2.C: Ecosystem Dynamics, Functioning, and Resilience LS2.D: Social Interactions and Group Behavior **LS3: Heredity: Inheritance and Variation of Traits** LS3.A: Inheritance of Traits LS3.B: Variation of Traits **LS4: Biological Evolution: Unity and Diversity** LS4.A: Evidence of Common Ancestry and Diversity LS4.B: Natural Selection LS4.C: Adaptation LS4.D: Biodiversity and Humans	**ESS1: Earth's Place in the Universe** ESS1.A: The Universe and Its Stars ESS1.B: Earth and the Solar System ESS1.C: The History of Planet Earth **ESS2: Earth's Systems** ESS2.A: Earth Materials and Systems ESS2.B: Plate Tectonics and Large-Scale System Interactions ESS2.C: The Roles of Water in Earth's Surface Processes ESS2.D: Weather and Climate ESS2.E: Biogeology **ESS3: Earth and Human Activity** ESS3.A: Natural Resources ESS3.B: Natural Hazards ESS3.C: Human Impacts on Earth Systems ESS3.D: Global Climate Change	**ETS1: Engineering Design** ETS1.A: Defining and Delimiting an Engineering Problem ETS1.B: Developing Possible Solutions ETS1.C: Optimizing the Design Solution **ETS2: Links Among Engineering, Technology, Science, and Society** ETS2.A: Interdependence of Science, Engineering, and Technology ETS2.B: Influence of Engineering, Technology, and Science on Society and the Natural World

Source: Willard 2015, p. 3.

address in our lessons for grades K–2: reading (literature and informational text), writing, speaking and listening, and language. You can access the complete *Common Core State Standards ELA* at *www.corestandards.org/ELA-Literacy.*

Figure 4.1. Sample CCSS ELA Box

Common Core State Standards, Mathematics

The *CCSS Mathematics* (NGAC and CCSO 2010) are divided into two parts: eight mathematical practices that apply to every grade level and grade-specific standards of mathematical content. Many of these grade-specific standards are used in *Picture-Perfect STEM Lessons* as students measure, graph, compare, and design. In the boxes

titled "Connecting to the Common Core," you will find the *CCSS Mathematics* domain the activity addresses, the grade level(s), and standard number(s) (see Figure 4.2).

Because the *CCSS Mathematics* codes are listed in the lessons instead of the actual standards statements, we have included the *CCSS Mathematics* grade-level standards in Table 4.4 (pp. 36–41). This table is not a complete version of the *CCSS Mathematics*. Rather, it includes only the domains we address in our lessons for grades K–2. You can access the complete *CCSS Mathematics* at *www. corestandards.org/Math.*

Figure 4.2. Sample CCSS Mathematics Box

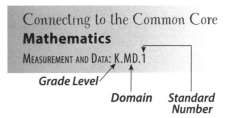

Table 4.3. Common Core State Standards for English Language Arts and Literacy in History/Social Studies, Science, and Technical Subjects

Reading Standards for Literature, K–2

Kindergartners	Grade 1 Students	Grade 2 Students
Key Ideas and Details		
1. With prompting and support, ask and answer questions about key details in a text.	1. Ask and answer questions about key details in a text.	1. Ask and answer such questions as *who, what, where, when, why,* and *how* to demonstrate understanding of key details in a text.
2. With prompting and support, retell familiar stories, including key details.	2. Retell stories, including key details, and demonstrate understanding of their central message or lesson.	2. Recount stories, including fables and folktales from diverse cultures, and determine their central message, lesson, or moral.
3. With prompting and support, identify characters, settings, and major events in a story.	3. Describe characters, settings, and major events in a story, using key details.	3. Describe how characters in a story respond to major events and challenges.
Craft and Structure		
4. Ask and answer questions about unknown words in a text.	4. Identify words and phrases in stories or poems that suggest feelings or appeal to the senses.	4. Describe how words and phrases (e.g., regular beats, alliteration, rhymes, repeated lines) supply rhythm and meaning in a story, poem, or song.
5. Recognize common types of texts (e.g., storybooks, poems).	5. Explain major differences between books that tell stories and books that give information, drawing on a wide reading of a range of text types.	5. Describe the overall structure of a story, including describing how the beginning introduces the story and the ending concludes the action.
6. With prompting and support, name the author and illustrator of a story and define the role of each in telling the story.	6. Identify who is telling the story at various points in a text.	6. Acknowledge differences in the points of view of characters, including by speaking in a different voice for each character when reading dialogue aloud.
Integration of Knowledge and Ideas		
7. With prompting and support, describe the relationship between illustrations and the story in which they appear (e.g., what moment in a story an illustration depicts).	7. Use illustrations and details in a story to describe its characters, setting, or events.	7. Use information gained from the illustrations and words in a print or digital text to demonstrate understanding of its characters, setting, or plot.
8. (Not applicable to literature)	8. (Not applicable to literature)	8. (Not applicable to literature)
9. With prompting and support, compare and contrast the adventures and experiences of characters in familiar stories.	9. Compare and contrast the adventures and experiences of characters in stories.	9. Compare and contrast two or more versions of the same story (e.g., Cinderella stories) by different authors or from different cultures.
Range of Reading and Level of Text Complexity		
10. Actively engage in group reading activities with purpose and understanding.	10. With prompting and support, read prose and poetry of appropriate complexity for grade 1.	10. By the end of the year, read and comprehend literature, including stories and poetry, in the grades 2–3 text complexity band proficiently, with scaffolding as needed at the high end of the range.

Table 4.3. *(continued)*

Reading Standards for Informational Text, K–2

Kindergartners	Grade 1 Students	Grade 2 Students
Key Ideas and Details		
1. With prompting and support, ask and answer questions about key details in a text.	1. Ask and answer questions about key details in a text.	1. Ask and answer such questions as *who, what, where, when, why,* and *how* to demonstrate understanding of key details in a text.
2. With prompting and support, identify the main topic and retell key details of a text.	2. Identify the main topic and retell key details of a text.	2. Identify the main topic of a multiparagraph text as well as the focus of specific paragraphs within the text.
3. With prompting and support, describe the connection between two individuals, events, ideas, or pieces of information in a text.	3. Describe the connection between two individuals, events, ideas, or pieces of information in a text.	3. Describe the connection between a series of historical events, scientific ideas or concepts, or steps in technical procedures in a text.
Craft and Structure		
4. With prompting and support, ask and answer questions about unknown words in a text.	4. Ask and answer questions to help determine or clarify the meaning of words and phrases in a text.	4. Determine the meaning of words and phrases in a text relevant to a grade 2 topic or subject area.
5. Identify the front cover, back cover, and title page of a book.	5. Know and use various text features (e.g., headings, tables of contents, glossaries, electronic menus, icons) to locate key facts or information in a text.	5. Know and use various text features (e.g., captions, bold print, subheadings, glossaries, indexes, electronic menus, icons) to locate key facts or information in a text efficiently.
6. Name the author and illustrator of a text and define the role of each in presenting the ideas or information in a text.	6. Distinguish between information provided by pictures or other illustrations and information provided by the words in a text.	6. Identify the main purpose of a text, including what the author wants to answer, explain, or describe.
Integration of Knowledge and Ideas		
7. With prompting and support, describe the relationship between illustrations and the text in which they appear (e.g., what person, place, thing, or idea in the text an illustration depicts).	7. Use the illustrations and details in a text to describe its key ideas.	7. Explain how specific images (e.g., a diagram showing how a machine works) contribute to and clarify a text.
8. With prompting and support, identify the reasons an author gives to support points in a text.	8. Identify the reasons an author gives to support points in a text.	8. Describe how reasons support specific points the author makes in a text.
9. With prompting and support, identify basic similarities in and differences between two texts on the same topic (e.g., in illustrations, descriptions, or procedures).	9. Identify basic similarities in and differences between two texts on the same topic (e.g., in illustrations, descriptions, or procedures).	9. Compare and contrast the most important points presented by two texts on the same topic.
Range of Reading and Level of Text Complexity		
10. Actively engage in group reading activities with purpose and understanding.	10. With prompting and support, read informational texts appropriately complex for grade 1.	10. By the end of year, read and comprehend informational texts, including history/ social studies, science, and technical texts, in the grades 2–3 text complexity band proficiently, with scaffolding as needed at the high end of the range.

Table 4.3. *(continued)*

Writing Standards, K–2

Kindergartners	Grade 1 Students	Grade 2 Students
Text Types and Purposes		
1. Use a combination of drawing, dictating, and writing to compose opinion pieces in which they tell a reader the topic or the name of the book they are writing about and state an opinion or preference about the topic or book (e.g., *My favorite book is …*).	1. Write opinion pieces in which they introduce the topic or name the book they are writing about, state an opinion, supply a reason for the opinion, and provide some sense of closure.	1. Write opinion pieces in which they introduce the topic or book they are writing about, state an opinion, supply reasons that support the opinion, use linking words (e.g., *because, and, also*) to connect opinion and reasons, and provide a concluding statement or section.
2. Use a combination of drawing, dictating, and writing to compose informative/explanatory texts in which they name what they are writing about and supply some information about the topic.	2. Write informative/explanatory texts in which they name a topic, supply some facts about the topic, and provide some sense of closure.	2. Write informative/explanatory texts in which they introduce a topic, use facts and definitions to develop points, and provide a concluding statement or section.
3. Use a combination of drawing, dictating, and writing to narrate a single event or several loosely linked events, tell about the events in the order in which they occurred, and provide a reaction to what happened.	3. Write narratives in which they recount two or more appropriately sequenced events, include some details regarding what happened, use temporal words to signal event order, and provide some sense of closure.	3. Write narratives in which they recount a well-elaborated event or short sequence of events, include details to describe actions, thoughts, and feelings, use temporal words to signal event order, and provide a sense of closure.
Production and Distribution of Wrting		
4. (Begins in grade 3)	4. (Begins in grade 3)	4. (Begins in grade 3)
5. With guidance and support from adults, respond to questions and suggestions from peers and add details to strengthen writing as needed.	5. With guidance and support from adults, focus on a topic, respond to questions and suggestions from peers, and add details to strengthen writing as needed.	5. With guidance and support from adults and peers, focus on a topic and strengthen writing as needed by revising and editing.
6. With guidance and support from adults, explore a variety of digital tools to produce and publish writing, including in collaboration with peers.	6. With guidance and support from adults, use a variety of digital tools to produce and publish writing, including in collaboration with peers.	6. With guidance and support from adults, use a variety of digital tools to produce and publish writing, including in collaboration with peers.
Research to Build and Present Knowledge		
7. Participate in shared research and writing projects (e.g., explore a number of books by a favorite author and express opinions about them).	7. Participate in shared research and writing projects (e.g., explore a number of "how-to" books on a given topic and use them to write a sequence of instructions).	7. Participate in shared research and writing projects (e.g., read a number of books on a single topic to produce a report; record science observations).
8. With guidance and support from adults, recall information from experiences or gather information from provided sources to answer a question.	8. With guidance and support from adults, recall information from experiences or gather information from provided sources to answer a question.	8. Recall information from experiences or gather information from provided sources to answer a question.
9. (Begins in grade 4)	9. (Begins in grade 4)	9. (Begins in grade 4)
Range of Writing		
10. (Begins in grade 3)	10. (Begins in grade 3)	10. (Begins in grade 3)

Table 4.3. (continued)
Speaking and Listening Standards, K–2

Kindergartners	Grade 1 Students	Grade 2 Students
Comprehension and Collaboration		

1. Participate in collaborative conversations with diverse partners about kindergarten topics and texts with peers and adults in small and larger groups.
 	
  a. Follow agreed-upon rules for discussions (e.g., listening to others and taking turns speaking about the topics and texts under discussion).
 	
  b. Continue a conversation through multiple exchanges.
	1. Participate in collaborative conversations with diverse partners about grade 1 topics and texts with peers and adults in small and larger groups.
	
	  a. Follow agreed-upon rules for discussions (e.g., listening to others with care, speaking one at a time about the topics and texts under discussion).
	
	  b. Build on others' talk in conversations by responding to the comments of others through multiple exchanges.
	
	  c. Ask questions to clear up any confusion about the topics and texts under discussion.
		1. Participate in collaborative conversations with diverse partners about grade 2 topics and texts with peers and adults in small and larger groups.
		
		  a. Follow agreed-upon rules for discussions (e.g., gaining the floor in respectful ways, listening to others with care, speaking one at a time about the topics and texts under discussion).
		
		  b. Build on others' talk in conversations by linking their comments to the remarks of others.
		
		  c. Ask for clarification and further explanation as needed about the topics and texts under discussion.

2. Confirm understanding of a text read aloud or information presented orally or through other media by asking and answering questions about key details and requesting clarification if something is not understood.	2. Ask and answer questions about key details in a text read aloud or information presented orally or through other media.	2. Recount or describe key ideas or details from a text read aloud or information presented orally or through other media.
3. Ask and answer questions in order to seek help, get information, or clarify something that is not understood.	3. Ask and answer questions about what a speaker says in order to gather additional information or clarify something that is not understood.	3. Ask and answer questions about what a speaker says in order to clarify comprehension, gather additional information, or deepen understanding of a topic or issue.
Presentation of Knowledge and Ideas		
4. Describe familiar people, places, things, and events and, with prompting and support, provide additional detail.	4. Describe people, places, things, and events with relevant details, expressing ideas and feelings clearly.	4. Tell a story or recount an experience with appropriate facts and relevant, descriptive details, speaking audibly in coherent sentences.
5. Add drawings or other visual displays to descriptions as desired to provide additional detail.	5. Add drawings or other visual displays to descriptions when appropriate to clarify ideas, thoughts, and feelings.	5. Create audio recordings of stories or poems; add drawings or other visual displays to stories or recounts of experiences when appropriate to clarify ideas, thoughts, and feelings.
6. Speak audibly and express thoughts, ideas clearly.	6. Produce complete sentences when appropriate to task and situation. (See grade 1 Language standards 1 and 3 on pages 34–35 for specific expectations.)	6. Produce complete sentences when appropriate to task and situation in order to provide requested detail or clarification. (See grade 2 Language standards 1 and 3 on pages 34–35 for specific expectations.)

Table 4.3. *(continued)*

Language Standards, K–2

Kindergartners	Grade 1 Students	Grade 2 Students
Conventions of Standard English		
1. Demonstrate command of the conventions of standard English grammar and usage when writing or speaking. a. Print many upper- and lowercase letters. b. Use frequently occurring nouns and verbs. c. Form regular plural nouns orally by adding /s/ or /es/ (e.g., *dog, dogs; wish, wishes*). d. Understand and use question words (interrogatives) (e.g., *who, what, where, when, why, how*). e. Use the most frequently occurring prepositions (e.g., *to, from, in, out, on, off, for, of, by, with*). f. Produce and expand complete sentences in shared language activities.	1. Demonstrate command of the conventions of standard English grammar and usage when writing or speaking. a. Print all upper- and lowercase letters. b. Use common, proper, and possessive nouns. c. Use singular and plural nouns with matching verbs in basic sentences (e.g., *He hops; We hop*). d. Use personal, possessive, and indefinite pronouns (e.g., *I, me, my; they, them, their; anyone, everything*). e. Use verbs to convey a sense of past, present, and future (e.g., *Yesterday I walked home; Today I walk home; Tomorrow I will walk home*). f. Use frequently occurring adjectives. g. Use frequently occurring conjunctions (e.g., *and, but, or, so, because*). h. Use determiners (e.g., articles, demonstratives). i. Use frequently occurring prepositions (e.g., *during, beyond, toward*). j. Produce and expand complete simple and compound declarative, interrogative, imperative, and exclamatory sentences in response to prompts.	1. Demonstrate command of the conventions of standard English grammar and usage when writing or speaking. a. Use collective nouns (e.g., group). b. Form and use frequently occurring irregular plural nouns (e.g., *feet, children, teeth, mice, fish*). c. Use reflexive pronouns (e.g., *myself, ourselves*). d. Form and use the past tense of frequently occurring irregular verbs (e.g., *sat, hid, told*). e. Use adjectives and adverbs, and choose between them depending on what is to be modified. f. Produce, expand, and rearrange complete simple and compound sentences (e.g., *The boy watched the movie; The little boy watched the movie; The action movie was watched by the little boy*).
2. Demonstrate command of the conventions of standard English capitalization, punctuation, and spelling when writing. a. Capitalize the first word in a sentence and the pronoun *I*. b. Recognize and name end punctuation. c. Write a letter or letters for most consonant and short-vowel sounds (phonemes). d. Spell simple words phonetically, drawing on knowledge of sound-letter relationships.	2. Demonstrate command of the conventions of standard English capitalization, punctuation, and spelling when writing. a. Capitalize dates and names of people. b. Use end punctuation for sentences. c. Use commas in dates and to separate single words in a series. d. Use conventional spelling for words with common spelling patterns and for frequently occurring irregular words. e. Spell untaught words phonetically, drawing on phonemic awareness and spelling conventions.	2. Demonstrate command of the conventions of standard English capitalization, punctuation, and spelling when writing. a. Capitalize holidays, product names, and geographic names. b. Use commas in greetings and closings of letters. c. Use an apostrophe to form contractions and frequently occurring possessives. d. Generalize learned spelling patterns when writing words (e.g., *cage → badge; boy → boil*). e. Consult reference materials, including beginning dictionaries, as needed to check and correct spellings.

Table 4.3. (continued)

Language Standards, K–2 (continued)

Chapter
4

Kindergartners	Grade 1 Students	Grade 2 Students
Knowledge of Language		
3. (Begins in grade 2)	3. (Begins in grade 2)	3. Use knowledge of language and its conventions when writing, speaking, reading, or listening. a. Compare formal and informal uses of English.
Vocabulary Acquisition and Use		
4. Determine or clarify the meaning of unknown and multiple-meaning words and phrases based on kindergarten reading and content. a. Identify new meanings for familiar words and apply them accurately (e.g., knowing *duck* is a bird and learning the verb *to duck*). b. Use the most frequently occurring inflections and affixes (e.g., *-ed, -s, re-, un-, pre-, -ful, -less*) as a clue to the meaning of an unknown word.	4. Determine or clarify the meaning of unknown and multiple-meaning words and phrases based on grade 1 reading and content, choosing flexibly from an array of strategies. a. Use sentence-level context as a clue to the meaning of a word or phrase. b. Use frequently occurring affixes as a clue to the meaning of a word. c. Identify frequently occurring root words (e.g., *look*) and their inflectional forms (e.g., *looks, looked, looking*).	4. Determine or clarify the meaning of unknown and multiple-meaning words and phrases based on grade 2 reading and content, choosing flexibly from an array of strategies. a. Use sentence-level context as a clue to the meaning of a word or phrase. b. Determine the meaning of the new word formed when a known prefix is added to a known word (e.g., *happy/unhappy, tell/retell*). c. Use a known root word as a clue to the meaning of an unknown word with the same root (e.g., *addition, additional*). d. Use knowledge of the meaning of individual words to predict the meaning of compound words (e.g., *birdhouse, lighthouse, housefly; bookshelf, notebook, bookmark*). e. Use glossaries and beginning dictionaries, both print and digital, to determine or clarify the meaning of words and phrases.
5. With guidance and support from adults, explore word relationships and nuances in word meanings. a. Sort common objects into categories (e.g., shapes, foods) to gain a sense of the concepts the categories represent. b. Demonstrate understanding of frequently occurring verbs and adjectives by relating them to their opposites (antonyms). c. Identify real-life connections between words and their use (e.g., note places at school that are *colorful*). d. Distinguish shades of meaning among verbs describing the same general action (e.g., *walk, march, strut, prance*) by acting out the meanings.	5. With guidance and support from adults, demonstrate understanding of word relationships and nuances in word meanings. a. Sort words into categories (e.g., colors, clothing) to gain a sense of the concepts the categories represent. b. Define words by category and by one or more key attributes (e.g., a *duck* is a bird that swims; a *tiger* is a large cat with stripes). c. Identify real-life connections between words and their use (e.g., note places at home that are *cozy*). d. Distinguish shades of meaning among verbs differing in manner (e.g., *look, peek, glance, stare, glare, scowl*) and adjectives differing in intensity (e.g., *large, gigantic*) by defining or choosing them or by acting out the meanings.	5. Demonstrate understanding of word relationships and nuances in word meanings. a. Identify real-life connections between words and their use (e.g., describe foods that are *spicy* or *juicy*). b. Distinguish shades of meaning among closely related verbs (e.g., *toss, throw, hurl*) and closely related adjectives (e.g., *thin, slender, skinny, scrawny*).
6. Use words and phrases acquired through conversations, reading and being read to, and responding to texts.	6. Use words and phrases acquired through conversations, reading and being read to, and responding to texts, including using frequently occurring conjunctions to signal simple relationships (e.g., *because*).	6. Use words and phrases acquired through conversations, reading and being read to, and responding to texts, including using adjectives and adverbs to describe (e.g., *When other kids are happy, that makes me happy*).

Table 4.4. Common Core State Standards for Mathematics, K–2

Counting and Cardinality	K.CC

Know number names and the count sequence.

1. Count to 100 by ones and by tens.
2. Count forward beginning from a given number within the known sequence (instead of having to begin at 1).
3. Write numbers from 0 to 20. Represent a number of objects with a written numeral 0–20 (with 0 representing a count of no objects).

Count to tell the number of objects.

4. Understand the relationship between numbers and quantities; connect counting to cardinality.
   a. When counting objects, say the number names in the standard order, pairing each object with one and only one number name and each number name with one and only one object.
   b. Understand that the last number name said tells the number of objects counted. The number of objects is the same regardless of their arrangement or the order in which they were counted.
   c. Understand that each successive number name refers to a quantity that is one larger.
5. Count to answer "how many?" questions about as many as 20 things arranged in a line, a rectangular array, or a circle, or as many as 10 things in a scattered configuration; given a number from 1–20, count out that many objects.

Compare numbers.

6. Identify whether the number of objects in one group is greater than, less than, or equal to the number of objects in another group, e.g., by using matching and counting strategies.[1]
7. Compare two numbers between 1 and 10 presented as written numerals.

Operations and Algebraic Thinking	K.OA

Understand addition as putting together and adding to, and under- stand subtraction as taking apart and taking from.

1. Represent addition and subtraction with objects, fingers, mental images, drawings[2], sounds (e.g., claps), acting out situations, verbal explanations, expressions, or equations.
2. Solve addition and subtraction word problems, and add and subtract within 10, e.g., by using objects or drawings to represent the problem.
3. Decompose numbers less than or equal to 10 into pairs in more than one way, e.g., by using objects or drawings, and record each decomposition by a drawing or equation (e.g., $5 = 2 + 3$ and $5 = 4 + 1$).
4. For any number from 1 to 9, find the number that makes 10 when added to the given number, e.g., by using objects or drawings, and record the answer with a drawing or equation.
5. Fluently add and subtract within 5.

[1]Include groups with up to ten objects.

[2]Drawings need not show details, but should show the mathematics in the problem. (This applies wherever drawings are mentioned in the Standards.)

Copyright 2010. National Governors Association Center for Best Practices and Council of Chief State School Officers. All rights reserved.

Table 4.4. (continued)

Number and Operations in Base Ten	K.NBT

Work with numbers 11–19 to gain foundations for place value.

1. Compose and decompose numbers from 11 to 19 into ten ones and some further ones, e.g., by using objects or drawings, and record each composition or decomposition by a drawing or equation (e.g., 18 = 10 + 8); understand that these numbers are composed of ten ones and one, two, three, four, five, six, seven, eight, or nine ones.

Measurement and Data	K.MD

Describe and compare measurable attributes.

1. Describe measurable attributes of objects, such as length or weight.
   Describe several measurable attributes of a single object.

2. Directly compare two objects with a measurable attribute in common, to see which object has "more of"/"less of" the attribute, and describe the difference. *For example, directly compare the heights of two children and describe one child as taller/shorter.*

Classify objects and count the number of objects in each category.

3. Classify objects into given categories; count the numbers of objects in each category and sort the categories by count.[3]

Geometry	K.G

Identify and describe shapes (squares, circles, triangles, rectangles, hexagons, cubes, cones, cylinders, and spheres).

1. Describe objects in the environment using names of shapes, and describe the relative positions of these objects using terms such as *above, below, beside, in front of, behind,* and *next to.*

2. Correctly name shapes regardless of their orientations or overall size.

3. Identify shapes as two-dimensional (lying in a plane, "flat") or three- dimensional ("solid").

Analyze, compare, create, and compose shapes.

4. Analyze and compare two- and three-dimensional shapes, in different sizes and orientations, using informal language to describe their similarities, differences, parts (e.g., number of sides and vertices/"corners") and other attributes (e.g., having sides of equal length).

5. Model shapes in the world by building shapes from components (e.g., sticks and clay balls) and drawing shapes.

6. Compose simple shapes to form larger shapes. *For example, "Can you join these two triangles with full sides touching to make a rectangle?"*

[3]Limit category counts to be less than or equal to 10.

Table 4.4. *(continued)*

| **Operations and Algebraic Thinking** | **1.OA** |

Represent and solve problems involving addition and subtraction.

1. Use addition and subtraction within 20 to solve word problems involving situations of adding to, taking from, putting together, taking apart, and comparing, with unknowns in all positions, e.g., by using objects, drawings, and equations with a symbol for the unknown number to represent the problem.[2]

2. Solve word problems that call for addition of three whole numbers whose sum is less than or equal to 20, e.g., by using objects, drawings, and equations with a symbol for the unknown number to represent the problem.

Understand and apply properties of operations and the relationship between addition and subtraction.

3. Apply properties of operations as strategies to add and subtract.[3] *Examples: If 8 + 3 = 11 is known, then 3 + 8 = 11 is also known. (Commutative property of addition.) To add 2 + 6 + 4, the second two numbers can be added to make a ten, so 2 + 6 + 4 = 2 + 10 = 12. (Associative property of addition.)*

4. Understand subtraction as an unknown-addend problem. *For example, subtract 10 – 8 by finding the number that makes 10 when added to 8.*

Add and subtract within 20.

5. Relate counting to addition and subtraction (e.g., by counting on 2 to add 2).

6. Add and subtract within 20, demonstrating fluency for addition and subtraction within 10. Use strategies such as counting on; making ten (e.g., 8 + 6 = 8 + 2 + 4 = 10 + 4 = 14); decomposing a number leading to a ten (e.g., 13 – 4 = 13 – 3 – 1 = 10 – 1 = 9); using the relationship between addition and subtraction (e.g., knowing that 8 + 4 = 12, one knows 12 – 8 = 4); and creating equivalent but easier or known sums (e.g., adding 6 + 7 by creating the known equivalent 6 + 6 + 1 = 12 + 1 = 13).

Work with addition and subtraction equations.

7. Understand the meaning of the equal sign, and determine if equations involving addition and subtraction are true or false. *For example, which of the following equations are true and which are false? 6 = 6, 7 = 8 – 1, 5 + 2 = 2 + 5, 4 + 1 = 5 + 2.*

8. Determine the unknown whole number in an addition or subtraction equation relating three whole numbers. *For example, determine the unknown number that makes the equation true in each of the equations 8 + ? = 11, 5 = □ – 3, 6 + 6 = □.*

| **Number and Operations in Base Ten** | **1.NBT** |

Extend the counting sequence.

1. Count to 120, starting at any number less than 120. In this range, read and write numerals and represent a number of objects with a written numeral.

Understand place value.

2. Understand that the two digits of a two-digit number represent amounts of tens and ones. Understand the following as special cases:
   a. 10 can be thought of as a bundle of ten ones — called a "ten."
   b. The numbers from 11 to 19 are composed of a ten and one, two, three, four, five, six, seven, eight, or nine ones.
   c. The numbers 10, 20, 30, 40, 50, 60, 70, 80, 90 refer to one, two, three, four, five, six, seven, eight, or nine tens (and 0 ones).

3. Compare two two-digit numbers based on meanings of the tens and ones digits, recording the results of comparisons with the symbols >, =, and <.

[2]See Glossary, Table 1.

[3]Students need not use formal terms for these properties.

Copyright 2010. National Governors Association Center for Best Practices and Council of Chief State School Officers. All rights reserved.

Table 4.4. (continued)

Number and Operations in Base Ten (*continued*)	**1.NBT**

Use place value understanding and properties of operations to add and subtract.

4. Add within 100, including adding a two-digit number and a one-digit number, and adding a two-digit number and a multiple of 10, using concrete models or drawings and strategies based on place value, properties of operations, and/or the relationship between addition and subtraction; relate the strategy to a written method and explain the reasoning used. Understand that in adding two-digit numbers, one adds tens and tens, ones and ones; and sometimes it is necessary to compose a ten.

5. Given a two-digit number, mentally find 10 more or 10 less than the number, without having to count; explain the reasoning used.

6. Subtract multiples of 10 in the range 10–90 from multiples of 10 in the range 10–90 (positive or zero differences), using concrete models or drawings and strategies based on place value, properties of operations, and/or the relationship between addition and subtraction; relate the strategy to a written method and explain the reasoning used.

Measurement and Data	**1.MD**

Measure lengths indirectly and by iterating length units.

1. Order three objects by length; compare the lengths of two objects indirectly by using a third object.

2. Express the length of an object as a whole number of length units, by laying multiple copies of a shorter object (the length unit) end to end; understand that the length measurement of an object is the number of same-size length units that span it with no gaps or overlaps. *Limit to contexts where the object being measured is spanned by a whole number of length units with no gaps or overlaps.*

Tell and write time.

3. Tell and write time in hours and half-hours using analog and digital clocks.

Represent and interpret data.

4. Organize, represent, and interpret data with up to three categories; ask and answer questions about the total number of data points, how many in each category, and how many more or less are in one category than in another.

Geometry	**1.G**

Reason with shapes and their attributes.

1. Distinguish between defining attributes (e.g., triangles are closed and three-sided) versus non-defining attributes (e.g., color, orientation, overall size); build and draw shapes to possess defining attributes.

2. Compose two-dimensional shapes (rectangles, squares, trapezoids, triangles, half-circles, and quarter-circles) or three-dimensional shapes (cubes, right rectangular prisms, right circular cones, and right circular cylinders) to create a composite shape, and compose new shapes from the composite shape.[4]

3. Partition circles and rectangles into two and four equal shares, describe the shares using the words *halves, fourths,* and *quarters,* and use the phrases *half of, fourth of,* and *quarter of.* Describe the whole as two of, or four of the shares. Understand for these examples that decomposing into more equal shares creates smaller shares.

[4]Students do not need to learn formal names such as "right rectangular prism."

Table 4.4. *(continued)*

Operations and Algebraic Thinking	2.OA

Represent and solve problems involving addition and subtraction.

1. Use addition and subtraction within 100 to solve one- and two-step word problems involving situations of adding to, taking from, putting together, taking apart, and comparing, with unknowns in all positions, e.g., by using drawings and equations with a symbol for the unknown number to represent the problem.[1]

Add and subtract within 20.

2. Fluently add and subtract within 20 using mental strategies.[2] By end of Grade 2, know from memory all sums of two one-digit numbers.

Work with equal groups of objects to gain foundations for multiplication.

3. Determine whether a group of objects (up to 20) has an odd or even number of members, e.g., by pairing objects or counting them by 2s; write an equation to express an even number as a sum of two equal addends.

4. Use addition to find the total number of objects arranged in rectangular arrays with up to 5 rows and up to 5 columns; write an equation to express the total as a sum of equal addends.

Number and Operations in Base Ten	2.NBT

Understand place value.

1. Understand that the three digits of a three-digit number represent amounts of hundreds, tens, and ones; e.g., 706 equals 7 hundreds, 0 tens, and 6 ones. Understand the following as special cases:
   a. 100 can be thought of as a bundle of ten tens — called a "hundred."
   b. The numbers 100, 200, 300, 400, 500, 600, 700, 800, 900 refer to one, two, three, four, five, six, seven, eight, or nine hundreds (and 0 tens and 0 ones).

2. Count within 1000; skip-count by 5s, 10s, and 100s.

3. Read and write numbers to 1000 using base-ten numerals, number names, and expanded form.

4. Compare two three-digit numbers based on meanings of the hundreds, tens, and ones digits, using >, =, and < symbols to record the results of comparisons.

Use place value understanding and properties of operations to add and subtract.

5. Fluently add and subtract within 100 using strategies based on place value, properties of operations, and/or the relationship between addition and subtraction.

6. Add up to four two-digit numbers using strategies based on place value and properties of operations.

7. Add and subtract within 1000, using concrete models or drawings and strategies based on place value, properties of operations, and/or the relationship between addition and subtraction; relate the strategy to a written method. Understand that in adding or subtracting three- digit numbers, one adds or subtracts hundreds and hundreds, tens and tens, ones and ones; and sometimes it is necessary to compose or decompose tens or hundreds.

8. Mentally add 10 or 100 to a given number 100–900, and mentally subtract 10 or 100 from a given number 100–900.

9. Explain why addition and subtraction strategies work, using place value and the properties of operations.[3]

[1] See Glossary, Table 1.

[2] See standard 1.OA.6 for a list of mental strategies.

[3] Explanations may be supported by drawings or objects.

Table 4.4. *(continued)*

Measurement and Data	2.MD

Measure and estimate lengths in standard units.

1. Measure the length of an object by selecting and using appropriate tools such as rulers, yardsticks, meter sticks, and measuring tapes.

2. Measure the length of an object twice, using length units of different lengths for the two measurements; describe how the two measurements relate to the size of the unit chosen.

3. Estimate lengths using units of inches, feet, centimeters, and meters.

4. Measure to determine how much longer one object is than another, expressing the length difference in terms of a standard length unit.

Relate addition and subtraction to length.

5. Use addition and subtraction within 100 to solve word problems involving lengths that are given in the same units, e.g., by using drawings (such as drawings of rulers) and equations with a symbol for the unknown number to represent the problem.

6. Represent whole numbers as lengths from 0 on a number line diagram with equally spaced points corresponding to the numbers 0, 1, 2, ..., and represent whole-number sums and differences within 100 on a number line diagram.

Work with time and money.

7. Tell and write time from analog and digital clocks to the nearest five minutes, using a.m. and p.m.

8. Solve word problems involving dollar bills, quarters, dimes, nickels, and pennies, using $ and ¢ symbols appropriately. *Example: If you have 2 dimes and 3 pennies, how many cents do you have?*

Represent and interpret data.

9. Generate measurement data by measuring lengths of several objects to the nearest whole unit, or by making repeated measurements of the same object. Show the measurements by making a line plot, where the horizontal scale is marked off in whole-number units.

10. Draw a picture graph and a bar graph (with single-unit scale) to represent a data set with up to four categories. Solve simple put-together, take-apart, and compare problems[4] using information presented in a bar graph.

Geometry	2.G

Reason with shapes and their attributes.

1. Recognize and draw shapes having specified attributes, such as a given number of angles or a given number of equal faces.[5] Identify triangles, quadrilaterals, pentagons, hexagons, and cubes.

2. Partition a rectangle into rows and columns of same-size squares and count to find the total number of them.

3. Partition circles and rectangles into two, three, or four equal shares, describe the shares using the words *halves, thirds, half of, a third of,* etc., and describe the whole as two halves, three thirds, four fourths. Recognize that equal shares of identical wholes need not have the same shape.

[4]See Glossary, Table 1.

[5]Sizes are compared directly or visually, not compared by measuring.

References

National Governors Association Center for Best Practices and Council of Chief State School Officers (NGAC and CCSSO). 2010. *Common core state standards.* Washington, DC: NGAC and CCSSO.

National Research Council. 2012. *A framework for K–12 science education: Practices, crosscutting concepts, and core ideas.* Washington DC: National Academies Press.

NGSS Lead States. 2013. *Next Generation Science Standards: For states, by states.* Washington, DC: National Academies Press. *www.nextgenscience. org/next-generation-science-standards.*

Willard, T., ed. 2015. *The NSTA quick-reference guide to the NGSS: Elementary school.* Arlington, VA: NSTA Press.

Science and Engineering Practices

Picture-Perfect STEM Lessons incorporates all three dimensions of *A Framework for K–12 Science Education* (*Framework;* NRC 2012). However, one dimension stands out as key to developing a successful STEM classroom—the science and engineering practices. Our previous *Picture-Perfect Science* books emphasized scientific inquiry as a key component, but we think the science and engineering practices allow for a broader implementation of inquiry by expanding the inquiry process into the world of engineering. We like how Mariel Milano, a member of the *Next Generation Science Standards* (*NGSS;* NGSS Lead States 2013) writing team, describes the shift from inquiry to the practices. Milano (2013, pp. 15–16) says, "The perspective presented in the Framework is not one of replacing inquiry; rather it is one of expanding and enriching the teaching and learning of science and engineering. The practices are in some ways inquiry unpacked."

The practices go well beyond the facts of science to help students understand how scientific knowledge develops and how it can be applied to solving real-world problems through engineering. The *Framework* states, "Any education that focuses predominantly on the detailed products of scientific labor—the facts of science—without developing an understanding of how those facts were established or that ignores the many important applications of science in the world misrepresents science and marginalizes the importance of engineering" (NRC 2012, p. 43). Simply put, the practices embody two aspects: (1) how we know what we know in science and (2) how to apply what we know in science.

Engineering is receiving more attention than ever before in elementary school. It is sometimes referred to as the "stealth" profession because, although we use thousands of designed objects each day, we seldom think about the engineering practices involved in the creation and production of those objects. From the pen you write with, to the window you look through, to the cell phone in your pocket, all of these objects were most likely designed by engineers. For the first time ever, we are working with national standards that include engineering as a disciplinary core idea and the practices of engineers as a key component. Milano (2013, pp. 10–11) says, "The NGSS demonstrates a commitment to fully integrating engineering and technology into the structure of science education by elevating engineering design to the same level as scientific inquiry in classroom instruction."

In this chapter, we describe the scientific and engineering practices, show how they apply to all of the components of STEM, and explain how K–2 students can use these practices in the classroom. Focusing on practices rather than discrete skills or methods helps teachers and students understand that there is more than one approach to doing science and engineering. In other words, there is no set "scientific method" or "design process" that all scientists and engineers use in lockstep. Instead, scientists and engineers engage in a wide variety of practices as part of their work. The *Framework* identifies eight science and engineering practices that students should engage in throughout grades K–12. These practices are not meant to be a linear sequence of steps to be taken in a specific order; rather, they are to be used iteratively and in combination with each other (see p. 25 for a list of the practices).

All four components of STEM—science, technology, engineering, and mathematics—are included in these practices. Although in name the science and engineering practices seem to include only the *S* and *E* components of STEM, through reading these practices one can see that technology and mathematics are integral parts. The science and engineering practices are closely tied to science content but go well beyond knowing scientific facts; they are based on the idea that "students cannot understand scientific and engineering ideas without engaging in the practices of inquiry and the discourses by which such ideas are developed and refined" (NRC 2012, p. 218).

Science and Engineering Practices in the K–2 Classroom

So what do the science and engineering practices look like in the K–2 classroom? Table 5.1 shows the components of the science and engineering practices specific to grades K–2.

On the first page of each lesson in this book, the science and engineering practice(s) addressed are identified. Although several of the practices might be addressed in a particular lesson, we chose to emphasize two to four practices in each lesson. Next, we discuss a few examples of how these practices are incorporated into the K–2 lessons in this book.

In Chapter 12, "Get the Message," students learn about communication technologies and how they have improved over time. Then, they have the opportunity to use simple materials to design their own devices that use light or sound to communicate over a distance. This design activity incorporates practice 6, constructing explanations and designing solutions. Specifically, students use tools and materials to design and build a device that solves a specific problem. After students build their devices, they test them, improve their designs, and then compare them with others. Next, they rate their devices based on evidence of effectiveness, which provides experience with practice 7, engaging in argument from evidence. Students make a claim about the effectiveness of

TESTING COMMUNICATION DEVICES

the solution and support it with evidence. In this lesson, and in several others in this book, students learn that scientists and engineers must support their claims with evidence.

In Chapter 18, "Flight of the Pollinators," students engage in practice 4, analyzing and interpreting data, as they observe the structures of flowers and record their observations in words and pictures. Then, they use practice 8, obtaining, evaluating, and communicating information, as they read grade-appropriate texts and watch videos that explain how plants are pollinated and show the features of pollinators. Next, they apply what they have learned by building a simple model that mimics the function of an animal pollinating plants. This model building activity engages students in practice 2, developing and using models. In this case, the model is a three-dimensional physical model, but it is important that students understand that a model can take other forms, such as a diagram, drawing, physical replica, diorama, dramatization, storyboard, or even a mental model.

Table 5.1. Science and Engineering Practices for Grades K–2

Asking Questions and Defining Problems for Grades K–2

Asking questions and defining problems in K–2 builds on prior experiences and progresses to simple descriptive questions that can be tested.

- Ask questions based on observations to find more information about the natural and/or designed world(s).
- Ask and/or identify questions that can be answered by an investigation.
- Define a simple problem that can be solved through the development of a new or improved object or tool.

Developing and Using Models for Grades K–2

Modeling in K–2 builds on prior experiences and progresses to include using and developing models (i.e., diagram, drawing, physical replica, diorama, dramatization, or storyboard) that represent concrete events or design solutions.

- Distinguish between a model and the actual object, process, and/or events the model represents.
- Compare models to identify common features and differences.
- Develop and/or use a model to represent amounts, relationships, relative scales (bigger, smaller), and/or patterns in the natural and designed world(s).
- Develop a simple model based on evidence to represent a proposed object or tool.

Planning and Carrying Out Investigations for Grades K–2

Planning and carrying out investigations to answer questions or test solutions to problems in K–2 builds on prior experiences and progresses to simple investigations, based on fair tests, which provide data to support explanations or design solutions.

- With guidance, plan and conduct an investigation in collaboration with peers (for K).
- Plan and conduct an investigation collaboratively to produce data to serve as the basis for evidence to answer a question.
- Evaluate different ways of observing and/or measuring a phenomenon to determine which way can answer a question.
- Make observations (firsthand or from media) and/or measurements to collect data that can be used to make comparisons.
- Make observations (firsthand or from media) and/or measurements of a proposed object or tool or solution to determine if it solves a problem or meets a goal.
- Make predictions based on prior experiences.

Analyzing and Interpreting Data for Grades K–2

Analyzing data in K–2 builds on prior experiences and progresses to collecting, recording, and sharing observations.

- Record information (observations, thoughts, and ideas).
- Use and share pictures, drawings, and/or writings of observations.
- Use observations (firsthand or from media) to describe patterns and/or relationships in the natural and designed world(s) in order to answer scientific questions and solve problems.
- Compare predictions (based on prior experiences) to what occurred (observable events).
- Analyze data from tests of an object or tool to determine if it works as intended.

Using Mathematics and Computational Thinking for Grades K–2

Mathematical and computational thinking in K–2 builds on prior experience and progresses to recognizing that mathematics can be used to describe the natural and designed world(s).

- Use counting and numbers to identify and describe patterns in the natural and designed world(s).
- Describe, measure, and/or compare quantitative attributes of different objects and display the data using simple graphs.
- Use quantitative data to compare two alternative solutions to a problem.

Source: Willard 2015, pp. 88–89.

Table 5.1. *(continued)*

Constructing Explanations and Designing Solutions for Grades K–2

Constructing explanations and designing solutions in K–2 builds on prior experiences and progresses to the use of evidence and ideas in constructing evidence-based accounts of natural phenomena and designing solutions.

- Use information from observations (firsthand and from media) to construct an evidence-based account for natural phenomena.
- Use tools and/or materials to design and/or build a device that solves a specific problem or a solution to a specific problem.
- Generate and/or compare multiple solutions to a problem.

Engaging in Argument From Evidence for Grades K–2

Engaging in argument from evidence in K–2 builds on prior experiences and progresses to comparing ideas and representations about the natural and designed world(s).

- Identify arguments that are supported by evidence.
- Distinguish between explanations that account for all gathered evidence and those that do not.
- Analyze why some evidence is relevant to a scientific question and some is not.
- Distinguish between opinions and evidence in one's own explanations.
- Listen actively to arguments to indicate agreement or disagreement based on evidence, and/or to retell the main points of the argument.
- Construct an argument with evidence to support a claim.
- Make a claim about the effectiveness of an object, tool, or solution that is supported by relevant evidence.

Obtaining, Evaluating, and Communicating Information for Grades K–2

Obtaining, evaluating, and communicating information in K–2 builds on prior experiences and uses observations and texts to communicate new information.

- Read grade-appropriate texts and/or use media to obtain scientific and/or technical information to determine patterns in and/or evidence about the natural and designed world(s).
- Describe how specific images (e.g., a diagram showing how a machine works) support a scientific or engineering idea.
- Obtain information using various texts, text features (e.g., headings, tables of contents, glossaries, electronic menus, icons), and other media that will be useful in answering a scientific question and/or supporting a scientific claim.
- Communicate information or design ideas and/or solutions with others in oral and/or written forms using models, drawings, writing, or numbers that provide detail about scientific ideas, practices, and/or design ideas.

Source: Willard 2015, pp. 88–89.

OBSERVING FLOWER STRUCTURES

USING GOOGLE EARTH

We do not think that every STEM lesson needs to include a specific design challenge. In some lessons in this book, students can engage in the science and engineering practices by using technologies that apply scientific concepts and developing an understanding of how the technologies work. For example, in Chapter 20, "Our Blue Planet," students engage in practice 8, obtaining, evaluating, and communicating information, as they use the Google Earth tool to explore Earth's water. Then, they learn how satellite technology allows us to capture images of our planet. Students are also involved in practice 2, developing and using models, as they begin to realize that maps are considered models that can be used to learn more about our planet. So although students are not designing a solution to a problem, they are learning about a technology that has been developed to help us make models of our planet, and they are using that technology to learn more about the Earth.

The Differences Between Science and Engineering

Science and engineering are closely related and interdependent. As stated in the *Framework,* "It is impossible to do engineering today without applying science in the process and, in many areas of science, designing and building new experiments requires scientists to engage in some engineering practices" (NRC 2012, p. 32). However, it is helpful to understand the difference between what scientists do and what engineers do. You can begin to see a key difference between science and engineering by the way practice 1 is written: "Asking questions (for science) and defining problems (for engineering)." Science begins with a question and engineering begins with a problem. The rest of the practices follow accordingly. Table 5.2 (p. 48) shows how the eight science and engineering practices apply differently to the fields of science and engineering.

Some lessons in this book emphasize the engineering side of the practices. For example, in Chapter 6, "The Handiest Things," students are deeply immersed in the practices of engineers as they design solutions to everyday problems. In Chapter 7, "Build It!," students learn about architecture and apply engineering practices to build a model of a famous building. These lessons not only give students an awareness of the work of engineers but also provide them with opportunities to think like

Table 5.2. Science Practices and Engineering Practices

Science Practices	Engineering Practices
1. **Asking questions**	1. **Defining problems**
2. **Developing and using models** to understand natural phenomena	2. **Developing and using models** to analyze systems and test solutions
3. **Planning and carrying out investigations** to answer a question about the natural world	3. **Planning and carrying out investigations** to collect data to specify design criteria or test a solution
4. **Analyzing and interpreting data** from an investigation to identify patterns and derive meaning	4. **Analyzing and interpreting data** from an investigation to compare different solutions to see which best solves the problem
5. **Using mathematics and computational thinking** to represent variables and their relationships and to predict natural phenomena	5. **Using mathematics and computational thinking** to calculate and simulate different designs to see which are best
6. **Constructing explanations** of natural phenomena	6. **Designing solutions** to solve problems
7. **Engaging in argument from evidence** to evaluate different lines of reasoning in searching for an explanation of a natural phenomenon	7. **Engaging in argument from evidence,** using a systematic method to find the best solution for a problem
8. **Obtaining, evaluating, and communicating information** by listing and reading others' ideas critically and communicating one's own ideas clearly	8. **Obtaining, evaluating, and communicating information** to learn how others have solved a problem and to present persuasive arguments in favor of a given solution

Source: Adapted from Milano 2013.

Note: A more detailed version of this table can be found on pages 50–53 in *A Framework for K–12 Science Education* (NRC 2012).

engineers. However, lessons such as Chapter 19, "A Birthday Is No Ordinary Day," and Chapter 13, "Science Mysteries," focus more on the science side of the practices: Students are carrying out investigations, identifying patterns in the natural world, and constructing explanations of natural phenomena.

In most of the lessons, however, science and engineering are closely tied together. For example, in Chapter 9, "Feel the Heat," students investigate how the Sun warms different surfaces on Earth and then design and build a structure that will reduce the warming effect of sunlight in an area. In Chapter 17, "Pillbots," students directly observe the structures and behaviors of pill bugs and apply their learning to design a robot that mimics pill bug structures and behaviors. In both of these lessons, scientific understanding is essential to the design challenge. These experiences can help students see the interdependent relationship between science and engineering.

The Engineering Design Process

There are many approaches to the engineering design process, but all of them follow the same basic pattern—a series of steps completed iteratively to solve a problem. In these lessons, we use the simple, three-component model described in the *NGSS* as our framework (see Figure 5.1).

The *NGSS* make it clear that these component ideas do not always follow in order and that "at any stage a problem solver can redefine the problem or generate new solutions to replace an idea that is just not working out" (NGSS Lead States 2013, Appendix I).

Figure 5.1. Engineering Design in K–2

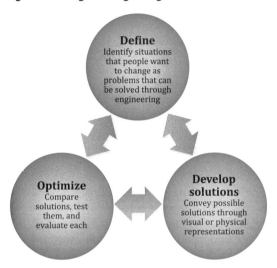

Source: NGSS Lead States 2013, Appendix I.

The *NGSS* also provide the following explanation of engineering design in K–2:

Engineering design in the earliest grades introduces students to "problems" as situations that people want to change. They can use tools and materials to solve simple problems, use different representations to convey solutions, and compare different solutions to a problem and determine which is best. Students in all grade levels are not expected to come up with original solutions, although original solutions are always welcome. Emphasis is on thinking through the needs or goals that need to be met and on which solutions best meet those needs and goals. (NGSS Lead States 2013, Appendix I)

Picture-Perfect STEM Lessons integrates the three component ideas of engineering throughout the book. Students are provided with opportunities to define problems, develop solutions, and optimize solutions. For example, in Chapter 8, "Robots Everywhere," students learn how various types of robots are used every day to make our lives better. Next, they define a problem they have that

a robot could solve, design a robot to solve that problem, and express their designs through words and pictures. Although students are not designing and building actual robots, they are learning about how technologies are designed to solve problems. In Chapter 10, "Move It!," students learn about force and motion, design a way to get a toy dog and toy car into a plastic-cup "dog house," and then compare, test, and optimize their designs.

A DESIGN CHALLENGE

Student-Directed Exploration With the Practices

In *Picture-Perfect STEM Lessons,* students are engaged in science and engineering practices in a guided manner throughout the lessons. At the end of each lesson, a "For Further Exploration" box is provided to help you encourage your students to use the science and engineering practices in a more student-directed format. This box lists questions and challenges related to the lesson that students may select to research, investigate, or innovate. Students may also use the questions as examples to help them generate their own questions. After selecting one of the questions in the box or formulating their own questions, students can individually or collaboratively make predictions, design investigations or surveys to test their predictions, collect evidence, devise explanations, design solutions, or examine related resources. They can communicate their findings through a science notebook, during a poster session or gallery walk, or by producing a media project.

For example, in Chapter 9, "Feel the Heat," students investigate how the Sun heats a variety of surfaces and are then challenged to design a shade structure to keep an ice cube from melting quickly. After this guided investigation, they can research information about how the Sun compares with other stars, plan and carry out their own investigations to find out which objects heat up fastest in the Sun, and apply what they have learned to design a drink holder to keep a drink cold on a sunny day. Students can choose a question from the box or brainstorm some questions of their own. We believe that once students have participated in the guided format of *Picture-Perfect STEM Lessons,* they are more likely to be able to apply the science and engineering practices on their own. The "For Further Exploration" box can help you provide those opportunities.

On the following pages, we have provided some "think sheets" to guide students as they approach the "For Further Exploration" questions (see pp. 51–54). The Innovation Think Sheet (pp. 53–54) is based on the design process offered by PBS's *Design Squad Global* (see Figure 5.3, p. 55). The *Design Squad Global* website suggests that "when you see the design process in action, you'll notice that it's rarely the smooth succession of steps that the diagram implies. The steps often overlap and blur, and their order is sometimes reversed— it's a creative, fluid way of working that has to be adapted to each individual situation. As you guide kids through the design process, you'll want to be flexible and receptive to the different approaches your kids may try" (PBS 2016).

We suggest that students share the results of their explorations with each other through a poster session. Scientists, engineers, and researchers routinely hold poster sessions to communicate their findings. Here are some suggestions for poster sessions:

- Posters should include a title, the researchers' names, a brief description of the investigation, and a summary of the main findings.

A GALLERY WALK

- Observations, data tables, and/or graphs should be included as evidence to justify conclusions.
- The print should be large enough that people can read it from a distance.
- Students should have the opportunity to present their posters to the class.
- The audience in a poster session should examine the evidence, ask thoughtful questions, identify faulty reasoning, and suggest alternative explanations to presenters in a polite, respectful manner.

Poster sessions not only mirror the work of real scientists but also provide excellent opportunities for authentic assessment. Another way to share students' posters is during a gallery walk. In a gallery walk, students put their posters on display for their classmates to view and critique. Students taking the gallery walk use sticky notes to post suggestions, questions, and praise directly on their classmates' posters. Writing on sticky notes encourages interaction, and the comments provide immediate feedback for the "exhibitors." Here are some guidelines for a gallery walk:

- All necessary information about the investigation should be included on the poster because students will not be giving an oral presentation.
- Like a visit to an art gallery, the gallery walk should be done quietly. Students should be respectful of their classmates' poster displays.
- Students should have the opportunity to read the comments about their own posters and make changes if necessary.

Name: _____   Date: _____

Research Think Sheet

1. My question: _____

2. My prediction: _____

3. How I will find information on the question:

_____

_____

_____

_____

4. My answer:

_____

_____

_____

_____

_____

5. My sources:

_____

_____

_____

_____

_____

_____

Name: _____   Date: _____

Investigation Think Sheet

1. My question: _____

2. My prediction: _____

3. My procedure and materials: _____

_____

_____

_____

4. My data (observations, measurements, graphs, etc.):

_____

5. My conclusion:

_____

_____

_____

Name: _____   Date: _____

Innovation Think Sheet

What is the problem or need?

_____

_____

Brainstorm! What are some ways to solve the problem or meet the need?

_____

_____

_____

Design it! Sketch your best design idea:

Build it! Sketch your solution:

Test it! How well did it solve the problem or meet the need?

_____

_____

_____

Redesign it! What can you change to improve your design?

_____

_____

Share it! Describe your final solution in words and pictures:

_____

_____

_____

Figure 5.3. Design Process From Design Squad Global

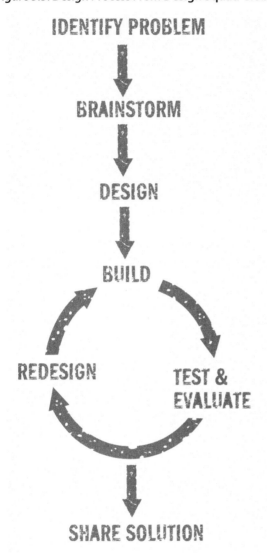

Source: PBS 2016.

Implementing the guided lessons in this book along with the "For Further Exploration" suggestions at the end of each lesson provides a framework for moving from teacher-guided to self-directed learning.

In summary, *Picture-Perfect STEM Lessons* engages students in these scientific and engineering practices to capture their interest, motivate their continued study, and above all instill in them a sense of wonder about the natural and designed world. The end result is that by actually doing science and engineering rather than merely learning about it, students will recognize that the work of scientists and engineers is creative and rewarding and deeply impacts their world.

References

Milano, M. 2013. The *Next Generation Science Standards* and engineering for young learners: Beyond bridges and egg drops. *Science and Children* 51 (2): 10–16.

National Research Council (NRC). 2012. *A framework for K–12 science education: Practices, crosscutting concepts, and core ideas.* Washington, DC: National Academies Press.

NGSS Lead States. 2013. *Next Generation Science Standards: For states, by states.* Washington, DC: National Academies Press. *www.nextgenscience. org/next-generation-science-standards.*

PBS. 2016. Design squad global. Parents and educators: Online workshop. *http://pbskids.org/designsquad/ parentseducators/workshop/process.html.*

Willard, T., ed. 2015. *The NSTA quick-reference guide to the NGSS: Elementary school.* Arlington, VA: NSTA Press.

The Handiest Things

Description

Students explore a variety of technologies—from chopsticks to calculators—that solve problems in our everyday lives. They learn that all technologies have various parts that work together to solve a problem, and then they brainstorm some new parts to improve an invention they use every day—a backpack.

Suggested Grade Levels: K–2

LESSON OBJECTIVES Connecting to the *Framework*		
Science and Engineering Practices	**Disciplinary Core Ideas**	**Crosscutting Concept**
Asking Questions and Defining Problems Constructing Explanations and Designing Solutions	**ETS1.A:** Defining and Delimiting Engineering Problems **ETS1.B:** Developing Possible Solutions **ETS2.B:** Influence of Engineering, Technology, and Science on Society and the Natural World	Structure and Function

Featured Picture Books

TITLE: ***The Handiest Things in the World***
AUTHOR: **Andrew Clements**
PHOTOGRAPHER: **Raquel Jaramillo**
PUBLISHER: **Atheneum Books for Young Readers**
YEAR: **2010**
GENRE: **Non-Narrative Information**
SUMMARY: *Simple rhyme and vivid photographs portray some of the everyday things we use to make life easier, including a dog leash, calculator, watering can, and umbrella. Each photograph on the left-hand page shows a child using his or her hands to do a task, while on the right-hand page is a photo of a "handy" invention completing the same task more efficiently.*

TITLE: ***Engineering in Our Everyday Lives***
AUTHOR: **Reagan Miller**
PUBLISHER: **Crabtree Publishing**
YEAR: **2014**
GENRE: **Non-Narrative Information**
SUMMARY: *Simple text and photographs explain that engineers design technologies to solve problems and try to improve existing technologies.*

Time Needed

This lesson will take several class periods. Suggested scheduling is as follows:

Day 1: Engage with *The Handiest Things in the World* Read-Aloud and **Explore** with One Handy Thing

Day 2: Explain with *Engineering in Our Everyday Lives* Read-Aloud and the Handiest Things in the Classroom

Day 3: Elaborate and **Evaluate** with Build a Better Backpack

Materials

- The Handiest Things Picture Cards (1 precut set per group of 3–4 students)
- 2 umbrellas—1 to demonstrate and 1 to take apart (both for teacher use only)
- Examples of some of the inventions featured in *The Handiest Things in the World*, such as the following:
  - Chopsticks
  - Dog leash
  - Calculator
  - Butterfly net
  - Watering can
  - Broom and dustpan
  - Comb
  - Paper fan
  - Earmuffs

SAFETY
- Remind students to use caution when working with chopsticks and to keep the chopsticks away from their eyes.
- Have children wear eye protection if appropriate.

Student Pages

- One Handy Thing
- Build a Better Backpack
- STEM at Home

Background for Teachers

The study of engineering is being emphasized more than ever before in elementary school. Engineering is sometimes referred to as the "stealth" profession because, although we use countless designed objects each day, we seldom think about the engineering practices involved in the creation and production of these objects. From the pen you write with, to the window you look through, to the cell phone in your pocket, many commonplace objects were designed by engineers.

This lesson not only raises awareness of the work of engineers, but also gives students the opportunity to think like engineers. Students are introduced to the term *technology,* which is anything made by people that meets a need or solves a problem. Then, they identify various technologies in books and in the classroom. They learn how technologies are made of parts that all work together to solve a problem. By identifying parts and purposes, students begin to learn about the crosscutting concept of structure and function. Students also learn that engineers do not just invent new technologies; they also improve on existing technologies. Finally, students come up with some ways to improve a technology they use every day, a backpack.

engage

The Handiest Things in the World Read-Aloud

Connecting to the Common Core
Reading: Informational Text
CRAFT AND STRUCTURE: K.5, 1.5, 2.5

Inferring

Show students the cover of *The Handiest Things in the World* and introduce the author, Andrew Clements, and the photographer, Raquel Jaramillo. *Ask*

? What do you think this book is about? (Answers will vary.)

Show students the back cover of the book as well as the front and back inside covers. They should notice all of the photographs of children's hands and be able to conclude that the book has something to do with hands.

INFERRING

Connecting to the Common Core
Reading: Informational Text
KEY IDEAS AND DETAILS: K.1, 1.1, 2.1

Give each group of three to four students a precut set of the Handiest Things Picture Cards. Tell students that all of these items appear in the book and that as you read the book aloud, you would like them to guess which object you are reading about. For each two-page spread, hide the photo as you read the rhyme and have students infer from the rhyme which of the objects the book is describing. When they think they know which one it is, they should hold that card up in the air. After students have guessed, reveal the illustration.

Connecting to the Common Core
Reading: Informational Text
CRAFT AND STRUCTURE: 2.6

Synthesizing

After reading, *ask*

? Why do you think the author titled this book *The Handiest Things in the World*? (The book features some handy things.)

Next, model how you can find out more information about a book and its author by reading the book jacket. Open to the front jacket flap and read it aloud: "Eight fingers. Two thumbs. Two flat palms. And all those knuckles. But our hands are so much more than that. They were once the first pair of earmuffs, a primitive visor, and a convenient set of chopsticks. The work done by hands centuries and centuries ago paved the way for many of our favorite and most useful tools. The always-clever Andrew Clements reminds us all that the mother of much invention is right at our fingertips."

Then, *ask*

? Now, why do you think the author decided to call the book *The Handiest Things in the World*? (Students should realize that all of the "handy things" in the book were first done with hands long ago and now they are done with tools.)

Revisit each two-page spread in the book. Show how the child on the left-hand page is using his or her hands to do a task, and the child on the right-hand page is using a tool to do the same task. For each page, discuss how the tool is better than using your hands (e.g., It would be hard to hold your dog with your hands, but a leash makes it easy for you to run and play together. You can't hold much water in your hands, but a watering can will hold a whole lot more.)

explore

One Handy Thing

Show students an umbrella, which is one of the objects featured in *The Handiest Things in the World*. (In advance, you may want to disassemble another umbrella to more clearly show students the parts). *Ask*

? What is an umbrella used for? (To keep you dry in the rain.)

OBSERVING AN UMBRELLA

**T-Chart**

Then, create a T-chart on the board with *Part* written on the left-hand side and *Purpose* on the right. *Ask*

? Look closely at the umbrella. What parts do you see? (handle, fabric, frame, button, strap, etc.)

On the left-hand side of the chart, list the umbrella parts that they observe. It is not important that they know the technical name of each part; a general term will be sufficient for this activity. Then, have students come up with a purpose for each part, and write that purpose on the right-hand side.

Example:

UMBRELLA

Part	Purpose
Handle	To hold it
Frame	To hold the fabric open
Fabric	To block the rain
Button	To open the umbrella
Fastener	To keep the umbrella closed

After you have filled in the T-chart, *ask*

? How do all of these parts work together to solve one problem? (All of the parts serve certain purposes but work together to keep someone from getting wet in the rain.)

Connecting to the Common Core
Writing
RESEARCH TO BUILD AND PRESENT KNOWLEDGE: K.8, 1.8, 2.8

Next, give each student the One Handy Thing student page, and give each group of three to four students one of the objects featured in *The Handiest Things in the World* (or a picture card of the object). Use objects that have multiple parts (e.g., dog leash, calculator, watering can, small broom and dustpan, baseball cap, comb, earmuffs). On the student page, they will draw a picture of their group's object with the parts labeled, fill out the part and purpose sections of the T-chart, identify the problem the object solves, and write about what life would be like without the object. Point out that even something as simple as a comb has parts (handle and tines) that work together to solve a problem—messy hair. When students are finished, discuss the various parts they labeled and how, just like with the umbrella, all of the parts work together to solve a problem.

Engineering in Our Everyday Lives Read-Aloud

Connecting to the Common Core
Language
VOCABULARY ACQUISITION AND USE: K.6, 1.6, 2.6

Questioning

Ask

? Where did all of the handy things from *The Handiest Things in the World* come from? (a store)

? Where do you think a store gets them? (from a factory)

? Where might a factory get the designs to make them? (Allow them to share their ideas.)

Show students the cover of *Engineering in Our Everyday Lives*. Tell students that this book is about engineers, people who design the handy things that we use everyday. Read the book aloud, pausing at pages 6–7 of the book, which explain that objects

designed by engineers to solve problems are called *technologies*.

After reading page 7, pause to ask students the questions on the inset:

? Which pictures show technologies? (soccer ball, backpack)

? Which pictures show things that are natural? (a bird's nest, lightning)

Continue reading through page 11, pausing to read the questions on the insets and allowing students to answer.

The Handiest Things in the Classroom

After reading page 11, refer to *The Handiest Things in the World* and explain that all of the objects in that book, including the umbrella, are *technologies*—things that have been designed to solve a problem. Objects that are not designed by humans are called *natural objects*.

LOOKING FOR TECHNOLOGIES IN OUR CLASSROOM

Next, give students a piece of paper, a pencil, and a clipboard. Ask them to walk around the room silently and write or draw a list of as many technologies as they can. Give them a few minutes to walk around and make their lists. You may want to play a song while they are making their lists and have them return to their seats when the song is over.

Students will quickly realize that almost everything in the room is a technology—from the chair they are sitting in, to pencils they use, to the clothes they are wearing. Have students share some items from their lists. For each technology, discuss what problem it was designed to solve.

Example:

Technology	Problem
Pencil sharpener	Pencil dull or broken
Chair	Legs tired
Desk	Need a place to work and write
Clock	Need to know what time it is
Computer	Need to store and locate data or information

Challenge students to find something that is not a technology, such as a classroom pet, plant, apple, rock, or even themselves! Students will likely notice that the technologies in the classroom greatly outnumber the natural objects.

Next, explain that technologies, such as the umbrella they examined in the explore section of the lesson, are made of parts. Engineers often refer to these parts as *structures* and the purpose of each part as its *function*. Refer to the T-chart you made in the explore phase and add the words *structure* and *function* above the appropriate columns. Next, have students add the words *structure* and *function* to the T-chart on the One Handy Thing student page. You may want to explain that living things also have structures and functions and that they will be exploring that concept in other lessons.

elaborate & evaluate

Build a Better Backpack

Connecting to the Common Core
Reading: Informational Text
KEY IDEAS AND DETAILS: K.1, 1.1, 2.1

Questioning

Read aloud pages 12–15 in *Engineering in Our Everyday Lives,* which explains, "Engineers not only create new technologies, they also improve them, or make the ones we have better." Show students the example of the Rain-or-Shine Rider on page 15. *Ask*

? What structure or part was added to improve the bicycle? (an umbrella)

? What is the function or purpose of that new structure? (keeps you dry in the rain or gives shade in the sunshine)

? How is the Rain-or-Shine Rider better than the original technology (the bicycle)? (You can ride it in any kind of weather.)

Read the section title "Your Turn!" and then tell students that they are going to have the opportunity to improve a technology they probably use every day—their backpacks. *Ask*

? What problem does a backpack solve? (School supplies are hard to carry; your hands are full.)

? How did people carry things before backpacks? (carried things in their hands, used a duffel bag)

You may want to show students the illustrations from NPR Ed's *Tools of the Trade* series about the backpack titled "From 'Book Strap' to 'Burrito': A History of the School Backpack" (see "Website" section) for some background and inspiration. Then, give each group of three to four students a backpack to observe. Ask students to examine the backpack, identify as many parts as they can, and discuss each part and its purpose. Students will notice that some backpacks have different parts than others, but all backpacks have some parts in common, such as straps, zippers, pockets, and so on.

Example:

BACKPACK

Structure (Part)	Function (Purpose)
Straps	To hold it on your back
Zipper	To keep things inside and take them out
Mesh side pocket	To hold a water bottle
Small outside zipper pocket	To hold small items

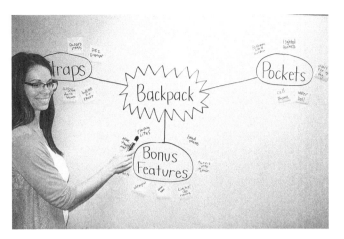

BUILD A BETTER BACKPACK WORD WEB

 ## Word Web

Next, students can brainstorm parts they could add to the backpack to improve it. Make a word web with the target word *Backpack* in the middle, and organize student ideas in circles that surround the target word. You may want to create categories for their suggestions, such as straps, pockets, bonus features, and so on. *Ask* guiding questions, such as the following:

? What are some problems you have with your backpack? What parts could you add to solve those problems?

? What part could you add to make it easier to carry?

? Is there something you would like to carry in it that needs a special place? What part could you add to carry it?

? What part or material could you add to make your backpack more fun or stylish?

Connecting to the Common Core
Writing
TEXT TYPES AND PURPOSES: K.2, 1.2, 2.2

 ### Writing

Give each student a copy of the Build a Better Backpack student page. Tell them that the Better Backpack Company would like them to improve on the company's standard backpack design, which is pictured on the student page. Have students brainstorm about how they would make this backpack better. They will give the new and improved backpack a catchy name, draw any new parts on the line drawing of the backpack, list each new structure (part) in the T-chart along with its function (purpose), and then explain why their design is better than the original backpack. Students can also create a song, rap, or advertisement to help "sell" their backpacks to consumers.

When students have completed their designs, explain that engineers have to be good communicators. An important part of an engineer's job is speaking or writing clearly to share ideas with peers and with companies or individuals who will be buying or using the technologies they design. Have students share their better backpack drawings

A BETTER BACKPACK

with the class. Encourage them to share any songs or advertisements they created as well.

STEM at Home

Have students complete the "I learned that …" and "My favorite part of the lesson was …" portions of the STEM at Home student page as a reflection on their learning. They may choose to do the following at-home activity with an adult helper and share their results with the class. If students do not have access to the internet or these materials at home, you may choose to have them complete this activity at school.

"At home, we can watch a short video called 'Preventing Back Pain From Backpacks' about the problems backpacks can cause."

Search "Inside Science Preventing Back Pain" to find the Inside Science video at https://www.insidescience.org/content/preventing-back-pain-backpacks/812.

"After we watch the video together, we can figure out if my backpack is too heavy! We will need a bathroom scale and a calculator for this part."

For Further Exploration

This section is provided to help you encourage your students to use the science and engineering practices in a more student-directed format. This box lists questions and challenges related to the lesson that students may select to research, investigate, or innovate. Students may also use the questions as examples to help them generate their own questions. After selecting one of the questions in the box or formulating their own questions, students can individually or collaboratively make predictions, design investigations or surveys to test their predictions, collect evidence, devise explanations, design solutions, or examine related resources. They can communicate their findings through a science notebook, at a poster session or gallery walk, or by producing a media project.

Research

Have students brainstorm researchable questions:

? Who invented the backpack?

? How are backpacks made?

? What are some of the latest improvements to the umbrella?

Investigate

Have students brainstorm testable questions to be solved through science or math:

? Which materials are the best for building a waterproof backpack?

? Which type of thread is the strongest (i.e., can support the most weight) for using in a backpack?

? What is the average weight of the backpacks in our class?

Innovate

Have students brainstorm problems to be solved through engineering:

? How could a pencil be improved?

? How could the classroom pencil sharpener be soundproofed or relocated so that the noise is less distracting?

? How could an umbrella be improved?

Website

"From 'Book Strap' to 'Burrito': A History of the School Backpack"
www.npr.org/sections/ed/2015/11/02/445339503/from-book-strap-to-burrito-a-history-of-the-school-backpack

More Books to Read

Beaty, A. 2013. *Rosie Revere, engineer.* New York: Harry N. Abrams.
Summary: Young Rosie dreams of being an engineer. Alone in her room at night, she constructs great inventions from odds and ends. Afraid of failure, Rosie hides her creations under her bed until a fateful visit from her great-great-aunt Rose, who shows her that a first flop isn't something to fear—it's something to celebrate.

Johnson, R. 2014. *How engineers find solutions.* New York: Crabtree Publishing.
Summary: Part of the *Engineering Up Close* series, this book uses simple text and photographs to describe the kinds of problems engineers solve and outlines the process they use to solve them. Other books in this series include *Engineers Build Models* by Reagan Miller and *Engineers Solve Problems* by Reagan Miller and Crystal Sikkens.

Novak, P. O. 2009. *Engineering the ABCs: How engineers shape our world.* Northville, MI: Ferne Press.
Summary: This engineering ABC book answers questions about how everyday things work and how engineering relates to so many parts of a child's daily life.

Picture Cards

Crayon

Dog leash

Earmuffs

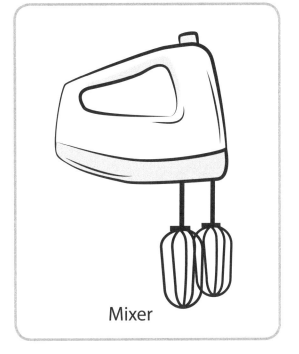

Mixer

Picture Cards

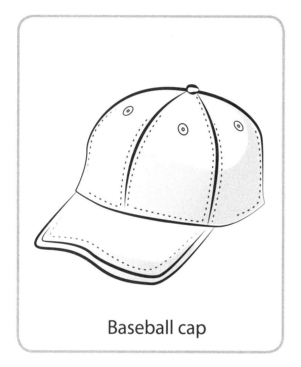

Baseball cap

Calculator

Watering can

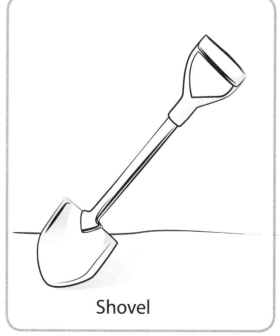

Shovel

National Science Teachers Association

Picture Cards

Broom

Drumsticks

Paper fan

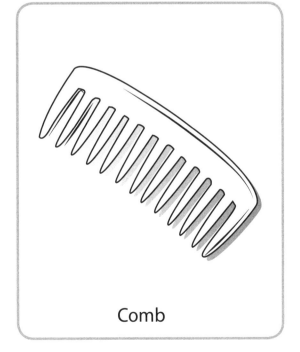

Comb

Picture Cards

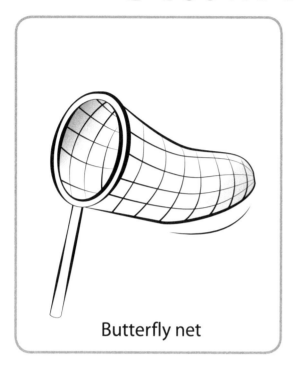

Butterfly net

Meterstick

Umbrella

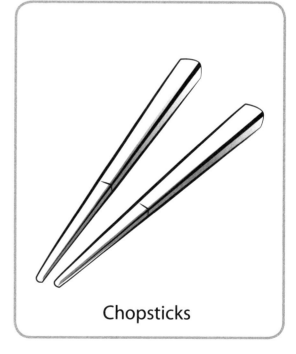

Chopsticks

Name: _____

One Handy Thing

1. Name of object: _____

2. Labeled sketch of object:

3. What are the object's parts and their purposes?

Part	Purpose

4. What problem does this handy thing solve? _____

_____

_____

5. What would life be like without it? _____

_____

_____

Name: _____

Build a Better Backpack

1. Name of your improved backpack: _____

2. Draw and label the new structures on the picture below.

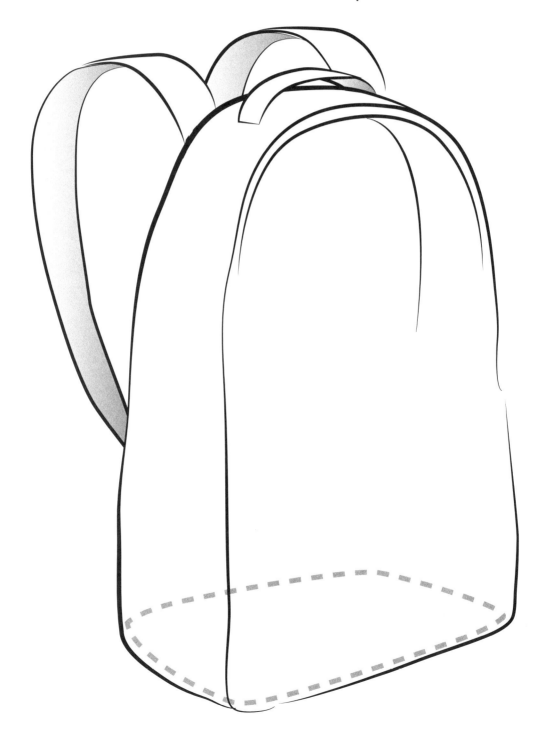

3. What does each new structure do? Fill out the T-chart below.

Structure	Function

4. How is your improved backpack better than the original?

_____

_____

_____

_____

_____

_____

5. Create a song, rap, or advertisement to sell your new and improved backpack!

Name: _____

STEM at Home

Dear _____,

At school, we have been learning that engineers design many of the things we use in our daily lives. These things are called **technologies.**

I learned that: _____

_____

My favorite part of the lesson was: _____

_____

At home, we can watch a short video called "Preventing Back Pain From Backpacks" about the problems backpacks can cause.

Search "Inside Science Preventing Back Pain" to find the Inside Science video at *www.insidescience.org/content/preventing-back-pain-backpacks/812.*

After we watch the video together, we can figure out if my backpack is too heavy! We will need a bathroom scale and a calculator for this part.

_____ lbs. = weight of my full backpack

_____ lbs. = my weight

_____ = 10% of my weight (my weight x .10)

Conclusion: Is my full backpack heavier than 10% of my weight?

☐ Yes   ☐ No

If yes, my backpack is too heavy!

What I can do to help make my backpack safer for me to carry:

_____

_____

_____

Build It!

Description

Children love to build. In this lesson, they use their creativity to build structures out of everyday materials. Next, they are introduced to a variety of iconic buildings and learn about the architects who designed them. Finally, students design and build architectural models of some of these famous structures.

Suggested Grade Levels: K–2

LESSON OBJECTIVES Connecting to the *Framework*		
Science and Engineering Practices	**Disciplinary Core Ideas**	**Crosscutting Concept**
Asking Questions and Defining Problems Developing and Using Models	**PS1.A:** Structure and Properties of Matter **ETS1.B:** Developing Possible Solutions **ETS2.B:** Influence of Engineering, Technology, and Science on Society and the Natural World	Structure and Function

Featured Picture Books

TITLE: *Iggy Peck, Architect*
AUTHOR: **Andrea Beaty**
ILLUSTRATOR: **David Roberts**
PUBLISHER: **Abrams**
YEAR: **2007**
GENRE: **Story**
SUMMARY: *Iggy Peck spends every waking hour building things, until second grade, when his teacher forbids it. He finally wins her over by using his skills to save the day on his class field trip.*

TITLE: *Dreaming Up: A Celebration of Building*
AUTHOR: **Christy Hale**
ILLUSTRATOR: **Christy Hale**
PUBLISHER: **Lee & Low Books**
YEAR: **2012**
GENRE: **Non-Narrative Information**
SUMMARY: *This book is a unique celebration of children's playtime explorations and the surprising ways childhood experiences find expression in the dreams and works of innovative architects. Each spread features illustrations of children building various structures as they play paired with a photograph of an actual building that uses the same basic ideas and principles. Information on each featured building and its architect is contained in the end matter.*

Time Needed

This lesson will take several class periods. Suggested scheduling is as follows:

Day 1: **Engage** with *Iggy Peck, Architect* Read-Aloud and **Explore** with Free Build

Day 2: **Explain** with *Dreaming Up* Read-Aloud and Famous Buildings and Structures Video

Day 3: **Elaborate** with Iggy's Models and Architecture Journal

Day 4 and beyond: **Evaluate** with Build It! and Architecture Expo

Materials

For Free Build (per group of 4–6 students)

Each group receives a different set of building materials modeled after the book *Dreaming Up,* such as the following:

- Group 1: Small paper or plastic cups and masking tape
- Group 2: Empty tissue or other small boxes, masking tape, and scissors
- Group 3: Playing cards and masking tape
- Group 4: Toothpicks and packing peanuts
- Group 5: Cardboard tubes, brown paper grocery or lunch bags, masking tape, and scissors
- Group 6: Craft sticks, index cards, and masking tape

SAFETY
- Use caution with scissors to avoid puncturing skin or eyes.
- Use eye protection when working with craft sticks.

For Iggy's Models

- Images of the Gateway Arch, Golden Gate Bridge, Great Sphinx of Giza, Hōryū-ji Temple, Leaning Tower of Pisa, and Neuschwanstein Castle

For Build It!

- Bins of the supplies used in the Free Build activity (above)

Student Pages

- Architecture Journal
- STEM at Home

Background for Teachers

In this lesson, students are introduced to the fascinating world of architecture, a discipline that combines science, engineering, and art in the design of buildings. A Roman architect and engineer named Vitruvius, who lived in the first century BC, asserted that there were three principles of good architecture:

- Durability—It should be made of the right materials to stand up, be safe, and remain in good condition.
- Utility—It should be useful and function well for the people using it.

- Beauty—It should delight people and raise their spirits.

Although these principles originated thousands of years ago, they still hold true today. To achieve these goals, architects plan the overall appearance of buildings, while ensuring that they are safe, functional, and economical. Sketches, plans, elevation drawings, and architectural models are important tools in communicating an architect's ideas.

The *Framework* suggests that throughout K–12, students have opportunities to design and use models. In the early grades, these models progress from making diagrams and replicas to developing models to represent a new object or tool. This lesson uses models in the context of architecture. The lesson begins with a "free build" activity where students work with building materials, such as cups, craft sticks, boxes, and cardboard tubes, to make them into something new. Young children need time to "tinker" with a variety of materials to construct their own understandings of how small pieces can be built into objects and structures and how objects and structures can be disassembled into smaller pieces.

Next, students are exposed to some iconic buildings from a range of historical periods, learn about famous architects and their inspirations, and reuse some of the materials they worked with during the explore phase to create sketches and design architectural models of buildings. An architectural model is a type of scale model—a physical representation of a structure—that is used to study aspects of architectural design or to communicate design ideas. Architects construct these models using a variety of materials, including blocks, paper, and wood, just as the students do in the elaborate phase of the lesson. This activity provides opportunities for students to create drawings and physical models just as real architects do.

engage

Iggy Peck, Architect Read-Aloud

 **Inferring**

Show students the cover of *Iggy Peck, Architect* and introduce the author, Andrea Beaty, and the illustrator, David Roberts. *Ask*

? From looking at the cover and title, what do you think this book is about?

? What do you think an architect does? (Students may know that architects are involved in designing buildings.)

> Connecting to the Common Core
> **Reading: Literature**
> KEY IDEAS AND DETAILS: K.1, 1.1, 2.1

 **Questioning**

Read the book aloud. Then, *ask*

? What kinds of materials did Iggy Peck use to build the structures in the book? (chalk, pancakes, apples, dirt, etc.)

? How did Iggy's teacher feel about his passion for building? (She did not like it.) What evidence from the text makes you think that? (She would not allow him to build at school.)

? What happened to his teacher that made her dislike architecture? (She got lost on an architect's tour and was stuck in an elevator with a French circus troupe.)

? How did Iggy finally win his teacher over? (He used his building expertise to build a bridge to rescue the class.)

Making Connections: Text to Self

Ask

? Do you like to build things like the character Iggy Peck?

? What materials have you used to build something? (Have students share with a partner.)

Tell students that the author, Andrea Beaty, was inspired to write this book because her son had a passion for building when he was young. He would build with anything he could get his hands on; he built towers out of soup cans from their pantry and houses out of jelly packets at restaurants.

explore

Free Build

Tell students that they are going to have the opportunity to be like Iggy Peck and use their imaginations and some everyday materials to create a structure. Divide students into groups of three to six, and explain that each group will receive different supplies for building. Each student will build his or her own structure, but the group will share the supplies. Afterward, students will have a chance to share their structures. Give each group a container with the supplies listed in the "Materials" section (p. 78). Set a time limit and let them build!

FREE BUILD

When students are finished, have them clean up their supplies and display their structures on their tables or desks. Visit each group and observe the structures. Point out that there was no right or wrong way to build these structures. Each person used his or her imagination and had a different vision for how to build the structures. A great variety of objects can be built from a small set of pieces.

You may want to set up an area to display each structure or take photographs of each one and hang them in the classroom to create a class display. You can refer to this display during the activities in the explain phase of the lesson.

explain

Dreaming Up Read-Aloud

Determining Importance

Show students the cover of *Dreaming Up: A Celebration of Building* and introduce Christy Hale, the author and illustrator of this book. Tell students that the supplies that were used in the free build activity were all inspired by this book. As you read the book aloud, have students signal (touch their noses) when you come to a page where the illustration on the left-hand side of each two-page spread shows the supplies students used, and compare the structure pictured with the structures they made. Explain that these different structures are examples of how a great variety of objects can be made from a small set of pieces.

> Connecting to the Common Core
> **Mathematics**
> GEOMETRY: K.G.2
> **Reading: Informational Text**
> INTEGRATION OF KNOWLEDGE AND IDEAS: K.7, 1.7, 2.7

Then, compare each structure with the photograph of the actual building on the right-hand page. Have students notice similarities in lines and shapes among the structures the children built and the lines and shapes found in the actual building. Some examples are as follows:

- Pages 3–4: The cups have a nearly cylindrical shape similar to the Petronas Towers.
- Pages 7–8: The box has a rectangular prism shape similar to the Box House.
- Pages 17–18: The playing cards are thin and straight, which is similar to the linear shapes on the Vitra Fire Station.
- Pages 19–20: The toothpicks and gumdrops form small triangles similar to the triangles that make up the large sphere of the Montreal Biosphere.
- Pages 25–26: The paper towel tubes are cylinders similar to the cylinders supporting the roofs and walls of the Paper Tube School.
- Pages 27–28: The shape of the craft sticks is similar to the wooden planks that make up the cylinder shape of Sclera Pavilion.

Next, *ask*

? Do you notice any patterns in this book? (Students may notice that on the left-hand side of each page is an illustration of kids building, and on the right-hand side is a photograph of an actual building. They may also notice that the way the text is arranged on the page is similar to the structures pictured.)

To show an example of this, use pages 13–14, which shows children building a sandcastle on the left-hand side of the page and a photograph of La Sagrada Família on the opposite side. Explain to students that Hale's poem compares children's building experiences (p. 13) to real buildings (p. 14).

 **Synthesizing**

Then, *ask*

? Why do you think the author of this book compared this famous building, La Sagrada Família, to a sandcastle? (It is the same color as sand and the same shape.)

COMPARING STRUCTURES

? Why do you think the author and illustrator of this book, Christy Hale, decided to create the book this way? (Answers will vary.)

 Features of Nonfiction

Connecting to the Common Core
Reading: Informational Text
CRAFT AND STRUCTURE: K.5, 1.5, 2.5

Model how to find information about the author by looking at the back flap of the book jacket. Read the section that explains Hale's vision for this book:

Her inspiration for Dreaming Up *dates back to her first encounter with Barcelona's La Sagrada Família. "I'm sure I made the sandcastle connection way back then," says Hale. From then on, "it became a fun challenge to think of the many ways kids build, and then buildings that correspond to their building play."*

Explain that this cathedral, La Sagrada Família, was her first inspiration for this book. After seeing how it resembled a child's sandcastle, she started to notice how other structures resembled things that children build.

Questioning

Explain that the very different buildings featured in this book were designed by different architects. Show students the last four pages that discuss the architects for each building. Read a few of the sections aloud. You may want to begin with Antoni Gaudi and La Sagrada Família. Allow students to suggest some other architects for you to read about aloud. *Ask*

? How are these architects different? (Some are men and some are women. They are different ethnicities, ages, and backgrounds. They have different inspirations. They designed with different materials and for different purposes.)

? What do all of these architects have in common? (They liked to build when they were young. They are creative.)

Synthesizing

Ask

? After reading both *Iggy Peck, Architect* and *Dreaming Up,* how have your ideas changed about what an architect does?

Famous Buildings and Structures Video

 Making Connections: Text to Text

Tell students that you have a video to show them called the "100 Most Famous Buildings/Structures of All Time." Explain that these particular buildings were chosen by the video's creator and that other people might have other ideas about the world's most famous buildings. Tell them that the video is set to music from the era or historical time period of each set of buildings. As you watch, have students signal when they see a building they recognize. It could be a building from *Dreaming Up,* a building they have visited, or a building they have seen in other books or videos (Many students will likely recognize the Taj Mahal, Leaning Tower of Pisa, Eiffel Tower, and Gateway Arch.)

After viewing, *ask*

? What buildings did you recognize from the book *Dreaming Up*? (Fallingwater, Habitat 67, Petronas Towers, Guggenheim Museum, and La Sagrada Família are all pictured.)

? What information was given for each building shown? (name, architect, and year built)

? What building materials did you recognize in the video? (stone, metal, concrete, etc.)

? Do you think those materials were the right choices for durability? (Yes, because all of these buildings are still standing.)

? Do all of the buildings look the same? (no)

? Why do you think the buildings look different? (They serve different purposes and were designed by different architects.)

? What are some of the uses for the different buildings in the video? (homes, churches, monuments, office buildings, etc.)

? Which buildings did you like the most? (Answers will vary.)

? Do you think that all of the buildings are beautiful? (Answers will vary.)

Explain that "beauty is in the eye of the beholder." Some people may criticize an architect's building, while other people may think the same building is very beautiful!

elaborate

Iggy's Models

Connecting to the Common Core
Reading: Informational Text
KEY IDEAS AND DETAILS: K.1, 1.1, 2.1

Revisit the book *Iggy Peck, Architect* and flip through the illustrations. Point out to students that Iggy is not just building random things in the book; he is actually creating models of famous buildings (some of which were in the video they just watched!). So Iggy not only likes to build but also likes to study architecture.

Show the following examples and have students compare Iggy's model with a photograph of the actual building (which can easily be found online):

- Page 4: He uses diapers to create a model of the Leaning Tower of Pisa.

- Page 7: He uses dirt clods to make a model of the Great Sphinx of Giza.

- Pages 8–9: He uses modeling clay and pencils to make a model of Hōryū -Ji Temple.

- Pages 10–11: He uses pancakes and pie to make a model of the Gateway Arch.

- Page 18: He uses chalk to build a model of Neuschwanstein Castle.

ARCHITECTURE EXPO

- Pages 28–29: The bridge he builds is modeled after the Golden Gate Bridge.

Architecture Journal

Connecting to the Common Core
Writing
TEXT TYPES AND PURPOSES: K.2, 1.2, 2.2

Writing

Give each student a copy of the Architecture Journal student page. Tell students that they are going to have another opportunity to build something. However, unlike the first time, when their challenge was just to build something creative out of the materials they were presented, this time they are going to build a model of an actual building. They will go through all the steps of the journal first, and then they will get to make a model of a building they choose.

- Cover: Students write their name and decorate the journal cover any way they like.

- Pages 1–2: Students glue or tape here pictures of some buildings they like. They can cut the pictures out of magazines or print them from Google images (search "famous buildings").

- Page 3: Students select the building they want to model and tape or glue a photo here.

- Page 4: Students research some information about the building: the name, architect, location, and fun facts.

- Page 5: Students think carefully about which materials would be best to represent their building and then circle the materials they plan to use to make their model.

- Page 6: Students sketch a plan of how they will use those materials to make a model of the building they chose.

evaluate

Build It!

As students are working on their journals, review their sketches, provide feedback on their choice of materials for their models, and *ask*

? Why did you choose that building?

? Why did you choose those materials?

Next, they can build their model! Provide all of the building supplies from the Free Build activity (explore phase) in bins for students to access as they build. Encourage students to look closely at the photo of their building. They may also use pencils, crayons, and markers to add details to their models.

Architecture Expo

Tell students that they are going to get to share their models to a visiting class at an Architecture Expo. Have students display their models on their desks. They should have their Architecture Journal open to pages 3–4 so that visitors can see a photograph of the building, its name, the architect, location, and

fun facts. Have students do a gallery walk through the classroom, where they use sticky notes to post suggestions, questions, and positive feedback on the desks next to the models. Writing on sticky notes encourages interaction, and the comments provide immediate feedback for the "exhibitors." A few guidelines for a gallery walk are as follows:

- All necessary information about the model should be provided in the display (pp. 3–4 of the Architecture Journal) because students will not be giving an oral presentation.

- Like a visit to an art gallery, the gallery walk should be done quietly. Students should be respectful of the displays. You may even want to play soft, classical music to set the tone.

STEM at Home

Have students complete the "I learned that …" and "My favorite part of the lesson was …" portions of the STEM at Home student page as a reflection on their learning. They may choose to do the following at-home activity with an adult helper and share their results with the class. If students do not have access to the internet or these materials at home, you may choose to have them complete this activity at school.

"At home, we can watch a short video together called 'Shape House' about drawing the shapes that make up a house."

 Search "Shape House Everyday Learning" to find the PBS video at http://cet.pbslearning-media.org/resource/7750bded-235c-4ac8-8a0e-bd8656e3d305/everyday-math-shape-house.

"After we watch the video, we can go outside together and look for the shapes that make up our own home or another building in our neighborhood!"

For Further Exploration

This section is provided to help you encourage your students to use the science and engineering practices in a more student-directed format. This box lists questions and challenges related to the lesson that students may select to research, investigate, or innovate. Students may also use the questions as examples to help them generate their own questions. After selecting one of the questions in the box or formulating their own questions, students can individually or collaboratively make predictions, design investigations or surveys to test their predictions, collect evidence, devise explanations, design solutions, or examine related resources. They can communicate their findings through a science notebook, at a poster session or gallery walk, or by producing a media project.

Research

Have students brainstorm researchable questions:

? What are the tallest buildings in the world, and who designed them?

? Who designed your school, and what year was it built?

? What materials were used to build your school, and why did the builder choose those materials?

Investigate

Have students brainstorm testable questions to be solved through science or math:

? What materials can hold the most weight without breaking: rubber bands, paper strips, or toothpicks?

? What materials could be used to make a model of a geodesic dome?

? Which shape can support the most weight: a triangular prism, a rectangular prism, or a cylinder?

Innovate

Have students brainstorm problems to be solved through engineering:

? What structure could you design for your school playground?

? What structure could you design to represent your school spirit?

? What would your dream house look like? What features would it have and what materials would you use?

Website

"100 Most Famous Buildings/Structures of All Time" (video)
www.youtube.com/watch?v=dA3Ak-FLk_A

More Books to Read

Ames, L. 2013. *Draw 50 buildings and other structures: The step-by-step way to draw castles and cathedrals, skyscrapers and bridges, and so much more …* New York: Watson-Guptill.
Summary: This step-by-step book filled with black-and-white line drawings reduces famous buildings such as the Taj Mahal and the Eiffel Tower (and other buildings such as igloos and castles) to basic lines and shapes. It then shows young artists how to put the shapes together and add details to represent each building.

Guarnaccia, S. 2010. *The three little pigs: An architectural tale.* New York: Abrams Books for Young Readers.
Summary: In this quirky retelling of the three little pigs, the pigs and their homes are nods to three famous architects—Frank Gehry, Philip Johnson, and Frank Lloyd Wright—and their signature homes. Each house is filled with clever details, including furnishing by the architects and their contemporaries. Of course, not all the houses are going to protect the pigs from the wolf's huffing and puffing. The wolf, and readers, are in for a clever surprise ending.

Hayden, K. 2003. *Amazing buildings.* DK Readers, Level 2. New York: DK Children.
Summary: Simple text and vivid photographs depict how some of the world's most famous buildings were made.

Ritchie, S. 2011. *Look at that building: A first book of structures.* Tonawanda, NY: Kids Can Press.
Summary: Come along as the five friends from *Follow That Map!* start a whole new adventure. Max the dog needs a new doghouse to live in, so the gang is on a quest to find out all it can about buildings and how they are constructed.

Roeder, A. 2011. *13 buildings children should know.* New York: Prestel Verlag.
Summary: From the Great Pyramid of Giza to the Beijing National Stadium, this book presents 13 famous buildings from around the world. It includes information about the architect, location, materials, and special features of each building.

Stevenson, R. L., and D. Heston. 2012. *Block city.* New York: Simon & Schuster Books for Young Readers.
Summary: This illustrated version of Robert Louis Stevenson's classic poem also includes folk songs, building projects, and math activities.

Architecture Journal

Name: _____

Buildings I Like

Tape or glue some photographs of buildings you like.

Sketch

What will your model look like if you build it using only those materials? Make a sketch.

National Science Teachers Association

Materials

Cups

Tubes

Playing cards

Index cards

Toothpicks

Craft sticks

Packing peanuts

Paper bags

Boxes

Other (draw):

Photo

Tape or glue a photograph of the building you want to model.

Research

Record some details about the building.

Name of Building: _____

Architect: _____

Location: _____

Fun Facts: _____

_____

_____

_____

Name: _____

STEM at Home

Dear _____,

At school, we have been learning about how **architects** use different shapes and materials in their designs.

I learned that: _____

_____

My favorite part of the lesson was: _____

_____

At home, we can watch a short video together called "Shape House" about drawing the shapes that make up a house.

 Search "Shape House Everyday Learning" to find the PBS video at *http://cet.pbslearningmedia.org/resource/7750bded-235c-4ac8-8a0e-bd8656e3d305/everyday-math-shape-house.*

After we watch the video, we can go outside together and look for the shapes that make up our own home or another building in our neighborhood!

Sketch of Building	Shapes We Found (color in)
	Triangle Square Circle Arc Rectangle Cylinder

Robots Everywhere

Description

After sharing what they know about different types of robots, students model how robots are programmed to perform tasks. They learn that every robot is designed for a specific job, and that job determines what a robot looks like. They also make a labeled drawing of a robot that could complete a particular task in their own home or at school, and they compare it with another technology designed to solve the same problem.

Suggested Grade Levels: K–2

LESSON OBJECTIVES Connecting to the *Framework*		
Science and Engineering Practices	**Disciplinary Core Ideas**	**Crosscutting Concept**
Developing and Using Models	**ETS1.B:** Developing Possible Solutions	Structure and Function
Constructing Explanations and Designing Solutions	**ETS2.B:** Influence of Engineering, Technology, and Science on Society and the Natural World	

Featured Picture Books

TITLE: ***Beep! Beep! Go to Sleep!***
AUTHOR: **Todd Tarpley**
ILLUSTRATOR: **John Rocco**
PUBLISHER: **Little, Brown Books for Young Readers**
YEAR: **2015**
GENRE: **Story**
SUMMARY: *This fun, rhyming story will have kids giggling as a little boy tries everything to get his household robots to power down.*

TITLE: ***National Geographic Kids: Robots***
AUTHOR: **Melissa Stewart**
PUBLISHER: **National Geographic Children's Books**
YEAR: **2014**
GENRE: **Non-Narrative Information**
SUMMARY: *Young readers will learn about the most fascinating robots of today and tomorrow in this colorful, photo-packed book.*

Time Needed

This lesson will take several class periods. Suggested scheduling is as follows:

Day 1: **Engage** with *Beep! Beep! Go to Sleep!* Read-Aloud, **Explore** with Robot Arms, and **Explain** with Robot Arms Discussion and Chocolate Factory Video

Day 2: **Explain** with *National Geographic Kids: Robots* Read-Aloud and Robot Jobs Card Sort

Day 3: **Elaborate** with Robots of the Future and **Evaluate** with My Robot

Materials

For Robot Arms (per pair)

- 9 × 12 in. two-pocket folder with a mouse-hole-shaped opening (large enough for a student's arm to reach through) cut in the bottom center
- 1 small bowl
- Plastic sandwich bag with about 10 pieces of spiral-shaped pasta and about 10 pieces of tube-shaped or bowtie pasta
- 1 precut Robot Arm Program Card

Optional: For My Robot Advertisement (per student)

- White poster board or large construction paper
- Markers

SAFETY
- Check with your school nurse about wheat allergies, and substitute wheat-free pasta if necessary.
- Remind students not to eat any food used in the lab or activity.

Student Pages

- Robot Jobs Card Sort
- Robot Job Descriptions
- My Robot and My Robot Advertisement
- STEM at Home

Background for Teachers

What do you think of when you hear the word *robot*? Most likely, you have a mental image of a walking, talking, blinking, and thinking humanoid machine. But most robots don't really look like people at all. Robots come in every shape and size you can think of and perform more jobs than you can imagine. If it seems as if robots are everywhere today, that's because they are! In this lesson, students learn about the influence of engineering, technology, and science on society by studying how people have come to depend on robots to do many jobs they could not (or would not) do.

So what exactly is a robot? Oddly enough, there is no widely accepted, standard definition of a robot. Even Joseph Engelberger, often referred to as the "father" of the modern robotics industry, was said to have remarked, "I can't define a robot, but I know one when I see one." In *National Geographic Kids: Robots,* author Melissa Stewart proposes this definition: "A robot, or bot, is a *machine* that has movable parts and can make decisions. People design it to do a job by itself." Although some robots lack computers and perform only simple, motor-driven tasks, the book explains that most robots have three main types of parts: a computer, sensors, and actuators. A robot's *computer* contains programs to help it make decisions. It makes these decisions based on data collected by its *sensors*. Some common robot sensors are video cameras to "see"; microphones to "hear"; pressure and temperature sensors to "feel"; ultrasound, infrared, and laser sensors to measure distance, navigate, and avoid obstacles; and even sensors that detect magnetic fields and certain types of chemicals.

INDUSTRIAL ROBOT ARM

To be called a robot, a machine must move. *Actuators,* also known as drives, are devices that receive messages from the computer and control the robot's movements. Most actuators are powered by pneumatics (air pressure), hydraulics (fluid pressure), or motors (electric current), but they all convert one kind of energy into motion energy. Actuators help the robot make sounds, flash lights, pick things up, move, and so on. Sometimes the whole robot moves, like the rovers that are rolling around the surface of Mars collecting rock samples and other data. Sometimes the robot is stationary with moving parts, like the robotic arms commonly used in industry for many different kinds of jobs. Welding or spray-painting robots don't have to move from place to place, but when a robot's job does require movement, robotics engineers (or *roboticists*) usually design it to have tracks, wheels, or legs (and some robots can even swim or fly). Robots need energy to move. They might be plugged in, battery powered, or even solar powered, depending on what they are designed to do.

In this lesson, students learn that a robot can only do things that engineers and roboticists *program* it to do. They learn that a robot's programming must be very detailed; each and every step must be spelled out for a robot to do its job properly. They model how a "pick-and-place" industrial robot arm needs a very precise and logical *program* to follow in order to complete a task, such as picking things up and sorting them. To model this, each student "programs" his or her partner's "robot arm" to pick up and sort pasta shapes into separate piles.

Students also learn that most robots are designed to do jobs that are too repetitive or dangerous for humans to do. Robots can explore places that humans can't go, such as Mars, the deepest trenches of the sea, or the craters of active volcanoes. But some of the handiest robots have less glamorous jobs: they are the domestic, or household, robots. There are robots to mow your lawn, clean your gutters, scoop out your cat's litterbox, entertain you, and even wake you up! Caregiving robots are being designed to help people with physical challenges move from a chair to a bed, fetch household items, or take a bath.

In this lesson, students look around their homes and classrooms and brainstorm problems that robots could solve. They design a robot and then compare its strengths and weaknesses with those of the technology (or the person!) currently solving the problem. Students share their designs through labeled drawings. Finally, they create an advertisement to "sell" their robot, explaining how it is a better solution than the technology (or person) currently solving the problem. The concept of structure and function is woven throughout the lesson as students explore how a robot's job determines what it looks like.

In the explore phase, students will get a sense of how robots are programmed by being exposed to simple IF-THEN-ELSE statements. Programming is a great way to teach problem-solving, creativity, and communication skills, and even very young children can be taught simple coding. To find out more about teaching young students to code, visit Reading Rockets (see "Websites" section) to view the article "IF kids code, THEN … what?" There are several suggested websites and apps listed at the end of the article, including Code, a nonprofit organization working to ensure that every student in every school has the opportunity to learn computer science. Its completely free curriculum for ages 4 and up consists of multiple courses, each of which has about 20 lessons that may be implemented as one unit or over the course of a school year. We hope that by learning about "robots everywhere" you and your students will be inspired to learn more about the wonderful world of coding!

engage

Beep! Beep! Go to Sleep!
Read-Aloud

Connecting to the Common Core
Reading: Literature
KEY IDEAS AND DETAILS: K.1, 1.1, 2.1

ENGAGING WITH BEEP! BEEP! GO TO SLEEP!

 **Inferring**

Show students the cover of *Beep! Beep! Go to Sleep!* and introduce the author, Todd Tarpley, and illustrator, John Rocco. *Ask*

? Based on the cover, what do you think this book might be about? (a boy and some robots)

? How do you know? (The boy is reading a book called *3 Little Robots,* and there are three robots on the cover.)

Then, read the book aloud.
Questioning

After reading, *ask*

? What kinds of jobs do robots do? (Answers will vary.)

? What job do you think the robots in the book were designed to do? (entertain the boy or take care of the boy; students may notice that the first two-page spread has pictures on the wall showing that the robots have been with the boy since he was a baby)

? Do most robots look like the ones in the book? (Answers will vary.)

explore

Robot Arms

Tell students that most robots look nothing like the cute, funny ones featured in the book *Beep! Beep! Go to Sleep!* In fact, robots that consist of just a moving "arm" are among the most common robots used. Show students the robot arm on pages 22 and 23 of *National Geographic Kids: Robots.* Tell students they are going to do a fun activity to model how one of these robot arms works.

Before beginning the activity, divide students into teams of two. Tell students that one member of each pair is going to be the "robot arm" and the other member is going to be the "programmer." (They will be switching roles after the first trial.)

Robot Arms activity

Explain that all robots need to be *programmed* to do their job. This means that engineers must write a very specific set of instructions called a *computer program* and then upload, or transfer, the program to a robot's computer. The student who is the programmer will be reading these instructions to the student who is modeling the robot arm so that this student knows how to do his or her job. (You may want to read the Robot Program together if your students are not yet reading independently.)

Give a sandwich bag of pasta (spirals and either tubes or bowties) and a precut folder (to act as a screen) to each pair. Give a Robot Arm Program Card to each programmer. Then, read aloud the directions below:

Directions for Robot Arms Activity

1. Stand the folder on the table. The first person to be the robot should place one hand through the hole in the folder and lean over until his or her forehead is touching the folder. The robot should not be able to see his or her own hand (but may use the other hand to keep the folder standing up).

2. The programmer should dump the pasta into a bowl in front of the folder, within reach of the robot arm.

3. The programmer will tell the robot how to do its job by reading a set of instructions called the *Robot Program.*

When all pairs are set up and ready to go, call out, "START!"

Robot Program

1. Pick up a piece of pasta from the bowl.
2. IF the pasta feels like a spiral, THEN place it to the left of the bowl, or ELSE place it to the right of the bowl.
3. IF any pasta is still in the bowl, THEN GO TO step 1, or ELSE END program.

After a few minutes of pasta sorting (or more if necessary), call out, "STOP!" Next, have the programmers remove the folder so their partners can see the results. Then, have students trade roles and repeat the activity.

explain

Robot Arms Discussion and Chocolate Factory Video

 Questioning

After everyone has had a chance to be both a programmer and a robot arm, *ask*

? What was the job the robot arms had to do? (sort the pasta)

? How well did the robot arms do their job? (Answers will vary.)

? Is this a job you would want to do? (Students will most likely answer no.)

? Why or why not? (It would be boring or too repetitive, and your arm would get tired.)

? What parts or structures on the robot arms helped them do their job? (movable elbows, wrists, hands, fingers, etc.)

? Did the programmer ever have to give the robot additional instructions? (Answers will vary.)

Explain that real robots can *only* do what they are programmed to do. Every step of a task must be spelled out in the robot's program. If the program is not detailed and exact, the robot won't be able to do its job very well or at all. Discuss the Robot Program used in the model. Point out that many types of computer programs are similar to

this one: They are made up of a series of logical statements that include the words IF, THEN, ELSE, GO TO, and END. You may want to give students the opportunity to write another simple program for a robotic arm, such as a program for sorting and placing different-shaped blocks into containers.

Next, explain that robot arms are typically used in factories, doing jobs that people might not want to do because they are so repetitive (meaning they are repeated over and over). There are many different types of robot arms used in industry. One kind is designed to spray paint cars. Another kind welds metal together. One of the most common kinds found in factories and warehouses is called a *pick-and-place robot* because it is designed to pick things up and place them somewhere else, usually into some sort of package. The robot arm they modeled is a type of pick-and-place robot.

After completing the Robot Arms activity, tell students that they will have an opportunity to see some real pick-and-place robot arms in action. The "M-430iA Robots in Food Industry: Pick&Place of Chocolates" video (see "Websites" section) features two FANUC Robotics robot arms in a chocolate factory "picking and placing" different kinds of chocolate truffles into blister packs. Have students watch the video carefully to observe the robot arms doing their jobs.

After watching, point out that these robots have vision sensors, which are cameras that help them "see" the chocolates. Also, explain that although the robots are automatically doing their jobs, a machine operator nearby is controlling the settings on the robots' computers. Robots can only do jobs they are programmed to do, and often their programs need to be changed or adjusted for them to do their jobs properly.

 Questioning

After watching the video, discuss the following:

? Is packaging chocolate a job that a person could do? (yes)

? Would you want to do that job? (Answers will vary.)

? Why do you think the chocolate factory uses robots instead of people to pick and place chocolates? (The job is boring, it is repetitive, the robots are faster, the robots never get tired, etc.)

 Making Connections: Text to Self

Then, help students make connections between the video and the robot arms activity. *Ask*

? How were the chocolate factory robot arms like the robot arms we modeled? (They were picking up food and sorting it, they stayed in one place, and they had to be programmed.)

? How were they different? (The factory robots were picking the food from a moving conveyor belt instead of a bowl, they were putting the chocolates into different kinds of packages instead of piles, they could "see" the objects whereas our robots could only feel the objects, they could work a lot faster, etc.)

Tell students that they are going to learn much more about what robots look like and the many kinds of jobs they do.

explain

National Geographic Kids: Robots Read-Aloud

Turn and Talk

Show students the cover of the book *National Geographic Kids: Robots,* and *ask*

? What's a robot? (Students will likely provide a variety of responses—even engineers don't always agree on the definition of *robot.*)

Making Connections: Text to World

Read and discuss pages 4–7, which describe these characteristics of a robot:

- Has movable parts or structures
- Can make decisions
- Is designed by people to do a job by itself

Remind students of the Robot Arm activity. Ask them to think about the pick-and-place robot arm that was programmed to sort the pasta. *Ask*

? If that had been a real robotic arm, and not a kid's arm, would it meet the characteristics of a robot?

Go through each characteristic, asking students to give a thumbs-up or thumbs-down to show whether they think their pick-and-place robot arms meets each characteristic. Then, ask them to explain why.

? Does it have movable parts or structures? (Yes, the arm moved at the elbow and wrist joints, and the fingers also moved.)

? Can it make decisions? (Yes, when it felt a spiral-shaped piece of pasta, it placed it to the left of the bowl. When the bowl was empty, it stopped.)

? Is it designed by people to do a job by itself? (Yes, it could do the job by itself with the right programming.)

Read pages 10–11 about the parts of a robot, and *ask*

? What part of a robot is like a person's brain? (computer)

? What parts of a robot receive messages from the computer and control the robot's movements? (actuators)

? What parts of a robot collect information about its surroundings? (sensors)

Explain that many robots have vision sensors— cameras that help them "see" and recognize the shapes or even the colors of objects. These sensors help the robot make decisions such as what object to pick up, where to put it, where to paint or weld on a car, and so on. *Ask*

? What kind of sensor did your robot arm have in the pasta sorting activity? (touch)

? What kind of sensors do you think the chocolate factory robots had? (touch, sight, or both)

Making Connections: Text to Text

The little blue robot in *Beep! Beep! Go to Sleep!* said, "My sensor aches!" *Ask*

? What kind of sensor do you think it had? (Answers will vary.)

Robot Jobs Card Sort

Explain that every robot is designed for a specific job, and that job determines what a robot looks like. Tell students that in the book *National Geographic Kids: Robots,* they will learn about the jobs that robots do at work, at home, and in space. Before reading, pass out the Robot Jobs student pages, and have the students cut out the pictures of the robots. Read each robot job description aloud, and then have students place their cards where they think the cards go. Students will have the opportunity to move their cards as you read the book.

Connecting to the Common Core
Reading: Informational Text
KEY IDEAS AND DETAILS: K.1, 1.1, 2.1

Explain that, because this book is nonfiction, you can enter the text at any point. You don't have to read the book from cover to cover if you are looking for specific information. Tell students that parts of this book will help them match their robot cards with the robot jobs. Ask students to signal (by giving a thumbs-up, making "robot arms," or using some other method) when they see or hear one of the robots from the picture cards. Stop each time you read about a robot from the Robot Jobs Card Sort student page, and have students move their cards if necessary.

 Chunking

Follow the steps below to "chunk" the book into the following sections: Robots at Work, Robots at Home, and Robots in Space. Note that you will not read the entire book aloud.

1. Robots at Work: Read pages 22–25, featuring factory robots and the volcano-exploring robot.
2. Robots at Home: Read pages 26–29, featuring the robot alarm clock and the fetch bot.
3. Robots in Space: Read pages 38–41, featuring the robonaut and the Mars rovers.

After reading, students may glue the picture cards onto the Robot Job Descriptions student page once they are all in the correct spaces. The answers to the Robot Jobs Card Sort are as follows:

1. F (Factory Robot)
2. E (Dante II)
3. A (Robot Alarm Clock)
4. C (Fetch Bot)
5. B (Robonaut)
6. D (Curiosity Rover)

 Questioning

After reading, ask students to fill in the blanks as you make the following statements:

? Every robot is designed for a specific _____. (job)

? What a robot looks like depends on _____. (the job it was designed for or built to do)

 Turn and Talk

Ask

? What was your favorite robot in the book, and why? (Answers will vary.)

elaborate

Robots of the Future

Read pages 44–45 about robots of the future. *Ask*

? After learning about robots and the jobs they can do, would you want to be a person who designs or builds robots? (Answers will vary.)

? Would you want a robot in your home? (Students will likely say yes!)

Tell students they are going to have the opportunity to be roboticists—engineers who design, program, and test robots! They will be designing their very own robot with the purpose of solving a human problem or meeting a human need in their own home or classroom. Tell students that in the not-so-distant future, robots in homes and schools may be commonplace. For inspiration, you can show students the first two-page spread of *Beep! Beep! Go to Sleep!* and have them imagine what it would be like to have a friendly robot in their home or school like the ones pictured.

 Word Web

Next, students can brainstorm jobs a robot could help them do. Make a word web with the target words *Robot Jobs* in the middle, and organize student ideas in circles that surround it. Ask guiding questions, such as the following:

? What are some jobs that you do around your home or at school?

? What tools or machines do you or your parents or teachers use to help get the jobs done?

? Are there any jobs that a robot could do around your home or school that you could not?

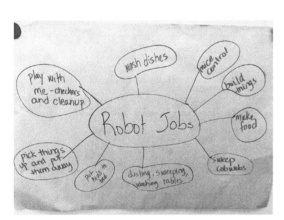

ROBOT JOBS WORD WEB

? Are there any jobs that a robot could do around your home or school better than you could do them?

? What are some ways that a robot might entertain you or teach you better than another toy or game that you play with?

Then, brainstorm some robot ideas together. Examples might include a robot designed to take out the trash that can carry heavier trash bags than you can carry and can see in the dark to take out the trash at night; a robot designed to play chess that can teach you to play better than your brother or sister and can also put away the chess pieces when you are finished; or a robot that can feed the classroom fish during weekends or vacations and can give the fish exactly the right amount of food every time.

evaluate

My Robot

Connecting to the Common Core
Writing
TEXT TYPES AND PURPOSES: K.1, 1.1, 2.1

Writing

Next, have each student select an idea from your brainstorming session, or come up with an idea of his or her own. Give each student a copy of the My Robot student page. Read the first page together.

You may choose to have students use the My Robot Advertisement student page, or have them draw their robot on construction paper or poster board. You can have students present their robots to the class, have a "Robotics Fair," invite other classes to attend a gallery walk, or display the posters in the classroom or hallway.

OUR ROBOT DESIGNS

STEM at Home

Have students complete the "I learned that …" and "My favorite part of the lesson was …" portions of the STEM at Home student page as a reflection on their learning. They may choose to do the following at-home activity with an adult helper and share their results with the class. If students do not have access to the internet at home, you may choose to have them complete this activity at school.

"At home, we can watch a short video together called 'Sandeep Yayathi: Robotics Engineer' about Robonaut 2, or R2, a human-like robot designed to assist astronauts in space."

Search "Sandeep Yayathi: Robotics Engineer" at www.pbslearningmedia.org *to find the video at* http://cet.pbslearningmedia.org/resource/mss13.sci.engin.design.robeng/sandeep-yayathi-robotics-engineer.

"If you were a robotics engineer, what kinds of robots would you want to design and why?"

For Further Exploration

This section is provided to help you encourage your students to use the science and engineering practices in a more student-directed format. This box lists questions and challenges related to the lesson that students may select to research, investigate, or innovate. Students may also use the questions as examples to help them generate their own questions. After selecting one of the questions in the box or formulating their own questions, students can individually or collaboratively make predictions, design investigations or surveys to test their predictions, collect evidence, devise explanations, design solutions, or examine related resources. They can communicate their findings through a science notebook, at a poster session or gallery walk, or by producing a media project.

Research

Have students brainstorm researchable questions:

? What is the world's largest walking robot?

? How did the Mars rovers get onto the surface of Mars?

? What is biomimicry, and what are some examples of it in robot design?

Investigate

Have students brainstorm testable questions to be solved through science or math:

? How many pieces of pasta can your partner's "robot arm" sort in 1 min. without looking?

? Survey your friends: Would you rather have a robot take care of you if you were sick, or would you prefer a human nurse? Graph the results, then analyze your graph. What can you conclude?

? Survey your friends: What household chore would you most want a robot to do? Graph the results, then analyze your graph. What can you conclude?

Innovate

Have students brainstorm problems to be solved through engineering:

? Can you write a code to program your partner's "robotic arm" to sort blocks by their shape or color?

? What kind of robot would you design to help you at school?

? What kind of robot would you design to explore a volcano, the deep ocean, or outer space?

Websites

"IF Kids Code, THEN … What?" (article)
www.readingrockets.org/article/if-kids-code-thenwhat

"M-430iA Robots in Food Industry: Pick&Place of Chocolates" (video)
www.youtube.com/watch?v=ZSbFW_ncldU

More Books to Read

Becker, H. 2014. *Zoobots: Wild robots inspired by real animals.* Toronto: Kids Can Press.
Summary: This book for older readers (grades 3–6) explores the world of robo-animals, or "zoobots." Twelve two-page spreads reveal vivid, Photoshop-rendered illustrations of robot prototypes such as the bacteria-inspired Nanobot, which can move through human blood vessels, and the OLE pill bug, which can fight fires. Each spread shows a smaller illustration of the animal on which the zoobot is based.

Fliess, S. 2013. *Robots, robots, everywhere.* New York: Golden Books.
Summary: This delightful rhyming picture book for very young readers features robots of all kinds, from the ones up in space to the ones we use at home.

Shulman, M. 2014. *TIME for Kids: Explorers—Robots.* New York: TIME for Kids.
Summary: Full of facts and photos, this book in the popular *TIME for Kids* series shows young readers just how useful robots are and why we need them.

Swanson, J. 2016. *National Geographic Kids: Everything robotics—All the photos, facts, and fun to make you race for robots.* Washington, DC: National Geographic Children's Books.
Summary: With stunning visuals and an energetic design, this book for grades 3–7 reveals everything kids want to know about robotics.

Robot Arm Program Cards

ROBOT PROGRAM

1. Pick up a piece of pasta from the bowl.

2. IF the pasta feels like a spiral, THEN place it to the left of the bowl, or ELSE place it to the right of the bowl.

3. IF any pasta is still in the bowl, THEN GO TO step 1, or ELSE END program.

ROBOT PROGRAM

1. Pick up a piece of pasta from the bowl.

2. IF the pasta feels like a spiral, THEN place it to the left of the bowl, or ELSE place it to the right of the bowl.

3. IF any pasta is still in the bowl, THEN GO TO step 1, or ELSE END program.

Robot Jobs Card Sort

Robots do many different kinds of jobs. They often do jobs that people don't want to do or can't do. What a robot looks like depends on the job it was designed to do.

Directions: Cut out the robot cards below and match each robot to its job description on the next page. Then, listen as your teacher reads the book *National Geographic Kids: Robots*. You will have the chance to move the cards again as your teacher reads the book.

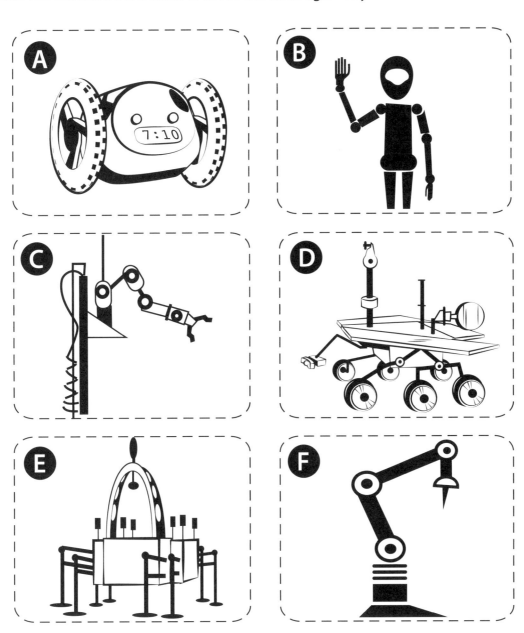

Name: _____

Robot Job Descriptions

Match the robot picture with the right description.

1 This robot arm welds together metal parts in a factory.

2 This eight-legged robot was designed to explore an active volcano.

3 This robot alarm clock is on wheels and rolls around your room.

4 This robot can pick up an object you want and bring it to you.

5 This human-like robot works on the International Space Station.

6 This six-wheeled robot was designed to explore the surface of Mars.

National Science Teachers Association

My Robot

Challenge: Design a robot to do a job in your home or classroom.

Robot's name: _____

Robot's job: _____

_____

_____

Think about how your robot can do the job better than a person could do it, or how it can do the job better than another technology. Then, list some reasons that people should buy your robot.

_____

_____

_____

_____

_____

_____

Next, draw your robot and create an advertisement to sell it! Include the robot's name and its job, and label the parts of your robot that help it do its job.

My Robot Advertisement

National Science Teachers Association

Name: _____

STEM at Home

Dear _____,

At school, we have been learning about **robots.** Every robot is designed for a specific job, and that job determines what a robot looks like.

I learned that:

_____

_____

_____

My favorite part of the lesson was: _____

_____

At home, we can watch a short video together called "Sandeep Yayathi: Robotics Engineer" about Robonaut 2, or R2, a human-like robot designed to assist astronauts in space.

 Search "Sandeep Yayathi: Robotics Engineer" at *www. pbslearningmedia.org* to find the video at *http://cet. pbslearningmedia.org/resource/mss13.sci.engin.design. robeng/sandeep-yayathi-robotics-engineer.*

If you were a robotics engineer, what kinds of robots would you want to design and why?

_____

_____

_____

_____

Feel the Heat

Description

Students explore the warming effects of sunlight on Earth's surface by comparing the temperatures of sunny surfaces and shady surfaces on their school grounds. Then, they design, build, and test models of shade structures that could provide a place to cool off on the playground.

Suggested Grade Levels: K–2

LESSON OBJECTIVES Connecting to the *Framework*		
Science and Engineering Practices	**Disciplinary Core Ideas**	**Crosscutting Concepts**
Planning and Carrying Out Investigations Using Mathematics and Computational Thinking Constructing Explanations and Designing Solutions	**PS3.B:** Conservation of Energy and Energy Transfer **ETS1.B:** Developing Possible Solutions	Cause and Effect Scale, Proportion, and Quantity

Featured Picture Books

TITLE: **Summer Sun Risin'**
AUTHOR: **W. Nikola-Lisa**
ILLUSTRATOR: **Don Tate**
PUBLISHER: **Lee & Low Books**
YEAR: **2002**
GENRE: **Story**
SUMMARY: *Rhythmic poetry and beautiful paintings depict a little boy enjoying a summer day on his family's farm in Texas in the 1950s. The illustrations trace the Sun as it travels across the sky from sunrise to sunset, while the text describes the family's daily ritual of chores and how the hot Sun affects their lives.*

TITLE: **The Sun: Our Nearest Star**
AUTHOR: **Franklyn M. Branley**
ILLUSTRATOR: **Edward Miller**
PUBLISHER: **HarperTrophy**
YEAR: **2002**
GENRE: **Non-Narrative Information**
SUMMARY: *This book describes characteristics of the Sun and how it provides all of the light energy needed for life on Earth.*

Time Needed

This lesson will take several class periods and will need to be taught on sunny days during the warmer months of the school year. Suggested scheduling is as follows:

Day 1: Engage with *Summer Sun Risin'* Read-Aloud and **Explore** with Comparing Temperatures

Day 2: Explain with Comparing Temperatures Graph and *The Sun: Our Nearest Star* Anticipation Guide and Read-Aloud

Day 3: Elaborate with Keep It Cool Design Challenge: Building Our Models

Day 4: Evaluate with Keep It Cool Design Challenge: Testing Our Models

Materials

For Comparing Temperatures (for teacher use only)

- Infrared digital thermometer (non-contact, not designed for measuring body temperature) (*Note:* Infrared, non-contact digital thermometer "temperature guns" with laser pointers can be purchased at Amazon.com, Walmart, or hardware and home improvement stores for $20–$60.)

For Keep It Cool Design Challenge

- Cooler of ice (*Note:* Take the cooler of ice outside with you and hand out the ice cubes when it is time to begin testing designs.)
- 2 ice cubes of the same size and shape (per pair)
- Lunch-sized paper bag that includes a variety of shade-structure building supplies such as the following (per pair):
  - Construction paper
  - Index cards, cardboard, or both
  - Pieces of cloth or felt
  - 4 or more straws
  - 4 or more craft sticks
  - Roll of masking tape
  - Scissors

Student Pages

- Comparing Temperatures
- Let's Learn About the Sun
- Keep It Cool Design Challenge
- STEM at Home

SAFETY

INFRARED THERMOMETER

An *infrared laser thermometer* is a device that can measure the temperature of an object or surface. The laser beam included in this type of device does not measure the temperature; it helps the user aim the device at the desired object. Because a laser beam is involved, you should be very cautious when using it.

- Follow all usage and safety guidelines included in the packaging.
- Do not allow students to use the device. Do not point it toward people.
- Do not point it at a highly reflective surface, such as a mirror.
- Some school districts and states prohibit the use of lasers in the classroom or field. Always check school district policy and state regulations relative to laser use before doing this activity.
- Use caution in working with scissors, sticks, and so on. They can be sharp and cut or puncture eyes and skin.
- Immediately wipe up any spilled water to avoid a slip-and-fall hazard.

Background for Teachers

The Sun, our nearest star, is the source of virtually all energy on our planet. Without the Sun's energy, there would be no light, no heat, and no life on Earth. The Sun is an enormous burning ball of gases nearly a million miles across. In terms of scale, if Earth were the size of a pea, the Sun would be about the size of a beach ball! By studying the color and brightness of the light emitted from the Sun, scientists have concluded that the surface of the Sun is about 10000°F. The Sun is very far from Earth—about 93 million miles away—but it appears so big and bright to us because it is much closer than neighboring stars.

We can feel the Sun's heat warm our skin and the sand at the beach, we can see the visible light that comes from the Sun, and we can see the effects of damaging ultraviolet light on our skin. But how do all these types of energy get to the Earth when the Sun is so far away? The Sun transfers energy to Earth through empty space by *radiation,* a form of energy transfer that does not require direct contact. Traveling at the speed of light, energy released by the Sun reaches the Earth in a little more than 8 min. This energy is known as *electromagnetic radiation* and takes many forms, including visible light, ultraviolet light, radio waves, and even x-rays. Fortunately, the atmosphere prevents most of the dangerous forms of energy from the Sun from reaching Earth's surface. Different surfaces can either reflect or absorb sunlight to various degrees. As a surface (such as your skin or the sand at the beach) absorbs sunlight, the sunlight forces the molecules in the material to move faster, thus warming the surface. Lighter-colored surfaces tend to reflect more sunlight, whereas darker surfaces tend to absorb more sunlight. In general, the darker the surface, the faster it warms up and the hotter it gets relative to surrounding surfaces. The temperatures of land and water in the same area may differ, even when they are exposed to the same amount of energy from the Sun. Land warms up at a faster rate than water and gets hotter. It also cools down faster than water. Different types of land (green grass, beach sand, bare soil) can have different temperatures within the same area. It is this uneven heating of the Earth's surface that contributes to an imbalance of air pressure across the Earth, which in turn causes wind and weather.

The amount of energy from the Sun that reaches a single location on the surface of Earth over a given period of time is called *insolation* (incoming solar radiation). The intensity of insolation on Earth varies according to such factors as the time of year, the time of day, and the latitude. In places with high average temperatures, high insolation can be a big problem for city dwellers. Urban planners and architects are finding ways to make cities cooler by selecting building materials that are more reflective and by using trees and engineered shade structures. Creating shade over an area can greatly reduce the warming effects of insolation. Installing engineered shade structures in public areas can help lower insolation and keep people feeling more comfortable when it is very hot outside (as well as protect people from the Sun's damaging ultraviolet rays). Although the air temperature in the Sun is about the same as the air temperature in a shaded area nearby, shade blocks insolation, which in turn makes surfaces cooler.

For primary students, laying a foundation for eventually learning about sunlight, weather and climate, global warming, and other concepts pertaining to the transfer of the Sun's energy to Earth systems involves making simple observations about the warming effects of the Sun. In this lesson, students will make qualitative observations of how warm it "feels" in the Sun versus the shade and collect quantitative data by measuring the temperature of the same surfaces in the shade and then in the Sun. Temperature data is collected using a handheld device called an *infrared laser thermometer,* which measures surface temperatures more quickly and accurately than traditional classroom thermometers (see safety notes in the Materials section).

This lesson also incorporates the engineering design practice of building a model. A *model* is a representation of a real object. A model can show how a design will look and how different parts work together. Models can be maps, diagrams, blueprints, or three-dimensional physical models. Engineers use models to plan, test, and show others their ideas. Using their knowledge of the warming effects of sunlight, students build and test a physical model of a shade structure to keep cooler on the playground.

A simple extension of this lesson might be to walk around the school grounds and brainstorm ideas for keeping the area cooler during the hotter months (e.g., by replacing darker surfaces with lighter-colored materials and installing shade structures or planting trees in certain places). Exploring ways that scientists and engineers are working to design solutions for problems such as helping people stay cooler in outside areas brings science and engineering together in the classroom.

ENGAGING WITH SUMMER SUN RISIN'

engage

Summer Sun Risin' **Read-Aloud**

Connecting to the Common Core
Reading: Literature
KEY IDEAS AND DETAILS: K.1, 1.1, 2.1

 **Inferring**

Show students the cover of *Summer Sun Risin'* and introduce the author, W. Nikola-Lisa, and illustrator, Don Tate. Show them the front and back covers and *ask*

? Where do you think this story takes place? (Students will likely guess that the story takes place on a farm.)

? What clues from the cover make you think that? (There are chickens, crops, and a scarecrow.)

Read the book aloud, or share the pictures as you have the author sing the book aloud! You can find his SoundCloud version at *https://soundcloud. com/nikolaplays/summer-sun-risin.*

 Questioning

After reading, *ask*

? What did you notice about the pictures of the Sun in the book? (Answers will vary. Flip through the pages to show how the Sun starts on the left-hand page near the horizon, travels across the sky, and ends up on the right-hand side sinking down into the horizon.)

? Why do you think the Sun appears again in the very last picture? (It is the next day, so the Sun is rising again.)

? Why do you think the author used words such as *shinin', glarin', blazin',* and *burnin'* to describe the Sun? (The Sun is very hot. Heat comes from the Sun.)

? What do you think the author was trying to show about the Sun in his poem? (how the Sun makes things hot on a summer day; how it is a big part of our lives, especially in the summer; how it affects people all day long, etc.)

 **Making Connections:**
Text to Self

Ask

? Have you ever felt the Sun blazin', burnin', and glarin'? (Answers will vary. Remind students to never look directly at the Sun!)

? How do you keep cool on a hot summer day? (sit in the shade, drink cold water, swim, eat ice pops)

? Are some areas of the playground hotter than others? (Answers will vary. Students may have noticed that some places on the playground get hotter than others, such as the surface of the slide, the blacktop area, seats of the swings, etc.)

Tell students that, next, they are going to have the opportunity to explore how the Sun heats different surfaces in different ways.

**explore**

Comparing Temperatures

Ahead of time, identify four separate surfaces on the playground or elsewhere on school grounds that are partly shaded (e.g., grass, blacktop, cement, shade).

Give each student a copy of the Comparing Temperatures student page and a clipboard, and have them write the names of the four surfaces you have selected in the first column of the table. Tell them that they will be investigating the temperatures of these four surfaces. *Ask*

? What ways could we measure the temperatures of these four surfaces? (by feeling and then comparing them or by measuring their temperature with a thermometer)

Tell students that they will be comparing how warm these surfaces feel *and* measuring the surfaces' temperatures with a special type of thermometer. The temperatures will be recorded on their data tables in degrees Fahrenheit. Point out the °F symbol on the data table. Demonstrate how the infrared laser thermometer works by aiming it at the floor

COMPARING TEMPERATURES

and measuring the temperature (follow all usage and safety guidelines included in the packaging). Tell them that because the thermometer uses a laser beam for precise aiming, students may not use it. Laser beams, even small ones such as those used in classroom pointers, cat toys, and the infrared laser thermometer, can be dangerous if pointed at the eye.

 **Turn and Talk**

Before you take the students outside, *ask*

? Which surface do you think will be the warmest? (Answers will vary.)

? Why do you think so? (Students will likely have had prior experience with shady versus sunny surfaces and may also have noticed relative temperature differences between darker and lighter surfaces.)

Have students discuss their thoughts with a partner, then ask a few pairs to share with the entire class.

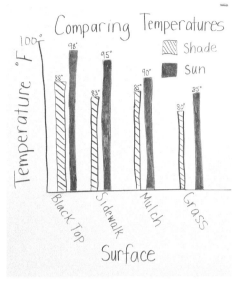

COMPARING TEMPERATURES BAR GRAPH

Next, take students outside with their clipboards. Visit the shaded part of the first area together, and have students place their hands on the surface. Ask them to describe how the temperature feels to the touch—cold, cool, warm, or hot. Measure the surface with the infrared laser thermometer, and have students record the temperature in the "Temperature in Shade" column.

Then, move to the sunny part of the same area and have students place their hands on the same surface in the Sun. Ask them to compare how the temperature of the same surface feels in the Sun. Is it colder, cooler, warmer, or hotter in the Sun than in the shade? Then, measure with the infrared laser thermometer, and have students record the temperature in the "Temperature in Sun" column. Repeat the procedure for the rest of the surfaces.

explain

Comparing Temperatures Graph

Connecting to the Common Core
Mathematics
MEASUREMENT AND DATA: K.MD.2, 1.MD.4, 2.MD.10

Next, return to the classroom and discuss the data together. Ask students to identify patterns in their data (i.e., Were the sunny surfaces typically warmer than the shaded surfaces? Were lighter surfaces cooler than darker surfaces? Was the blacktop in the Sun the warmest of all the surfaces?). Then, explain that

sometimes it is helpful to graph data to find patterns. Create a bar graph titled "Comparing Temperatures" to display the data with "Surface" on the x-axis and "Temperature" on the y-axis. For each surface, there will be two bars of data, so have students help you create a key for "Sun" and "shade" (e.g., yellow for Sun and a darker color for shade). Have students help you determine how to draw the bars on the graph.

After completing the graph together, *ask*

? Which surface was the warmest? What is your evidence? (Students should know to choose their answer by observing which bar is the highest.)

? Why do you think so? (Answers will vary.)

? Which surface was the coolest? What is your evidence? (Students should know to choose their answer by observing which bar is the lowest.)

? Why do you think so? (Answers will vary.)

? What other observations can you make about our graph? (Answers will vary.)

Then, *ask*

? What is warming these surfaces outside our school? (the Sun)

The Sun: Our Nearest Star Anticipation Guide and Read-Aloud

 Determining Importance

Connecting to the Common Core
Reading: Informational Text
KEY IDEAS AND DETAILS: K.1, 1.1, 2.1

Tell students that they are going to learn more about how the Sun warms the Earth by reading a nonfiction book titled *The Sun: Our Nearest Star*. Show students the cover and introduce the author, Franklyn M. Branley, and the illustrator, Edward Miller. Tell students that Dr. Branley is an astronomer, a scientist who studies stars, planets, and space.

Project a copy of *The Sun* anticipation guide, Let's Learn About the Sun. Pre-assess the students' understanding of the Sun by having them signal (thumbs-up or thumbs-down) to indicate whether they agree or disagree with each of the following statements. They should also write their guesses in the blanks on the student page. Tell them that at this point, they should just make their best guesses. After reading the book, they will be revisiting the anticipation guide to see if their guesses were correct.

1. The Sun is a star.
2. The Sun is much smaller than Earth.
3. The Sun is much farther away than the Moon.
4. A spaceship has been to the Sun.
5. Without the Sun, Earth would be cold and dark.

Have students signal when they hear evidence from the text for or against any of the five statements. Stop and discuss each one as you read the book aloud. The correct answers are as follows:

1. The Sun is a star. (true—p. 6)
2. The Sun is much smaller than Earth. (false—p. 9; the Sun is much bigger than Earth)
3. The Sun is much farther away than the Moon. (true—p. 10; the Sun is 93 million miles away)
4. A spaceship has been to the Sun. (false—p. 14; the Sun is so hot that a spaceship could not get close to it without burning up)
5. Without the Sun, Earth would be cold and dark. (true—p. 16)

Explain that although the Sun is so far away from us (93 million miles), we can feel the heat it produces. It heats us, the air, the ground—everything on Earth. Refer to the Comparing Temperatures activity in the explore section and *ask*

? Were all the surfaces the same temperature outside our school? (no)
? What was different about the surfaces? (They were in different places, some were in the Sun

and some were in the shade, and they were different textures and colors.)

Explain that some surfaces absorb more sunlight than others, and that makes them warmer than the surrounding surfaces. For example, darker colors (such as blacktop) *absorb,* or take in, more sunlight than lighter colors (such as concrete). *Ask*

? Why do you think the shade was cooler than the other surfaces? (The sunlight was blocked.)
? What was blocking the sunlight in the shady area? (Answers will vary.)

elaborate

Keep It Cool Design Challenge: Building Our Models

Ask

? Do you ever get hot playing on our school's playground?
? Where do you go to cool off?
? Do you think you could design a structure for the playground that would reduce the warming effect of the Sun on you and your classmates?
? What kind of structure would help you cool on the playground? (something that makes shade, something that is covered with a light-colored material)

Present the following problem to students by writing it on the board and reading it aloud: "Problem: We need a place to cool off on the playground."

Tell students that they are going to have the opportunity to solve this problem through engineering. They will be working with a partner to design a structure to provide a place to cool off when they are on the playground. Tell students that when engineers design something, they often build a model and test it before they build the real thing. Explain that a *model* is a representation of a real object. The model they build will not be big enough for real people to be underneath. It will be small, no bigger than a shoebox, but it will show

TESTING A SHADE STRUCTURE

the shape and features of a real structure. Explain that they will be testing their structure by placing one ice cube in the structure and another ice cube outside of it to see which melts first.

Next, show students the supplies they will be using to build their models. Show them an ice cube and tell them that they need to make sure that it can fit underneath their structure. Then, brainstorm some ideas together. Ask guiding questions, such as the following:

? What shape will your structure be?

? What materials will you use?

? What color will you use for the roof of the structure? Why?

? Where will you place the ice cubes?

Provide each pair of students with a bag of supplies (see Materials section), and let them begin building. Set a time limit, and visit groups as they work, reminding them that the structure must be tall enough for an ice cube to fit underneath.

evaluate

Keep It Cool Design Challenge: Testing Our Models

When all students have finished their structures, go outside on a sunny day to test them. Remember

to take a cooler of ice with you! Give each student the Keep It Cool Design Challenge student page and a clipboard. *Ask*

? How will we know if our models solved the problem of providing a place to cool off on the playground? (If it works, the ice cube inside the structure will stay frozen longer or be less melted than the one beside the structure.)

Have students set up their models in a sunny area. Encourage them to rotate their models and find the best angle to position it (the angle that provides the most shade). Then, give each pair two ice cubes of the same size and shape. Tell them to place one ice cube inside the model and one beside it. As students are waiting for the ice cubes to melt, have them each draw a picture of their model on the student page.

Connecting to the Common Core
Writing
TEXT TYPES AND PURPOSES: K.2, 1.2, 2.2

Writing

After waiting long enough to see a difference, have students compare the two ice cubes and answer the questions on the student page. For the first question, they need to circle which ice cube took longer to melt. For the second question, they need to write "yes" or "no" about whether their structure worked. For the third question, they need to write a sentence explaining how they know it did or didn't work. An example of an acceptable response would be "I know it worked because the ice cube in the model did not melt as fast as the ice cube in the Sun."

Have students compare their designs and discuss what they think worked the best. Then, have them brainstorm some ideas to improve their designs. If time allows, give students an opportunity to improve their designs and test the models again.

STEM at Home

Have students complete the "I learned that …" and "My favorite part of the lesson was …" portions of the STEM at Home student page as a reflection on their learning. They may choose to do the following at-home activity with an adult helper and share their results with the class. If students do not have access to the internet at home, you may choose to have them complete this activity at school.

"At home, we can experiment to find out which will melt faster: an ice cube on black paper or an ice cube on white paper. This experiment should be done outside in a sunny spot on a warm day. We will need the following materials:

- 2 clear plastic containers
- 1 sheet of black construction paper
- 1 sheet of white construction paper
- 2 ice cubes of the same size and shape
- 1 watch or timer

Lay the papers next to each other in the Sun. Put an ice cube in each container, and place the containers on the papers. Then, record the time it takes for each ice cube to melt completely."

For Further Exploration

This section is provided to help you encourage your students to use the science and engineering practices in a more student-directed format. This box lists questions and challenges related to the lesson that students may select to research, investigate, or innovate. Students may also use the questions as examples to help them generate their own questions. After selecting one of the questions in the box or formulating their own questions, students can individually or collaboratively make predictions, design investigations or surveys to test their predictions, collect evidence, devise explanations, design solutions, or examine related resources. They can communicate their findings through a science notebook, at a poster session or gallery walk, or by producing a media project.

Research

Have students brainstorm researchable questions:

? What is inside a glass thermometer? How does it work?

? What does the color of a star tell you about its temperature?

? What are some ways engineers are designing buildings and parking lots to keep cities cooler?

Investigate

Have students brainstorm testable questions to be solved through science or math:

? Does the shape or size of an ice cube affect how fast it melts?

? What heats up faster in the Sun: a cup of water or a cup of sand?

? Do different-colored T-shirts have different surface temperatures in the Sun?

Innovate

Have students brainstorm problems to be solved through engineering:

? Can you design a way to make s'mores with the Sun's energy?

? Can you design a cup to keep your drink cold on a hot day?

? Can you design a container to keep an ice pop frozen on a hot day?

More Books to Read

Miller, R. 2014. *Engineers build models.* New York: Crabtree.
Summary: Clear, concise text and photographs featuring child engineers introduce the importance of building models in engineering. Featured models include map models, diagrams, blueprints, and three-dimensional models.

Sherman, J. 2004. *Sunshine: A book about sunlight.* Minneapolis: Picture Window Books.
Summary: Simple text and colorful illustrations describe how the Sun heats Earth and causes our weather. It also explains rainbows, day and night, and moonlight.

Comparing Temperatures

Directions: Write the names of four different outside surfaces in the "Surface" column. Your teacher will measure the temperature of each surface in the shade and in the Sun. Write the temperatures in the chart.

Surface	Temperature in Shade (°F)	Temperature in Sun (°F)
1.		
2.		
3.		
4.		

Circle the highest temperature. Why do you think it was the highest?

_____

_____

_____

_____

Let's Learn About the Sun

Before Reading True or False		**After Reading** True or False
_____	1. The Sun is a star.	_____
_____	2. The Sun is much smaller than Earth.	_____
_____	3. The Sun is much farther away than the Moon.	_____
_____	4. A spaceship has been to the Sun.	_____
_____	5. Without the Sun, Earth would be cold and dark.	_____

Name: _____

Keep It Cool
Design Challenge

Challenge: Design a structure to provide a place to cool off on the playground.

Draw your model. Show the Sun in your picture.

Which ice cube took longer to melt? (circle)

In the model   In the Sun

Did your model work? _____

How do you know?

_____

_____

_____

_____

Name: _____

STEM at Home

Dear _____,

At school, we have been learning about how **the Sun warms the Earth.**

I learned that: _____

_____

My favorite part of the lesson was: _____

_____

_____

At home, we can experiment to find out which will melt faster: an ice cube on black paper or an ice cube on white paper. This experiment should be done outside in a sunny spot on a warm day. We will need the following materials:

- 2 clear plastic containers
- 1 sheet of black construction paper
- 1 sheet of white construction paper
- 2 ice cubes of the same size and shape
- 1 watch or timer

Lay the papers next to each other in the Sun. Put an ice cube in each container, and place the containers on the papers. Then, record the time it takes for each ice cube to melt completely.

Black Paper	White Paper
_____ min.	_____ min.

Our conclusion: The ice cube on _____ paper melted faster because

_____

_____

Move It!

Description

Students explore simple cause-and-effect relationships with forces and motion by experimenting with a toy dog (named Newton) and a toy car. They read about how pushes and pulls can stop and start motion and change an object's direction. Then, they apply their knowledge to complete a design challenge: getting Newton into his doghouse!

Suggested Grade Levels: K–2

LESSON OBJECTIVES Connecting to the *Framework*		
Science and Engineering Practices	**Disciplinary Core Ideas**	**Crosscutting Concepts**
Analyzing and Interpreting Data	**PS2.A:** Forces and Motion	Cause and Effect
Constructing Explanations and Designing Solutions	**ETS1.C:** Optimizing the Design Solution	Scale, Proportion, and Quantity

Featured Picture Books

TITLE: ***Newton and Me***
AUTHOR: **Lynne Mayer**
ILLUSTRATOR: **Sherry Rogers**
PUBLISHER: **Sylvan Dell**
YEAR: **2010**
GENRE: **Story**
SUMMARY: *Named an Outstanding Science Trade Book by the National Science Teachers Association and the Children's Book Council, this rhyming book about a boy and his dog, Newton, provides a fun introduction to forces and motion.*

TITLE: ***Move It! Motion, Forces and You***
AUTHOR: **Adrienne Mason**
ILLUSTRATOR: **Claudia Dávila**
PUBLISHER: **Kids Can Press**
YEAR: **2005**
GENRE: **Non-Narrative Information**
SUMMARY: *This fun-to-read and easy-to-understand book provides a simple introduction to forces and motion, with many opportunities to "stop and try it!"*

Time Needed

This lesson will take several class periods. Suggested scheduling is as follows:

Day 1: Engage with Picture Walk Through *Newton and Me* and **Explore** with Ride, Newton, Ride! and *Newton and Me* Read-Aloud

Day 2: Explain with *Move It!* Read-Aloud

Day 3: Elaborate with Newton's Doghouse Challenge and **Evaluate** with Our Best Design

Materials

For Ride Newton, Ride! (per group of 3–4 students)

- 1 small plastic dog figurine (*Note:* Safari Ltd TOOBS and other brands of dog figurines are available in packs of 12 from many retailers.)
- 1 small die-cast metal car (such as Hot Wheels or Matchbox)
- Tape
- 12 in. section of toy-car track to use as a ramp (or use a small wooden ramp)
- Books to change the height of the ramp
- Approximately 8 in. square of green felt or textured fabric to represent grass
- 2 plastic bingo markers
- 2 identical small plastic containers with lids, 1 empty and 1 filled with rocks or marbles

> **SAFETY**
> - Have students wear safety glasses or goggles for this activity.
> - Immediately pick up any marbles or other items that fall on the floor to avoid a slip-and-fall hazard.
> - Remind students to stay clear of objects rolling down inclined ramps onto the floor to avoid tripping.

For Move It! *Read-Aloud*

- 3 identical opaque plastic tubs with lids (prepared in advance):
  - 1 filled with rocks or marbles
  - 1 filled with uncooked macaroni
  - 1 filled with crumpled paper
- Cotton ball for each student
- Straw for each student
- Cutting board or other item that could be used as a smooth ramp
- Large eraser
- Small stone
- Small wooden block
- Ice cube
- Glue stick

For Newton's Doghouse Challenge (per group of 3–4 students)

- Same dog, car, track, books, felt or fabric, and containers as used in the Ride, Newton, Ride! activities

- Tape
- 16 oz. plastic cup with a half circle cut in the lip that is big enough for Newton and his car to fit through when the cup is upside down
- 12 in. ruler

Student Pages

- Ride, Newton, Ride!
- Move It!
- Our Best Design
- STEM at Home

Background for Teachers

This lesson provides students with opportunities to recognize the simple cause-and-effect relationships between force and motion. Students explore what happens when toy cars travel down ramps, move across different surfaces, and bump into objects of different weights. These explorations give them the opportunity to observe the effects of pushes, pulls, gravity, and friction before learning the names of these forces from a nonfiction read-aloud. Students learn that *forces* are pushes and pulls and can make objects start moving, slow down, speed up, change direction, or stop moving. *Gravity* is a force that pulls everything down toward the center of Earth. *Friction* is a force that occurs when two objects rub together. Friction can slow down an object that is moving. For example, when a toy car rolls from a tile floor onto a piece of felt, the car slows down because of the increased friction created by the rougher surface. This lesson explores basic cause-and-effect relationships between forces and motion. Once cause-and-effect relationships are recognized, students can begin to predict and explain events in new circumstances and apply their scientific understandings to solving problems. In this lesson, students apply what they have learned to complete a simple force and motion design challenge. *Note:* The activities in this lesson are ideally done on tile floors. If your classroom floors are carpeted, try to find other areas in your school that have smooth-surface floors, such as the hallways, gymnasium, or cafeteria.

engage

Picture Walk Through *Newton and Me*

 *Inferring*

Connecting to the Common Core
Reading: Literature
INTEGRATION OF KNOWLEDGE AND IDEAS: K.7, 1.7, 2.7

Show students the cover of *Newton and Me*. Tell them that you are going to take a "picture walk" through the book and you would like them to try to infer what the book is about. As you show the pictures, have them signal when they see an illustration of something moving, such as the truck rolling down the hill, the wagon full of rocks being pulled across the yard, or the ball rolling in the grass. Students will likely recognize that the book is about a boy and his dog observing how ordinary things move.

Show students a small, plastic dog figurine. Tell them that the plastic dog will represent Newton,

the dog from the story. This dog is a little bit different from the dog in the story, however, because this dog travels only by car! Then, show them a die-cast metal toy car. Explain that before you read the book to them, they are going to have a chance to experiment with Newton, his car, a ramp made from a toy-car track (or a wooden ramp), some roadblocks (plastic containers), and felt or fabric. Tape the dog securely to the car, and tell students that from now on you will be referring to Newton and the car as *Newton's car.* Place Newton's car on the floor and *ask*

? What could we do to get Newton's car to move? (Students will likely suggest you push it. Push the car and observe its motion.)

? What are some other ways to get Newton's car to move? (They might say pull it, blow air on it, wave a paper behind it, place it on a ramp, pull it with a magnet, etc.)

? Once Newton's car is moving, how could we get it to stop? (Block it with something, put it on a rough surface, etc.)

? How could we get it to change direction? (Push it in a different direction, pull it in another direction, etc.)

? How could we get it to speed up? (Push harder, make it go down a hill, etc.)

? How could we get it to slow down? (Put it on carpet, give it a lighter push, etc.)

explore

Ride, Newton, Ride!

Connecting to the Common Core
Mathematics
MEASUREMENT AND DATA: K.MD.2

Divide students into groups of three to four, and tell them that they are going to make Newton's car move in various ways. Give each group of students a toy car, a plastic dog (Newton), tape to attach

HIGH AND LOW RAMPS

Newton to the car, a 12 in. section of toy-car track to use as a ramp, some books to stack to change the height of the ramp, two plastic bingo markers for marking the car's location, a 8 in. square piece of felt or other textured material, an empty plastic container, an identical plastic container filled with rocks or marbles, and a copy of the Ride, Newton, Ride! student page. Lead the groups through the following activities, and have them record their results on the student page. At the end of each activity, have each group compare its results with the findings of other groups.

Part A: Low and High Ramps

Have each group use tape to securely attach the toy dog to the car. Then, have each group make an incline by placing one end of the toy-car track on a book. (A small piece of tape can be used to keep the ramp in place.) Have each group release Newton's car (they should not push it!) from the top of the ramp, observe how fast it moves, and record how far it moves by placing a plastic bingo marker next to where it stops. *Ask*

? Were you surprised by how far the car went? (Answers will vary.)

? How do you think you could make the car go faster and farther, without pushing it? (Students will likely suggest raising the height of the ramp.)

Allow students to experiment with changing the height of the ramp. Each time they change the height, they should compare the distance the

CHANGING THE SURFACE

HEAVY WEIGHT AND LIGHT WEIGHT

car rolled to the marker they placed on the first run. Then, *ask*

? How did changing the height of the ramp affect the distance and speed that Newton traveled? (Generally, the higher the ramp, the faster and farther the car goes. However, some students will notice that if the ramp becomes too high, the car crashes onto the floor and does not move as far.)

Have students circle their answer in Part A on the student page. They should realize that the car goes faster and farther after going down a higher ramp.

Part B: Changing the Surface

Have each group place a square of felt or textured fabric beneath the end of the ramp, release Newton's car from the top, and use a bingo marker to record how far Newton travels. Next, have the students place a smooth surface at the end of the ramp (or let it roll onto the floor if you have tile) and repeat. Have them use the two markers to compare how far the car traveled on each of the two surfaces. *Ask*

? Did the surface make a difference in how fast and far Newton traveled? (Students should notice that the car moves faster and farther on the smooth surface than it does on the rough surface.)

Have students circle the appropriate answer in Part B on the student page.

Part C: Light Weight Versus Heavy Weight

Note: Be sure to try this activity in advance with your materials to determine the best ramp height.

Give each group two identical plastic containers, one that is empty and one that is filled with rocks or marbles. Have each student hold the containers in their hands so they can feel that one is much heavier than the other. Have each group set up a ramp and then place the empty container at the end of the ramp. Have each group release Newton's car from the top of the ramp and mark how far the container moves. *Ask*

? Did the container move? (Answers will vary.)

? What made it move? (the car hitting it)

? What do you think will happen when we do the same thing but replace the lighter container with the heavier container? (Answers will vary.)

Have students place the heavier container at the end of the ramp and release the car again. Have them mark how far the heavier container moves. Have students use the two markers to compare how far each container moved. Have them circle their answer in Part C of the student page. Students should notice that the lighter container moves farther than the heavier one.

Newton and Me Read-Aloud

 Making Connections: Text to Self

> Connecting to the Common Core
> **Reading: Literature**
> KEY IDEAS AND DETAILS: K.1, 1.1, 2.1

Next, tell students that you are going to read the book *Newton and Me* and you would like them to signal when they hear something in the book that reminds them of one of the activities they did during the Ride, Newton, Ride! activities. When they signal, stop reading and ask them to share their connections. Following are some examples:

- Page 6 relates to Part B: "The ball won't roll far in the rough, grassy yard. It rolls much farther on a surface that's smooth and hard." Students should realize that the text and illustration on this page connects with the changing surface activity. The grass is like the felt or fabric they used. Things roll faster and therefore farther on a smooth surface than a rough surface.

- Page 11 relates to Part A: Students should relate the hill on page 11 to the low-and-high ramps activity and realize that the higher the hill, the faster and farther things move as they travel down it.

- Pages 15–17 relate to Part C: They should connect the heavy and light wagons on pages 15–17 to the heavy and light containers in the light weight versus heavy weight activity and recognize that the heavier something is, the harder it is to get it moving.

After reading, tell students that you have a nonfiction book to share with them that will introduce them to some new vocabulary they can use to describe the motion of objects.

explain

Move It! Read-Aloud

> Connecting to the Common Core
> **Reading: Informational Text**
> KEY IDEAS AND DETAILS: K.3, 1.3, 2.3

Ahead of time, gather the materials you need for this read-aloud so that you can easily flow back and forth between activities and explanations from the book (see Materials section). Show students the cover of *Move It!* and introduce the author, Adrienne Mason, and the illustrator, Claudia Dávila. Tell students that this book can help them learn more about forces and motion and the names of some of the different forces they observed when experimenting with Newton. The book is written in an interactive manner. You will be stopping to try different activities and asking questions as you read.

 *Move It! Cloze*

Before reading, pass out the Move It! student page. Directions for the students are as follows:

1. Cut out the words on the cards.

2. With a partner, take turns reading the words on the cards. Talk about each word and see if you can figure out what it means together.

3. Listen as your teacher reads the sentences aloud, and then place the cards in the blanks where you think they belong.

4. As your teacher reads the book *Move It!*, listen for the words on the cards.

5. After listening to the book, you will have a chance to move the cards again.

Have students place their cards in the blanks on the Move It! student page. They will have an opportunity to move them, if necessary, and glue them down after the read-aloud. Then, read the book aloud, pausing to respond to the questions posed by the author. Next, try the activities that follow.

PUSHING THE TUBS

 Stop and Try It

"Push It!" Activity

After reading through page 8, "Push It!," get out the three tubs you previously prepared and call on a few students to push the tubs. Then, *ask*

? Which tub needed the most force (the biggest push) to move?

? What do you think is in it?

? Which needed the least force (the smallest push) to move?

? What do you think is in it?

Remove the lids so that students can check their guesses, and then read the explanation on page 9 titled "What's Happening?," where students learn that it takes more force to move heavy things and less force to move lighter things.

PUFFING POWER

SLIDING ALONG

"Puffing Power" Activity

After reading through page 14, "Puffing Power," give each student a straw and a cotton ball. (We suggest using cotton balls instead of ping pong balls because cotton balls will not roll around the classroom.) Read through the procedure, and allow students to try each step. Then, read the explanation on page 14 titled "What's Happening?," where students learn that a smaller force causes the cotton ball to move slowly and a bigger force causes the cotton ball to move faster.

Read pages 16–25, pausing to ask the questions posed by the author. Skip the activity on pages 22–23 because it does not pertain to the activities in the explore phase.

"Sliding Along" Activity

When you get to pages 26–27, "Sliding Along," demonstrate the activity for the class. Follow the instructions step by step, and give students time to respond to the questions. Then, read the explanation on page 27 titled "What's Happening?" where students learn that there is more friction between some materials than others.

Finish reading the rest of the book aloud. Then, revisit the Move It! student page. Read through the sentences again, and give students the opportunity to move the cards if they need to. When they are satisfied with their choices, they can use a glue stick to glue the cards to the page. The sentences should read as follows:

Let's learn some new words about motion!

1. A push or a pull is called a **force**.
2. If you throw something in the air, it will fall back down. It is pulled down by a force called **gravity.**
3. Two surfaces rubbing together creates a force called **friction.**
4. A force is a push or a pull that starts an object moving or changes its **motion.**

Note: The ideas for parents and teachers shared on pages 30–31 of *Move It!* are simple ways to explore these concepts further in everyday situations, such as playing on the playground, kicking a ball, kicking a rolling ball to change its direction, dropping objects, lifting things, comparing the surfaces of everyday items, and dragging an object over different surfaces.

elaborate

Newton's Doghouse Challenge

Challenge students to apply what they have learned about force and motion to solve a problem. Tell students that Newton is having trouble parking his car in his doghouse without moving the doghouse or knocking it over. He needs their help! Give each group of three to four students a toy dog taped to a toy car, some tape, a piece of felt or fabric, a toy-car track, some books, the two containers of different weights, and a ruler. Make a "doghouse" for each group by cutting an opening in a plastic cup from the lip down (creating the "door"). The opening should be large enough for Newton and

NEWTON'S DOGHOUSE CHALLENGE

the car to go through. Have students place the cup upside down 1 ft. away from the end of the ramp with the door facing the ramp. Their challenge is to use the supplies to get Newton from the top of the ramp into the doghouse without touching the car *and* without moving the doghouse.

Encourage students to use what they learned from the books and activities to set up their design. Tell students that it might take a lot of tries to figure out the challenge. Remind them to not be discouraged if their design doesn't work right way. Remind them that real engineers spend a lot of time trying to figure out how to solve problems! Allow them several attempts, and encourage them to modify their designs until they get one that works. As you visit groups, ask guiding questions such as the following:

? What could you do to the ramp to make Newton's car go faster and farther or slower and not as far? (Make the ramp higher or lower by adding books.)

? How could you change the surface of what Newton's car is riding on to slow him down? (Place the felt or fabric on or near the ramp or in front of the doghouse.)

? What could you do to make the doghouse harder to move? (Make it heavier by putting the heavy plastic container on top of it.)

Students can solve the problem in three ways. (There are certainly other ways, but these three ways relate to the activities and reading they have done up to this point.) Students can do the following:

1. Change the angle of the ramp (e.g., add or remove books from the ramp).
2. Change the surface the car is rolling on (e.g., place the felt between the end of the ramp and the doghouse).
3. Make the doghouse heavier (e.g., place the heavy plastic container on top of the doghouse).

Their solution will likely be some combination of those three options.

When groups figure out a design that worked, have them demonstrate it for you. Then, *ask*

? Can you come up with a different way to meet the challenge?

After all groups have successfully met the challenge in at least two different ways, have them discuss what they thought was their best design. Groups should share with the rest of the class so that students can see that Newton's car can get into the doghouse multiple ways.

evaluate

Our Best Design

Connecting to the Common Core
Writing
TEXT TYPES AND PURPOSES: K.2, 1.2, 2.2

 **Writing**

Give each student the Our Best Design student page. Have students draw and label a picture of their team's best design. Their drawings should include Newton's car, the ramp, the doghouse (cup), and any other supplies they used.

Ask students the following questions about their design:

? How did you get Newton to start moving? (put him on top of the ramp)

? What force pulled Newton down the ramp? (gravity)

? What did you do to make Newton move faster? (raised the ramp)

? What did you do to make Newton move more slowly? (lowered the ramp or added a rough surface)

? How did you get Newton to stop moving? (put something in front of him, added a rough surface, and waited for him to stop)

? What force made Newton slow down on the rough surface? (friction)

? What problems did you encounter when designing your solution? (Answers will vary.)

? How did you solve those problems? (Answers will vary.)

? What is another solution you could try that might work? (Answers will vary.)

STEM at Home

Have students complete the "I learned that …" and "My favorite part of the lesson was …" portions of the STEM at Home student page as a reflection on their learning. They may choose to do the following at-home activity with an adult helper and share their results with the class. If students do not have access to these materials at home, you may choose to have them complete this activity at school.

"At home, we can test different objects to find out how they move down a ramp! To build a ramp, we will need some books to stack and a large, flat piece of wood or cardboard (a cutting board or cookie sheet without sides will work, too). Then, we can collect some small objects such as blocks, paper tubes, and balls and check (✓) whether they **roll, slide,** or **stay in place** when released from the top of the ramp. Predict, then try it!"

For Further Exploration

This section is provided to help you encourage your students to use the science and engineering practices in a more student-directed format. This box lists questions and challenges related to the lesson that students may select to research, investigate, or innovate. Students may also use the questions as examples to help them generate their own questions. After selecting one of the questions in the box or formulating their own questions, students can individually or collaboratively make predictions, design investigations or surveys to test their predictions, collect evidence, devise explanations, design solutions, or examine related resources. They can communicate their findings through a science notebook, at a poster session or gallery walk, or by producing a media project.

Research

Have students brainstorm researchable questions:

? Who was Isaac Newton, and what were some of his discoveries?

? Is the force of gravity different on the Moon?

? Are there other forces at work in the world besides gravity and friction?

Investigate

Have students brainstorm testable questions to be solved through science or math:

? Would adding weight to a toy car make a difference in how far it travels?

? What happens to the distance a toy car travels as you increase the height of the ramp? Is there a limit to how high you can make the ramp before the car falls off?

? Which surface slows the motion of a toy car more: construction paper, felt, or sandpaper?

Innovate

Have students brainstorm problems to be solved through engineering:

? Can you design a way for Newton's car to turn before it goes into the doghouse?

? Can you design a game with the supplies from Newton's Doghouse Challenge?

? Can you design a marble run using a box or piece of cardboard, straws or craft sticks, and tape?

More Books to Read

Bradley, K. B. 2005. *Forces make things move.* New York: HarperTrophy.
    Summary: Simple language and comical illustrations show how forces make things move, prevent them from starting to move, and stop them from moving.

Higgins, N. 2009. *Marvelous motion.* Edina, MN: Magic Wagon.
    Summary: Colorful cartoonish illustrations introduce the basics of force and motion.

Stille, D. 2004. *Motion: Push and pull, fast and slow.* Mankato, MN: Picture Window Books.
    Summary: Simple text and vivid illustrations offer an introduction to basic force and motion concepts, such as inertia, gravity, and friction.

Name: _____

Ride, Newton, Ride!

Part A: Low and High Ramps

| On which ramp did Newton go the fastest and farthest? | 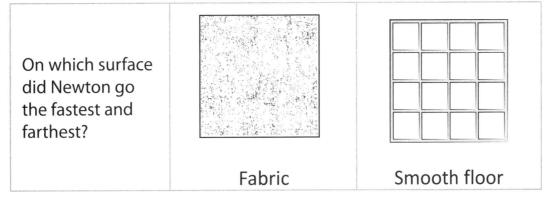 Low ramp | High ramp |

Part B: Changing the Surface

On which surface did Newton go the fastest and farthest?

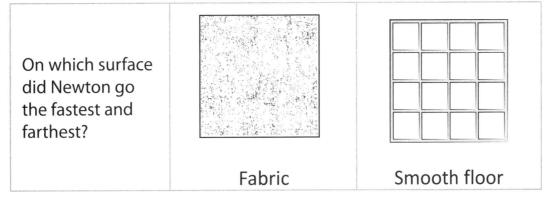

Fabric   Smooth floor

Part C: Light Weight Versus Heavy Weight

Which container moved the farthest when Newton's car hit it?

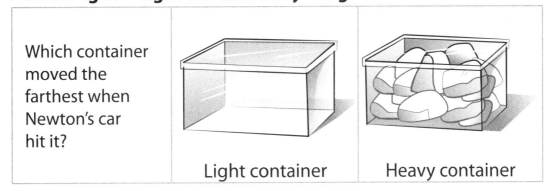

Light container   Heavy container

Name: _____

Move It!

Let's learn some new words about motion!

1. A push or a pull is called a _____.

2. If you throw something in the air, it will fall back down. It is pulled

   down by a force called _____.

3. Two surfaces rubbing together creates a force called

   _____.

4. A force is a push or pull that starts an object moving or changes its

   _____.

Directions: Cut out the cards and place them in the sentences
above. Then, listen as your teacher reads the book *Move It!*

force	gravity
motion	friction

Name: _____

Our Best Design

How did you get Newton's car into the doghouse? Draw and label your best solution in the box below.

Name: _____

STEM at Home

Dear _____,

At school, we have been learning about **forces and motion**—the ways pushes and pulls can stop and start motion as well as change an object's direction.

I learned that: _____

_____

My favorite part of the lesson was: _____

_____

At home, we can test different objects to find out how they move down a ramp! To build a ramp, we will need some books to stack and a large, flat piece of wood or cardboard (a cutting board or cookie sheet without sides will work, too). Then, we can collect some small objects such as blocks, paper tubes, and balls and check (✓) whether they **roll**, **slide**, or **stay in place** when released from the top of the ramp.

Predict, Then Try It!

Object	Rolls	Slides	Stays in Place

Let's Drum!

Description

After reading an inspirational story about a young female drummer, students learn about different types of drums, the basic parts of a drum, how drums make sound, and how repeated sound patterns are called *rhythms*. Students design and build their own drums out of everyday items, explain how they make sound, and create their own rhythms using their handmade drums.

Suggested Grade Levels: K–2

LESSON OBJECTIVES Connecting to the *Framework*		
Science and Engineering Practices	**Disciplinary Core Ideas**	**Crosscutting Concepts**
Constructing Explanations and Designing Solutions Obtaining, Evaluating, and Communicating Information	**PS4.A:** Wave Properties **ETS1.B:** Developing Possible Solutions	Patterns Scale, Proportion, and Quantity

Featured Picture Books

TITLE: ***Drum Dream Girl: How One Girl's Courage Changed Music***
AUTHOR: **Margarita Engle**
ILLUSTRATOR: **Rafael López**
PUBLISHER: **HMH Books for Young Readers**
YEAR: **2015**
GENRE: **Story**
SUMMARY: *Engle's beautiful, rhythmic poem tells the story of Millo Castro Zaldarriaga, a Chinese-African-Cuban girl who broke Cuba's traditional taboo against female drummers. It is an inspiring true story for dreamers everywhere.*

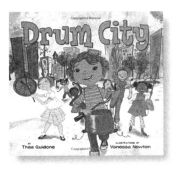

TITLE: ***Drum City***
AUTHOR: **Thea Guidone**
ILLUSTRATOR: **Vanessa Newton**
PUBLISHER: **Dragonfly Books**
YEAR: **2010**
GENRE: **Poetry**
SUMMARY: *A young boy begins banging on pots and pans in his front yard, enticing other children to join him. Before long, the entire city is feeling the beat.*

Time Needed

This lesson will take several class periods. Suggested scheduling is as follows:

Day 1: **Engage** with *Drum Dream Girl* Read-Aloud and **Explore** with Different Drums, Different Sounds

Day 2: **Explore** with Comparing Sounds and **Explain** with Drum Sounds Article

Day 3: **Elaborate** with *Drum City* Read-Aloud and Design a Drum

Day 4: **Evaluate** with My Drum Design

Materials

Per class

- World map or globe

For Different Drums, Different Sounds and Design a Drum

- 3 or more different types of drums, such as congas, bongos, timbales, snares, hand drums, and tubanos (Check with your school music teacher, high school band director, or local music school about borrowing drums, and possibly connecting you with a guest drummer, for this activity.)
- Clean cylindrical containers (with any sharp edges covered with duct tape or masking tape), such as the following:
  - Coffee cans
  - Popcorn tins
  - Cookie tins
  - Oatmeal containers
  - Plastic butter containers
- Items to use as drumsticks, such as the following:
  - Real wooden drumsticks (You can usually purchase inexpensive wooden drumsticks online for less than $1 each.)
  - Chopsticks
  - Dowel rods
  - Wooden spoons
  - Pencils

For Drum Sounds Article's Stop and Try It Activities

- Drumstick
- Drum (any type)
- Large bowl
- Plastic wrap
- Large rubber band or tape to attach plastic wrap to bowl
- 1 teaspoon dry rice grains

For Design a Drum

- Containers and items to use as drumsticks from earlier activities
- Materials to make drumheads, such as the following:
  - Duct tape
  - Packing tape
  - Heat-activated shrink wrap
  - Large balloons (nonlatex)
  - Large rubber bands or tape
  - Glue
- Art supplies to cover and decorate the drum shells, such as the following:
  - Construction paper
  - Markers
  - Crayons
  - Stickers
  - Patterned duct tape
  - Glitter

SAFETY
- Use safety glasses or goggles when constructing drums.
- Be sure that containers used did not previously hold food allergens (e.g., peanuts and tree nuts).

Student Pages

- Drum Sounds
- Design a Drum
- My Drum Design
- STEM at Home

Background for Teachers

The drum is probably the world's oldest musical instrument, yet the basic design has remained virtually unchanged to this day. A drum has three main parts: the head, rim, and shell. The *head* of a drum is the part that is struck with hands, sticks, or mallets. A drumhead is sometimes referred to as a *skin* because, for a long time, drumheads were made from stretched animal skins. Today, most drumheads are made of a synthetic polymer. The *rim* of a drum is the edge around the head. Drummers can play the rim of the drum to get a sound that is different from playing on the head. The *shell* of a drum is the part that has the head stretched over it. Most drum shells are wooden and have a cylindrical or truncated cone shape. However, some shells are bowl-shaped, such as timpani, and some are even six-sided and box-shaped.

A cylindrical shape helps the sound reverberate evenly inside the enclosed space when the drummer hits the drumhead, giving a fuller, richer sound. It is also easier to stretch a drumhead over a round shape than a rectangular or irregular shape. When a drumhead is struck, it *vibrates*, or moves up and down very quickly. The sound waves caused by the vibrations travel in all directions. When they reach your ears, you hear the drum. All sounds are caused by vibrations. The sound of a drum is affected by the size, shape, thickness, and material of the shell; the material and tightness of the head; and the object used to strike the drum. The sound can also be changed depending on where you hit the drum. Drums are typically played on their heads. But a drummer can also strike the rim or shell to add different sounds.

The difference between making noise on a drum and making music on a drum has to do with patterns. A drummer can keep a steady beat, or an unchanging tempo of a musical piece, but to really make music, a drummer also uses repeated patterns of sound called *rhythms*. A simple way to teach the concept of rhythm is to have students tap or clap out the rhythm of simple nursery rhymes. For example, clapping out each syllable of "Hickory Dickory Dock" (Hick/o/ry Dick/o/ry Dock) establishes a simple pattern that can be repeated to form a rhythm. The addition of sound patterns to make rhythms is just one example of how mathematics and music are related. It is interesting to note that many studies link musical training to both improved spatial-temporal reasoning skills and overall mathematics achievement.

In this lesson, students are introduced to the concept that vibrating materials make sound and sound can make materials vibrate. Then, they apply their knowledge of how drums make sound by making their own drums out of everyday materials. This activity incorporates the science and engineering practice of designing solutions. Students not only learn how drums make sound but also learn how music is made on drums by using repeated patterns of sound. The crosscutting concept of patterns is reinforced by students' creating rhythms on their own drums.

engage

Drum Dream Girl Read-Aloud

> Connecting to the Common Core
> **Reading: Literature**
> KEY IDEAS AND DETAILS: K.1, 1.1, 2.1

 Inferring

Show students the cover of *Drum Dream Girl* and introduce the author and illustrator. Read the title and subtitle aloud. Then, *ask*

? Based on the cover illustration and the title, what do you think this book is about? (Answers will vary.)

Next, show students the book trailer for *Drum Dream Girl* (see "Website" section). Explain that a book trailer is like a movie trailer; it gives you a preview of what the book is about. *Ask*

? Now, what do you think the book is about?

Read the subtitle of the book, *How One Girl's Courage Changed Music*, and *ask*

? What does *courage* mean? (bravery, the ability to do something you know is difficult)

 Determining Importance

Tell students that as you read the book aloud, you would like them to listen for examples of how the girl in the book showed courage and how she changed music in her country.

Then, read the book aloud, stopping periodically to ask guiding questions such as the following:

? How do you think the girl felt when she was told only boys should play drums? (disappointed, determined)

? What evidence from the text or illustrations made you think so? (She looks disappointed in the illustrations. She never gave up.)

? Do you think it was fair that only boys were allowed to play drums? (Answers will vary.)

? What happened when the girl was able to take lessons? (She learned more and practiced a lot.)

After reading, reread the title and subtitle, *Drum Dream Girl: How One Girl's Courage Changed Music*, and *ask*

How did the girl show courage? (She kept playing drums even though she was told girls could not play them. She practiced and practiced so that she could prove that girls can play as well as boys. She never gave up.)

How did the girl "change music"? (She proved that girls can play drums, and from then on, girls were allowed to play drums in her country.)

Finally, read the Historical Note at the end of the book, which reveals that this is the true story of a girl named Millo Castro Zaldarriaga, and that the "island of music" in the story is Cuba. Locate Cuba on a map or globe together. Tell students that Cuba is known for its lively, rhythmic music and that drums are a big part of Cuban music.

explore

Different Drums, Different Sounds

Connecting to the Common Core
Reading: Literature
KEY IDEAS AND DETAILS: K.1, 1.1, 2.1

Ask
? Can you recall the names of any of the drums from the book *Drum Dream Girl*? (congas, bongos, and timbales)

Refer to the author's descriptions of these drums: "tall conga drums, small bongo drums, and silvery moon-bright timbales." *Ask*

? Have you ever seen or heard these types of drums? (Answers will vary.)

? What other types of drums do you know of? (Answers will vary.)

 Making Connections:
Text to Text

If possible, bring in three or more different types of drums. The more variety in size and shape, the better. You may want to borrow them from your school music teacher, high school band director, or a local music school. Demonstrate how to play the drums, or, better yet, invite the music teacher or a drummer to your classroom to show students

EXPLORING DIFFERENT KINDS OF DRUMS

how various drums look and sound. Point out the different sizes and shapes of the drums, and have students listen for the different sounds that they make. Then, *ask*

? What were some differences among the drums? (They were different sizes and shapes. The drums made different sounds. Some were played with sticks, and some were played with hands.)

? How would you describe the shapes of the different drums you saw? (Answers will vary depending on the drums.)

? Do you notice a pattern in how drums are shaped? (They are usually a cylinder. They have something on top that you hit and a hollow area inside.)

? Why do you think most drums have round heads and are shaped somewhat like a cylinder? (They sound better, they can stand up on one end, etc.)

? Do you notice a pattern in how the size of the drum relates to the sound it makes? (Students should notice that larger drums typically make lower sounds, and smaller drums typically make higher sounds.)

? How do you make a drum sound louder? (Hit it harder.)

? How do you make a drum sound softer? (Hit it more lightly.)

Comparing Sounds

Next, tell students that they can make sounds similar to drums by using everyday objects that are shaped like drums. In advance, collect a variety of different-sized cylindrical containers such as metal or plastic coffee cans, popcorn canisters, cookie tins, cardboard oatmeal containers, plastic butter containers, and so on. Cover any sharp edges of metal containers with duct tape or masking tape. Be sure the containers have been cleaned, and confirm that there were no food allergens contained in them previously (e.g., do not use peanut butter containers or tree nut tins). Tell students that they are going to use these containers as models of (headless) drums, and you would like them to compare the different sounds the models make when they are struck. Give each student one of the containers and a drumstick, chopstick, dowel rod, wooden spoon, or pencil. Have them tap their containers in different places and notice the different sounds.

Then, reread the pages from *Drum Dream Girl* that describe how she played rhythms: "At home, her fingertips rolled out their own dreamy drum **rhythm** on tables and chairs," and "Her hands seemed to fly as they rippled, rapped, and pounded all the **rhythms** of her drum dreams." *Ask*

? What do you think it means to play rhythms? (Answers will vary.)

Teach students a simple rhythm. Practice the rhythm in unison several times, with each student playing his or her own container. Then, tell students that you would like each to play the rhythm on his or her container in turn. Everyone else should be silent and listen to the sound each type of container makes.

Afterward, collect the materials, and *ask*

? After playing some rhythms together, what do you think the word *rhythm* means? (Answers will vary.)

? Did all of the containers sound the same when you hit them? (no)

? What was different about the sounds? (Some were loud, some soft, some high, some low, etc.)

? Why do you think each container sounded different? (Answers will vary.)

explain

Drum Sounds Article

Connecting to the Common Core
Reading: Informational Text
KEY IDEAS AND DETAILS: K.1, 1.1, 2.1

Before reading the article together, *ask*

? What are the parts of a drum? (Answers will vary.)

? How does a drum make sound? (Answers will vary.)

? What do you think a rhythm is? (Answers will vary.)

? What is the difference between making noise with a drum and making music with a drum? (Answers will vary.)

Tell students that you have an article that will help them learn the answers to these and other questions about drums.

 Stop and Try It

Give each student a copy of the Drums Sounds student page. Have students follow along as you read the article aloud. Stop at the end of each section, and do the Stop and Try It activities together. Below are the instructions for each Stop and Try It activity and some explanations for you to adapt and share with students.

Parts of a Drum Activity

Identify the head, rim, and shell on a drum. Listen closely as each part is hit with a drumstick, and compare the sounds that are made. *Ask*

? Why do you think the sound is different when you hit the drumstick on the head, rim, and shell? (Those parts are made of different materials and are different sizes and shapes.)

Explanation: Students should be able to identify the three parts of a drum on several different drums and hear the different sounds made by hitting the head, rim, and shell. Although most of the drumming occurs on the head of the drum, drummers will sometimes strike the rim or shell to get a different sound.

OBSERVING SOUND MAKING OBJECTS VIBRATE

bowl will work best. Be sure the plastic wrap is stretched tightly and secured around the opening of the bowl, using tape or a large rubber band. A teaspoon of dry rice sprinkled on top should be sufficient.)

Explanation: Students should notice that the grains of rice vibrate even when the drum does not touch the plastic wrap or bowl. They vibrate more when the drum is hit harder and less when the drum is hit more softly. Explain to students that the sound vibrations are traveling through the air and making the plastic wrap vibrate, which causes the rice grains to move. Students may also notice that because the rice grains are moving, they are also making a faint sound.

How Drums Make Music Activity

Try tapping out the rhythm of a simple nursery rhyme with a pencil on your desk, such as "Hickory Dickory Dock" (Hick/o/ry Dick/o/ry Dock). Now, create your own rhythm and teach it to a partner. Play the rhythm together. You're making music!

Connecting to the Common Core
Mathematics
GEOMETRY: K.G.2

Have students recall the different shapes of the drums from the book *Drum Dream Girl* and the Different Drums, Different Sounds activity (conga: cylinder or barrel shape; bongo: cylinder or "cut-off-cone" shape; timbale: cylinder shape). Draw both a cylinder and a truncated cone on the board. Tell students that most drums are shaped roughly like a cylinder or cut-off cone because those shapes help the sound reverberate, or bounce around, inside the drum better when you hit the drumhead. It is also easier to stretch a drumhead evenly over a round shape as opposed to a rectangular or irregular shape. However, there are bowl-shaped drums such as timpani, and there is even a drum shaped like a box (rectangular prism) that is played with the drummer sitting on top of it!

How Drums Make Sound Activity

You can't see sound vibrations, but you can see how sound makes objects vibrate. Cover a bowl tightly with plastic wrap. Sprinkle some grains of rice on the plastic wrap. Observe the rice as a drum is hit near, but not touching, the bowl. What happens when the drum is hit harder? (*Note:* A large, sturdy

---

Connecting to the Common Core
Mathematics
OPERATIONS AND ALGEBRAIC THINKING: K.OA.1

Explanation: Banging on drums can sound quite noisy and chaotic, but when you play a rhythm on a drum, it becomes music. Explain that a rhythm is a repeating pattern and it can be simple or

Designing drums

complex. Grab a drum or container and demonstrate a simple pattern such as Hick/o/ry Dick/o/ry Dock. Repeat the pattern several times and have students play along. Explain that adding simple patterns together creates a rhythm. Then, demonstrate a rhythm that is a little more complicated, and have students repeat it. Next, allow students to come up with their own rhythm on a drum or container, and teach it to a partner or the class. Finally, explain that because a rhythm is a repeated pattern, or patterns added together, rhythm actually involves mathematics. In fact, there are many connections between music and math. Tell students that researchers have even discovered that learning to play music helps kids do better in math!

elaborate

Drum City Read-Aloud

> Connecting to the Common Core
> **Reading: Literature**
> Key Ideas and Details: K.1, 1.1, 2.1

 Determining Importance

Show students the cover of *Drum City* and introduce the author and illustrator. Tell students to look closely at the cover illustration, and then *ask*

? What do you think this book might be about? (Students will likely notice the kids on the cover banging on homemade drums and marching in a parade.)

Tell students that as you read the book aloud, you would like them to look and listen for all of the different types of homemade drums the children use in the book. Read the book aloud, being sure to demonstrate the intended rhythm of the book by emphasizing the larger words.

Design a Drum

Tell students that they are going to have the opportunity to design their own drums. Each student can use a container from the explore phase of the lesson as the shell of his or her drum. Provide a variety of different materials from which students can make drumheads, such as duct tape, packing tape, shrink wrap, or large balloons. Make sure they stretch their drumheads across the opening of the containers as tightly and as evenly as possible to ensure the best sound. They can use tape or rubber bands to fasten the head to the rim of the drum. Allow students time to tinker with the various supplies to make a drum that sounds the way they want it to sound. Provide supplies for them to make drumsticks, too, such as dowel rods, chopsticks, wooden spoons, or pencils. If desired, students can wrap duct tape on the ends to make them look more like drumsticks.

Encourage students to experiment with changing the sounds of their drums by using different sizes of cylinders and by stretching different materials across the opening to make the drumheads. When they are satisfied with their drum designs, they can cover the shells of their drums with construction paper and decorate them with markers, crayons, stickers, colorful duct tape, glitter, and so on.

If you prefer to have students design and build their drums at home, you can send home the Design a Drum student page, copied front-to-back with the My Drum Design student page. Be sure to have them write in the due date at the bottom.

COMPARING OUR DRUMS

evaluate

My Drum Design

Connecting to the Common Core
Writing
RESEARCH TO BUILD AND PRESENT KNOWLEDGE: K.8, 1.8, 2.8

 **Writing**

Give each student a copy of the My Drum Design student page. Have students sketch their drum and label the head, rim, and shell. They will also list the materials they used and explain why they chose those materials. Finally, they will explain how their drum makes sound using the word *vibrates, vibrating,* or *vibration.* For example, "My drum makes sound by *vibrating* when I strike the head with a wooden spoon."

 **Turn and Talk**

When students finish designing their drums, have each student find a partner and turn and talk. They can compare the materials they used and the sounds their drums make. Next, allow them to demonstrate the sounds for the class. They should explain what they used for the head and the shell and how they made the drumsticks (if applicable). Each student can demonstrate the unique sound of his or her drum by playing a short rhythm for the class. For fun, your students could parade through your school or playground, similarly to the children in the book *Drum City,* who all play the same rhythm on their drums as they march along.

STEM at Home

Have students complete the "I learned that ..." and "My favorite part of the lesson was ..." portions of the STEM at Home student page as a reflection on their learning. They may choose to do the following at-home activity with an adult helper and share their results with the class. If students do not have access to the internet or these materials at home, you may choose to have them complete this activity at school.

"At home, we can watch a video together called 'Stomp,' which is about using everyday objects to make patterns of sound that turn noise into music."

Search "STOMP" at pbslearningmedia.org *to find the video at* www.pbslearningmedia. org/resource/vtl07.math.algebra.pat.stomp/ stomp-cyberchase.

"After we watch the video, we can look around the house to find objects we can use to create rhythms. We can even invite friends and family to join in!"

For Further Exploration

This section is provided to help you encourage your students to use the science and engineering practices in a more student-directed format. This box lists questions and challenges related to the lesson that students may select to research, investigate, or innovate. Students may also use the questions as examples to help them generate their own questions. After selecting one of the questions in the box or formulating their own questions, students can individually or collaboratively make predictions, design investigations or surveys to test their predictions, collect evidence, devise explanations, design solutions, or examine related resources. They can communicate their findings through a science notebook, at a poster session or gallery walk, or by producing a media project.

Research

Have students brainstorm researchable questions:

? What were the first drums made of?

? What are some other types of drums from around the world?

? How do string instruments make sound?

Investigate

Have students brainstorm testable questions to be solved through science or math:

? Can sounds travel underwater?

? Can sounds travel through solids?

? What materials muffle sound the best?

Innovate

Have students brainstorm problems to be solved through engineering:

? What could you design to carry your drum as you play it?

? How can you build a rubber band guitar that plays different notes?

? How can you build a cup-and-string telephone to talk to a friend across the room?

Website

Drum Dream Girl (book trailer)
www.youtube.com/watch?v=_lruQabrUco

More Books to Read

Boothroyd, J. 2011. *Loud or soft? High or low? A look at sound.* Minneapolis: Lerner.
Summary: Part of the *Lightning Bolt Books* series, this book provides a simple introduction to sound—how sounds are made, how they travel, and how sounds compare.

Perkins, A. 1969. *Hand, hand, fingers, thumb.* New York: Random House.
Summary: This classic *Bright and Early Book for Beginning Readers* features lovable "monkeys" (chimpanzees, actually) who play a variety of drums with their hands, fingers, and thumbs. Readers will find themselves tapping out the infectious rhythms of the book: "Hand, hand, fingers thumb. One thumb, one thumb, drumming on a drum. One hand, two hands, drumming on a drum. Dum ditty, dum ditty, dum dum dum."

Pinkney, B. 1994. *Max found two sticks.* New York: Simon & Schuster Books for Young Readers.
Summary: Max doesn't feel like talking to anyone, but when he sees two heavy twigs fall to the ground, he picks them up and begins tapping out the rhythms of everything he sees and hears around him—the sound of pigeons startled into flight, rain against the windows, distant church bells, and the rumble of a subway. Then, when a marching band rounds Max's corner, something wonderful happens.

Name: _____

Drum Sounds

Since the beginning of history, people have been making and playing drums. There are many different kinds of drums, but they all work in the same basic way.

Parts of a Drum

A drum typically has three basic parts: head, rim, and shell. The **head** is the part you hit with your hand or a drumstick. The first drumheads were made out of animal skin, but now they are usually made from some kind of plastic. The **rim** is the edge around the head. Drummers can play the rim of the drum to get a sound that is different from playing on the head. The **shell** is the base of the drum. The size, shape, and material of the shell affect the sound of the drum. Most drum shells are wooden, roughly the shape of a **cylinder,** and hollow inside.

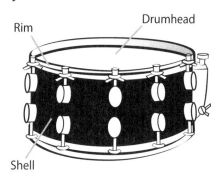

Rim · Drumhead · Shell

STOP and TRY IT: Identify the head, rim, and shell on a drum. Listen closely as each part is hit with a drumstick, and compare the sounds that are made.

How Drums Make Sound

When you hit a drum, the drumhead **vibrates**, or moves back and forth very quickly. These **vibrations** create sounds waves that travel through the air in all directions. When they reach your ears, you hear the sound made by the drum. All sounds are caused by vibrations.

STOP and TRY IT: You can't see sound vibrations, but you can see how sound makes objects vibrate. Cover a  bowl tightly with plastic wrap. Sprinkle some grains of rice on the plastic wrap. Observe the rice as a drum is hit near, but not touching, the bowl. What happens when the drum is hit harder?

How Drums Make Music

Banging on a drum might just sound like noise. In order to make music with a drum, you play a **rhythm**. A rhythm is a repeated pattern of sounds.

STOP and TRY IT: Try tapping out the rhythm of a simple nursery rhyme with a pencil on your desk, such as "Hickory Dickory Dock" (Hick/o/ry Dick/o/ry Dock) Now, create your own rhythm and teach it to a partner. Play the rhythm together. You're making music!

Name: _____

Design a Drum

Dear _____,

We have been learning about drums during a STEM unit on sound. We have studied the parts of a drum, how drums make sound through **vibration**, and how different kinds of drums produce different sounds. Your child will be designing and building his or her own drum by following the directions below.

Directions

1. Choose a clean cylinder-shaped container for the shell of the drum, such as a coffee can, cookie tin, or oatmeal container. Remove the lid from the container, and cover any sharp edges with duct tape or masking tape.

2. Test different materials for the drumhead. You can try duct tape, packing tape, shrink wrap, or even a large balloon.

3. Make the drumhead by taping or stretching the material tightly over the rim of the container. You may need to use large rubber bands to hold the material in place.

4. Tape or glue construction paper around your drum to completely cover the shell.

5. Decorate the paper with markers, crayons, stickers, colorful duct tape, glitter, or other materials.

6. Test different objects to use for drumsticks. Dowel rods, chopsticks, pencils, or wooden spoons will do.

7. Play your drum! Practice creating simple patterns of sound, or **rhythms**, on your drum.

Drums are due on_____.

Name: _____

My Drum Design

Sketch your drum in the box below and label the **head, rim,** and **shell.**

[blank box for sketch]

1. What materials did you use to make your drum?

_____

_____

_____

2. Why did you choose those materials?

_____

_____

_____

3. How does your drum make sound? Use the word **vibrates, vibrating,** or **vibration** in your explanation.

_____

_____

Name: _____

STEM at Home

Dear _____,

At school, we have been learning about drums. We have studied the parts of a drum, how they make sound through **vibrations**, and how **rhythms** can be played on drums.

I learned that: _____

_____

My favorite part of the lesson was: _____

_____

At home, we can watch a video together called "Stomp," which is about using everyday objects to make patterns of sound that turn noise into music.

 Search "STOMP" at *pbslearningmedia.org* to find the video at *www.pbslearningmedia.org/resource/vtl07.math.algebra.pat. stomp/stomp-cyberchase.*

After we watch the video, we can look around the house to find objects we can use to create rhythms. We can even invite friends and family to join in!

Object	How We Used It to Create Rhythms

Get the Message

Description

Students read a tall tale featuring the invention of the electric telegraph, learn how to decipher Morse code, and explore the influence of the telegraph and various other communication innovations over time. Then, they design and build devices that use sound or light to communicate over a distance and compare the strengths and weaknesses of each.

Suggested Grade Level: K–2

LESSON OBJECTIVES Connecting to the *Framework*		
Science and Engineering Practices	**Disciplinary Core Ideas**	**Crosscutting Concept**
Constructing Explanations and Designing Solutions Engaging in Argument From Evidence	**PS4.C:** Information Technologies and Instrumentation **ETS1.C:** Optimizing the Design Solution **ETS2.B:** Influence of Engineering, Technology, and Science on Society and the Natural World	Patterns

Featured Picture Books

TITLE: *Jackrabbit McCabe and the Electric Telegraph*
AUTHOR: **Lucy Margaret Rozier**
ILLUSTRATOR: **Leo Espinosa**
PUBLISHER: **Schwartz & Wade**
YEAR: **2015**
GENRE: **Story**
SUMMARY: *Jackrabbit McCabe's unusually long legs have made him the fastest thing around, and he uses his speed for everything from racing against horses to fetching the doctor. But when the electric telegraph arrives in Windy Flats, Jackrabbit may have met his match.*

TITLE: *Communication: Long Ago and Today*
AUTHOR: **Lindsy O'Brien**
PUBLISHER: **Capstone Press**
YEAR: **2013**
GENRE: **Non-Narrative Information**
SUMMARY: *Simple text and photographs describe the history of communication technologies, from ancient hieroglyphics to the computers of today.*

Time Needed

This lesson will take several class periods. Suggested scheduling is as follows:

Day 1: **Engage** with *Jackrabbit McCabe and the Electric Telegraph* Read-Aloud and **Explore** with Crack the Code

Day 2: **Explain** with Card Sequencing and *Communication: Long Ago and Today* Read-Aloud

Day 3: **Elaborate** with Get the Message Design Challenge

Day 4: **Evaluate** with Comparing Devices

Materials

For Card Sequencing

- Communication Innovation Cards (1 uncut set per pair of students)
- Sentence strips (optional, 2 per pair)
- Glue (optional)

For Get the Message Design Challenge

- Various materials to build a communication device that uses *light*, such as the following:
  - Flashlights, finger lights, and so on
  - Construction paper or index cards
  - Scissors
  - Opaque plastic cup
- Various materials to build a communication device that uses *sound*, such as the following:
  - Coffee cans (Cover sharp edges with duct tape or masking tape.)
  - Different-sized plastic cups
  - Pencils, spoons, and so on
  - Bells
  - Plastic eggs to fill with rice, beans, or popcorn
  - Coins and rubber bands to make homemade finger cymbals

SAFETY
- Use safety glasses or goggles when doing this activity.
- Use caution when working with scissors to avoid cutting or puncturing skin.
- Remind students never to eat food used in class activities.

Student Pages

- Morse Code Key (½ page, cut out)
- Crack the Code
- Get the Message Design Challenge
- Evaluating Your Design
- STEM at Home

Background for Teachers

In 1837, the *electric telegraph* was patented in the United States by American artist and inventor Samuel Morse. Before the telegraph, most messages sent over a distance were handwritten and had to be delivered on horseback. It could take days to carry a message a long distance. The telegraph allowed messages to be sent over great distances almost instantly by sending electrical pulses through wires. To send a telegraph, a handwritten message would be carried to a telegraph operator, who would then translate it into *Morse code,* a series of dots and dashes. The operator would tap the code on the telegraph, which would send electrical impulses through a wire to the receiving operator's location. There, the pulses were recorded as dots and dashes on a thin strip of paper. The receiving operator would translate the message from Morse code back into words, and that written message (called a *telegram*) would be delivered.

ELECTRIC TELEGRAPH

Telegraphs could even be sent across the ocean, after undersea cables were laid along the ocean floor. Newspapers, railroads, and government agencies used most telegraph wires, but the public also used them to share important personal news over long distances, such as marriages, births, and deaths. People would pay by the word to send a telegram, so the messages were usually short. The invention of the telegraph revolutionized communication. At last, people had a way to learn of important events soon after they happened. Although no longer widely used today, Morse code is still used by amateur radio operators and helps some people with disabilities communicate. The invention of the telegraph began the telecommunication age and led to many more innovations, such as the telephone. In the 1870s, inventor Alexander Graham Bell found a way to use a telegraph wire to send the sound of his voice. By the late 1800s, wires connected major cities around the world.

In this lesson, students learn about the telegraph's significant influence on society and how it paved the way for many other communication innovations. They read about the history of communication, from cave paintings to telephones to smartphones. Then, they are challenged to design and build devices that use light or sound to communicate over a distance and compare the strengths and weaknesses of those devices.

If students have not had experience learning about the science of light and sound, you might consider sharing two other *Picture-Perfect Science* lessons to introduce these concepts: Chapter 15, "Mirror, Mirror," from *More Picture-Perfect Science Lessons* (Morgan and Ansberry 2007), and Chapter 10, "Sounds All Around," from *Even More Picture-Perfect Science Lessons* (Morgan and Ansberry 2013).

engage

Jackrabbit McCabe and the Electric Telegraph Read-Aloud

Connecting to the Common Core
Reading: Literature
KEY IDEAS AND DETAILS: K.1, 1.1, 2.1

 **Inferring**

Show students the cover of *Jackrabbit McCabe and the Electric Telegraph* and introduce the author, Lucy Margaret Rozier, and illustrator, Leo Espinosa. *Ask*

? From looking at the cover and reading the title, what do you think this book is about? (Students might infer that some sort of race is going on and that the wires on the cover have something to do with the electric telegraph.)

? Have you ever heard of an electric telegraph? What do you think it does? (Answers will vary.)

 Questioning

Read the book aloud. Then, *ask*

? Do you think this book is fiction or nonfiction? (Fiction, because a man could not run as fast as a train or grow that fast.)

Explain that this story is a type of fiction story called a *tall tale*. A tall tale is a story that is told as if it were true but has exaggerated elements. Tall tales usually center around a main character who has unbelievable abilities. Students may be familiar with tall tales about Johnny Appleseed, Pecos Bill, Paul Bunyan, or John Henry. *Ask*

? Who is the main character in this story? (Jackrabbit McCabe)

? What unbelievable ability does he have? (to run incredibly fast—faster than horses and trains)

Explain that tall tales often also include some parts that are true. In this case, the invention of the electric telegraph really did happen, and it dramatically changed the speed at which people could communicate.

explore

Crack the Code

Read the Author's Note on page 31 about the invention of the telegraph and Morse code. Here, the author explains how a telegraph operator would tap out words in Morse code, which were sent as electrical pulses through a wire. On the other end of the wire, another person would change the codes into a written message called a *telegram*.

Tell students that they are going to have the opportunity to use Morse code to decode a message. Give each student the Crack the Code student page and the Morse Code Key (½ page sheet). Model how to use the key by deciphering the first word together. Then, have students use the code to figure out the rest of the message. The deciphered mes-

USING MORSE CODE

sage should read, "You got the message." Explain that this process mirrors what a telegraph operator would have to do when he or she *received* a message: The operator would translate the dots and dashes into words.

Next, tell students that the first thing a telegraph operator would need to do to *send* a message would be to take a written message and translate it into Morse code. Have students write their own messages using Morse code. Tell them that most telegrams were short because people who sent them had to pay by the word! Encourage them to keep their messages to five words or less. They must first write the message out on a separate piece of paper and then translate it into Morse code on the student page. This task can be challenging, so you may want to show students the Morse Code Machine from *Boys' Life* (see "Website" section) as an online tool to help them create their messages. The students can type in their letters, and the machine will show the Morse code. After students have completed their messages, they can trade with another student to decipher each other's messages.

After all students have had a chance to both decode a message and write their own messages in Morse code, *ask*

? Did you think it was easy or hard to use Morse code? (Answers will vary.)

? Was it harder to decipher a message with the code or write a message with the code? (Answers will vary.)

? What do you think it would have been like to be a telegraph operator? (Answers will vary.)

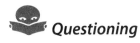explain

Card Sequencing

 *Questioning*

Connecting to the Common Core
Reading: Informational Text
KEY IDEAS AND DETAILS: K.3, 1.3, 2.3

Ask

? What does it mean to communicate? (to share information or ideas with other people)

? In what ways do people communicate? (talking, facial expressions, writing notes, texting, talking on the phone, etc.)

? How do you most often communicate with people when you are far apart? (phone, text messages, e-mail, FaceTime, Skype, etc.)

? Imagine a time when there were no phones, no computers, and no electricity. How would you have communicated with people when you were not with them? (Answers will vary.)

Show students the cover of *Communication: Long Ago and Today* and introduce the author, Lindsy O'Brien. Tell students that this book is going to take them through the history of communication so they can see how drastically it has changed over the years.

Give each pair of students an uncut set of Communication Innovation Cards. Explain that an *innovation* is a new idea, device, or method of doing something. As long as humans have been communicating, we have been trying to come up with better ways to do it. Each of the cards represents an innovation that changed the way people communicate. Explain that before you read, you would like the students to cut out the cards and place the innovations in order from earliest to most recent. Tell them that if they are not familiar with all of the innovations, it is OK to make their best guess using the pictures on the cards. Explain that they will learn about each innovation from the book and that, after the read-aloud, they will have a chance to reorder the cards.

Communication: Long Ago and Today Read-Aloud

Read the book aloud, discussing how each innovation made communication faster, more efficient, and more accessible to more people.

 *Card Sequencing (After Reading)*

After reading, have students go back to the Communication Innovation Cards and use what they learned to reorder the cards. Using the timeline on page 19, go through the correct sequence together. The correct order is as follows:

1. Cave Paintings
2. Paper
3. Printing Press
4. Pony Express
5. Telegraph
6. Telephone
7. Radio
8. Television
9. Internet
10. Smartphone

You may want to have students color the cards and glue them in the correct order on sentence strips so they can display their work in the classroom.

 *Turn and Talk*

Ask

? Now that we have the innovations in order, how does each innovation improve on the one before it? (Answers will vary.)

? What communication innovations do you think will come next? (Answers will vary.)

elaborate

Get the Message Design Challenge

Tell students that for hundreds of years, people have been using light and sound to send messages over distances, because sound and light can travel fast and far. For example, in ancient times, people would communicate by banging out specific rhythms on drums. These rhythms would relay messages to people far away. Before satellite communication, sailors used light to communicate with people on other ships. Bright signal lights would be used to send messages in Morse code by opening and closing shutters on the light. Short pulses of light represented the dots, and longer pulses of light represented the dashes.

Tell students that they are going to have the opportunity to use the design process to design and build a device that sends messages using codes. They will each work with a partner to design a device that uses either light or sound to send messages. Give each student the Get the Message Design Challenge student page. Although they will be working in pairs, each student will need his or her own student page. Explain the challenge, and show them the materials and tools you are providing. Encourage "out-of-the-box" thinking by asking students to consider other classroom materials that might be used. Have them follow along as you read the instructions on the student page. Brainstorm some possible designs together, such as the following:

Light

- A flashlight or finger light with construction paper or an index card that can cover the light to make patterns
- A flashlight or finger light in an opaque plastic cup with the bottom partially cut to make a flap

A COMMUNICATION DEVICE

Sound

- A cup or coffee can that could be hit with a pencil or spoon to make different patterns
- A bell that could be rung in different patterns
- A plastic egg that could be filled with rice, beans, or popcorn to make a rattling sound
- Finger cymbals made out of rubber bands and coins

Have students decide what kind of device they want to design and circle *light* or *sound*. Next, they will come up with a design and draw it. You will need to sign off on their design drawing (Teacher Checkpoint under step 1 on the student page) before they begin building. Students can now use the materials provided to build their devices. Once they finish building, they can write their codes. You will need to sign off on their codes (Teacher Checkpoint under step 3) before they test their device. Encourage students to keep their codes fairly simple. For example, two taps means "raise your hand," and three taps means "jump up." Once their codes are approved, they can test their design, recording their results in the Trial 1 column of the table. Students then give the device a rating from "Didn't Work" to "Worked Great" based on evidence of its effectiveness and explain why they gave it that rating. Next, the partners discuss how to improve their design, make any agreed changes, then trade places and repeart the test, recording their results in the Trial 2 column. Finally, students rate the device again and explain their rating.

Communicating with Light

Communicating with Sound

evaluate

Comparing Devices

Writing

After students have completed the design challenge, give them each a copy of the Evaluating Your Design student page. On this page, they will evaluate whether their device would work under different conditions and list the strengths and weaknesses of their device in the table provided. Then, they will compare the strengths and weaknesses of their design with another pair's device. Finally, they will share what changes they would make to

their device or code if they had the opportunity to redesign one more time.

STEM at Home

Have students complete the "I learned that …" and "My favorite part of the lesson was …" portions of the STEM at Home student page as a reflection on their learning. They may choose to do the following at-home activity with an adult helper and share their results with the class. If students do not have access to the internet or these materials at home, you may choose to have them complete this activity at school.

"At home, we can use an interactive website called Technology Over Time, which explores the innovations in technology since 1900."

Search "PBS Tech Over Time " to find the website at www.pbslearningmedia.org/resource/ate10.sci.engin.design.techover-time/technology-over-time.

"We can scroll through the years by dragging the rectangle across the timeline. Then, I can interview a parent, grandparent, or adult friend to see how technology has changed in his or her lifetime!"

For Further Exploration

This section is provided to help you encourage your students to use the science and engineering practices in a more student-directed format. This box lists questions and challenges related to the lesson that students may select to research, investigate, or innovate. Students may also use the questions as examples to help them generate their own questions. After selecting one of the questions in the box or formulating their own questions, students can individually or collaboratively make predictions, design investigations or surveys to test their predictions, collect evidence, devise explanations, design solutions, or examine related resources. They can communicate their findings through a science notebook, at a poster session or gallery walk, or by producing a media project.

Research

Have students brainstorm researchable questions:

? How is Morse code still used today?

? Who invented the printing press, and how did it change communication?

? What did the first cell phones look like, and how have they changed over the years?

Investigate

Have students brainstorm testable questions to be solved through science or math:

? Which materials are best for making a string-and-cup telephone?

? What is the longest distance you can send a clear message using a string-and-cup telephone?

? Survey your friends and family: How do they get news? Radio? Television? Newspaper? Internet? Graph the results, then analyze your graph. What can you conclude?

Innovate

Have students brainstorm problems to be solved through engineering:

? Can you make a "telephone" from two cups and a string?

? Can you and a friend design a code to send secret messages to each other?

? Can you design a stand to hold a cell phone?

References

Morgan, E., and K. Ansberry. 2007. *More picture-perfect science lessons: Using children's books to guide inquiry, K–4*. Arlington, VA: NSTA Press.

Morgan, E., and K. Ansberry. 2013. *Even more picture-perfect science lessons: Using children's books to guide inquiry, K–5*. Arlington, VA: NSTA Press.

Website

Morse Code Machine From *Boys' Life*
http://boyslife.org/games/online-games/575/morse-code-machine

More Books to Read

Kalman, B. 2014. *Communication: Then and now*. New York: Crabtree Publishing.
Summary: Part of the *From Olden Days to Modern Ways in Your Community* series, this book explores the various ways people communicate and how these ways have changed over time.

Yates, V. 2008. *Communication*. Chicago: Heinemann.
Summary: Part of the *Then and Now* series, this book uses simple text and photographs to compare communication methods from long ago with today's communication technologies.

Morse Code Key

A	● —	J	● — — —	S	● ● ●
B	— ● ● ●	K	— ● —	T	—
C	— ● — ●	L	● — ● ●	U	● ● —
D	— ● ●	M	— —	V	● ● ● —
E	●	N	— ●	W	● — —
F	● ● — ●	O	— — —	X	— ● ● —
G	— — ●	P	● — — ●	Y	— ● — —
H	● ● ● ●	Q	— — ●	Z	— — ● ●
I	● ●	R	● — ●		

Morse Code Key

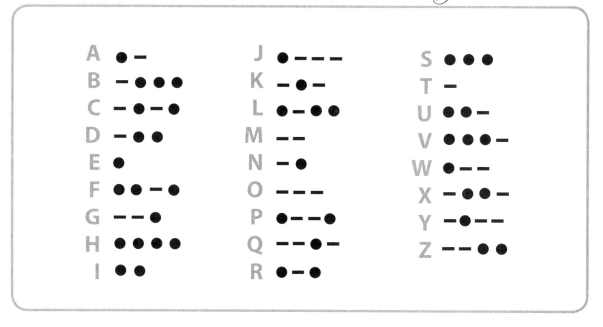

A	● —	J	● — — —	S	● ● ●
B	— ● ● ●	K	— ● —	T	—
C	— ● — ●	L	● — ● ●	U	● ● —
D	— ● ●	M	— —	V	● ● ● —
E	●	N	— ●	W	● — —
F	● ● — ●	O	— — —	X	— ● ● —
G	— — ●	P	● — — ●	Y	— ● — —
H	● ● ● ●	Q	— — ●	Z	— — ● ●
I	● ●	R	● — ●		

National Science Teachers Association

Crack the Code

1. Use the Morse Code Key to decode the message below.

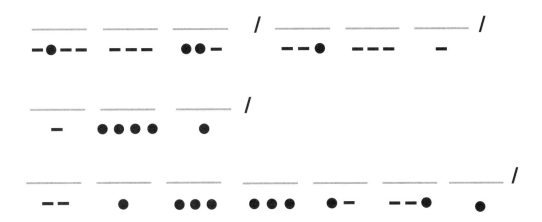

2. Now, write your own message in Morse code!

   a. Write your message out on a separate piece of paper.

   b. Use the Morse Code Key to write it in Morse code below. Use a slash "/" to separate words.

   c. Trade with a friend, and figure out each other's messages.

Communication Innovation Cards

Smartphone

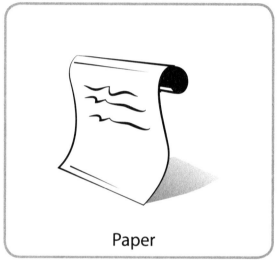

Paper

Cave paintings

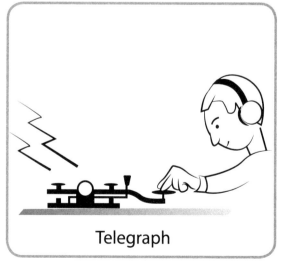

Telegraph

Printing press

Television

Pony Express

Radio

Internet

Telephone

Name: _____

Get the Message Design Challenge

Challenge: Design a device to communicate over a distance using light or sound.

Circle one:

Light

Sound

Step 1: Design the Device

Labeled Drawing

Teacher Checkpoint _____

Step 2: Build the Device

Build your device. You will need to figure out a way to send these messages to your partner:

- Raise your hand.
- Jump up.
- Touch the ground.

Step 3: Create the Codes

Together, create simple codes to send the messages across the room to your partner.

Message	Code	Trial 1 Record ✓ or ✗	Trial 2 Record ✓ or ✗
Raise your hand			
Jump up			
Touch the ground			

When you are finished creating the codes, signal your teacher.

Teacher Checkpoint _____

Step 4: Test the Device—Trial 1

One of you will use the codes to send the messages across the room to your partner. Do not send them in order.

Record your results: Put a checkmark ✓ in the **Trial 1** column above if it works or an ✗ if it doesn't work.

Step 5: Rate Your Device (circle one)

Didn't Work   Worked OK   Worked Great

Why did you give it that rating? _____

_____

_____

Step 6: Improve Your Design

Based on your first test, discuss how to improve your design. Should you modify your device, use it in a different way, change your code, make a completely different device? Then, make the changes you agreed on.

Labeled Drawing of Improved Device

Step 7: Test the Device—Trial 2

Trade jobs with your partner, repeat the test, and record your results in the **Trial 2** column of the chart.

Step 8: Rate Your Device Again (circle one)

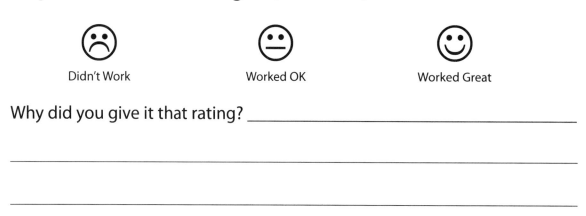

Didn't Work   Worked OK   Worked Great

Why did you give it that rating? _____

_____

_____

Name: _____

Evaluating Your Design

1. Would your design work if …

	Yes	No
the room was dark?		
the room was loud?		
you couldn't see your partner?		
you wanted to send a secret message?		

2. What are the strengths and weaknesses of your design?

Strengths	Weaknesses

3. Find another pair that used a different design. Compare the strengths and weaknesses of your design with the strengths and weaknesses of that pair's design.

4. If you had the chance to redesign your device or code, what would you change? Draw and write your ideas.

Name: _____

STEM at Home

Dear _____,

At school, we have been learning about the science and engineering behind **communication**. We have studied how messages were sent by telegraph using **Morse code** and how communication has changed over the years.

I learned that: _____

_____

My favorite part of the lesson was: _____

_____

At home, we can use an interactive website called Technology Over Time, which explores the innovations in technology since 1900.

Search "PBS Tech Over Time" to find the website at *www. pbslearningmedia.org/resource/ate10.sci.engin.design. techovertime/technology-over-time.*

We can scroll through the years by dragging the rectangle across the timeline. Then, I can interview a parent, grandparent, or adult friend to see how technology has changed in his or her lifetime!

Person's Name: _____ Year Born: _____

When you were younger, how did you do the following?

1. Listen to music: _____

2. Communicate with your friends: _____

3. Do your homework: _____

4. Enjoy your favorite shows: _____

Science Mysteries

Description

After reading a story about an extraordinary young scientist and then exploring the properties of matter, students learn that good scientists ask lots of questions and make careful observations. They also learn that scientists can use their skills to solve mysteries!

Suggested Grade Levels: K–2

LESSON OBJECTIVES Connecting to the *Framework*		
Science and Engineering Practices	**Disciplinary Core Ideas**	**Crosscutting Concepts**
Asking Questions and Defining Problems	**PS1.A:** Structure and Properties of Matter	Energy and Matter
Planning and Carrying Out Investigations	**ETS2.A:** Interdependence of Science, Engineering, and Technology	Patterns
Constructing Explanations and Designing Solutions		
Engaging in Argument From Evidence		

Featured Picture Books

TITLE: ***Ada Twist, Scientist***
AUTHOR: **Andrea Beaty**
ILLUSTRATOR: **David Roberts**
PUBLISHER: **Abrams Books for Young Readers**
YEAR: **2016**
GENRE: **Story**
SUMMARY: *In this charming story about a girl on a mission to use science to understand her world, young Ada discovers that her boundless curiosity can help her solve one smelly mystery!*

TITLE: ***Matter***
AUTHOR: **Abbie Dunne**
PUBLISHER: **Capstone Press**
YEAR: **2017**
GENRE: **Non-Narrative Information**
SUMMARY: *In this colorful, photo-packed book, young readers will learn about the properties of solids, liquids, and gases—how they can be mixed together and how they can change from one form to another.*

Time Needed

This lesson will take several class periods. Suggested scheduling is as follows:

Day 1: Engage with *Ada Twist, Scientist* Read-Aloud and Great Scientists Chart

Day 2: Explore with Properties of Matter and **Explain** with Our Results

Day 3: Explain with Properties of Matter Vocabulary and *Matter* Read-Aloud

Day 4: Elaborate with Mystery Mixtures

Day 5: Evaluate with Matter Quiz and Matter Mystery

Materials

For Ada Twist, Scientist *Read-Aloud (per pair of students)*

- 1 pack of sticky notes

For Properties of Matter (per student)

- Hand lens
- Safety goggles

For Properties of Matter (per group of 4 students)

Note: The quantities of salt, cornstarch, sand, and baking soda listed should be plenty for 4 classes.

- 1 lb. of salt
- 1 box of cornstarch (12 oz.)
- 1 lb. of white sand (Use a fine, crystalline sand for best results. Ashland decorative stone granules [1.75 lbs.] are available in white at Michaels craft stores.)
- 1 box of baking soda (12 oz.)
- Small tray containing the following materials:
    - 4 plastic 3 oz. cups, each half filled with a different substance: salt, cornstarch, white sand, and baking soda (Use a permanent marker to label each cup with the name of the substance.)
    - 1 small, plastic, lidded container filled with approximately ½ cup of water (labeled and closed)
    - 1 small, plastic, lidded container filled with approximately ¼ cup of vinegar (labeled and closed)
    - 2 plastic 5 ml eyedroppers (1 dedicated to each liquid)
    - 4 teaspoons (1 dedicated to each solid)
    - 16 wooden, noncolored craft sticks for stirring (4 per student)
    - 16 plastic 3 oz. bath cups (4 per student)

For New Vocabulary List (per student)

- Vocabulary Cards (1 strip of cards, precut)
- Tape or glue

For Mystery Mixtures (per group of 4 students)

- Small tray containing the following materials:

- 2 plastic 3 oz. bath cups, each half filled with a different "mystery mixture": equal parts cornstarch and sand (mixture A), and equal parts salt and baking soda (mixture B) (Use a permanent marker to label each cup "Mystery Mixture A" or "Mystery Mixture B.")
- 1 small, plastic, lidded container filled with approximately ½ cup of water (labeled and closed)
- 1 small, plastic, lidded container filled with approximately ¼ cup of vinegar (labeled and closed)
- 2 plastic eyedroppers (1 dedicated to each liquid)
- 2 teaspoons (1 dedicated to each mystery mixture)
- 8 wooden, noncolored craft sticks for stirring (2 per student)
- 8 plastic 3 oz. bath cups (2 per student)

Student Pages

- Properties of Matter data sheet
- Properties of Matter testing mat
- New Vocabulary List
- Mystery Mixtures data sheet
- Mystery Mixtures testing mat
- Matter Quiz
- Matter Mystery
- STEM at Home

Background for Teachers

Matter is all around us. *Matter* is defined as anything that has mass and takes up space. The paper this book is written on, the water in your bottle, the air you are breathing—they are all made of matter! So what is matter made of? All matter is made of tiny *atoms*. They are so small that you cannot see them with your eyes or even with a standard microscope. Atoms combine to form molecules, and these molecules make up a variety of substances. Matter can be described by its properties. Some properties of matter include color, texture, hardness, solubility (ability to dissolve in other substances), reactivity (ability to chemically react with other substances), and state.

Most matter on Earth is found in one of three states; solid, liquid, or gas. In this lesson, students find examples of all three states of matter as they observe common household substances such as salt, sand, baking soda, cornstarch, water, and vinegar. Each state of matter can be identified by its distinctive properties of shape and volume. A *solid* has a definite shape and a definite volume. Its molecules are the most tightly bound together of the three main states of matter. Solids can be poured only if they are made of very small particles such as salt crystals, grains of sand, or powdered substances. Salt crystals look like tiny cubes. Their flat surfaces reflect light, so they look somewhat shiny. Sand, depending on its mineral composition, may be a mixture of different-shaped crystals and more irregular grains. A powder, such as baking soda or cornstarch, is a dry solid composed of a large number of very fine particles that may flow freely when tilted or poured.

A *liquid* has a definite volume, but its shape changes more readily because its molecules are more loosely bound together than those of a solid. A liquid, whether it is thick or thin, is a wet substance that can be poured and always takes the shape of its container. A *gas* has no particular shape or volume. It will expand to fill the space it is in. It can also be compressed to fit a smaller container. Gas has this property because the distances between the molecules of a gas are relatively much greater than the distances between the molecules of a solid or liquid. A bubble is a thin sphere of liquid enclosing air or another gas, such as water vapor or carbon dioxide. Much of the universe is actually composed of a fourth state of matter known as *plasma*. Plasma has properties different from the other three fundamental states of matter. Scientists can generate plasma in a lab, and it naturally exists inside stars.

Matter can be combined in different ways. A *mixture* is made up of two or more different substances that are mixed but not combined chemically. Mixtures can be solids, liquids, or gases in any combination. Sand and salt stirred together creates a mixture. Food coloring in water is a mixture. Air is a mixture of gases. One particular type of mixture is called a *solution,* in which one substance is evenly mixed with another, making the particles of the substance too small to be seen or filtered out. Salt *dissolved* in water is a solution. The salt disappears, but it is still there. If you tasted the solution, it would taste salty. This mixture could be separated by heating the water until it evaporates, leaving behind the salt crystals.

Matter can also be combined chemically. When two or more substances are mixed, a new substance with different properties may be formed. This process is called a *chemical change.* Chemical changes create entirely new substances. After a chemical change occurs, physical methods, such as drying or filtering, cannot undo the change. In a chemical change, the molecules of different materials rearrange to form entirely new *compounds.* The new compounds have different properties. For example, when vinegar and baking soda are mixed, a chemical change occurs and a new substance—carbon dioxide gas—is formed.

In this lesson, students perform tests on some common household substances to observe their properties. In the process, they learn that matter can be described and classified by its observable properties and that matter can be a solid, liquid, or gas. An equally important component of this lesson is students learning about the practices of scientists. By engaging in scientific practices to observe the properties of matter (and eventually solving a mystery), students learn firsthand how scientists ask questions, carry out investigations, and support their claims with evidence. Students are also introduced to the crosscutting concept of energy and matter as they use their senses to make observations of different kinds of matter and the crosscutting concept of patterns as they recognize how patterns in certain substances appear and behave.

engage

Ada Twist, Scientist Read-Aloud

 **Inferring**

Show students the cover of *Ada Twist, Scientist* and introduce the author, Andrea Beaty, and illustrator, David Roberts. *Ask*

? Based on the cover, what do you think this book might be about? (a girl who likes science or is a scientist)

? How do you know? (from the title, the goggles she is wearing, or the pictures in the background)

? What do you think the tennis player on the cover has to do with the story? (Answers will vary.)

 **Questioning**

Connecting to the Common Core
Reading: Literature
Key Ideas and Details: K.1, 1.1, 2.1

After reading, *ask*

? Who is the tennis player on the cover? (Ada's brother)

? What mystery did Ada try to solve? (the source of the horrible stench)

? How did she try to solve it? (She wrote down lots of questions and then tested different smells with her homemade sniffing machine.)

? By the end of the story, did Ada solve the mystery? (no)

? Do you think scientists always find the answers to their questions? (Answers will vary.)

? The book says, "But this much was clear about Miss Ada Twist: She had all the traits of a great scientist." What are the traits of a great scientist? In other words, what are great scientists like? (Answers will vary.)

? How was Ada a great scientist? (Answers will vary but may include being passionate about understanding the world around you, being curious or asking questions that lead to more questions, making observations, doing research, performing tests and experiments, persevering, etc.)

? Look back at page 18. What safety equipment does Ada wear to help her do science safely? (She wears safety goggles and gloves and also has her hair pulled up.)

? Look back at page 29. What other tools or equipment do you see in the picture that Ada might use to help her do science? (books, models, beakers and flasks, microscope, screwdriver, etc.).

? Ada is holding one of the most important tools of a great scientist. What is it? (pen, pencil, or marker)

Explain that great scientists use pencils (or nowadays, computers or tablets!) to write down their questions, plan their investigations, record their data and conclusions, draw sketches and diagrams, make claims supported by evidence, and compose research papers to share with other scientists about their work. Good communication in all forms, not just writing, is one of the most important skills

ENGAGING WITH ADA TWIST, SCIENTIST

great scientists can have. They also need to be team players!

Great Scientists Chart

Make a whole-class chart titled "Great Scientists …," and *ask*

? What great scientists do you know of? (Answers will vary.)

? What are some of the skills or characteristics of great scientists? (Answers will vary.)

 ### *Turn and Talk*

Next, have students turn and talk with a partner to come up with a few words that describe what great scientists are like or what they do in their work. Pass out sticky notes, and have each pair of students write their words or phrases on separate sticky notes and put them on the chart. Then, put similar words and phrases together and look for common themes such as "Great scientists … make observations," "Great scientists … are curious,"

GREAT SCIENTISTS CHART

"Great scientists … ask questions," or "Great scientists … use safety equipment."

Next, *ask*

? Would *you* like to be a great scientist? (Answers will vary, but many students will likely say yes!)

explore

Properties of Matter

Tell students that you have a problem: You mixed some household substances for a science activity, but you forgot to label your mixtures. Show them two containers of white mixtures. Explain that Mystery Mixture A contains two substances, and Mystery Mixture B contains two other substances. Tell them you need the help of some great scientists to figure out what's what. Like Ada Twist, they are going to use the skills of a great scientist to solve this mystery! Tell them that the first thing they will need to do is find out more about the four substances that you used in the mixtures by observing each substance's individual properties.

Show students the labeled containers of salt, cornstarch, white sand, and baking soda. Tell them that these were the four household substances that you used in the mixtures. *Ask*

? What does "property of a substance" mean? (its characteristics or attributes)

? What properties of these substances could we safely observe? (what they look like [color, grains, etc.], and how they feel [texture, etc.])

? What are some ways that we can safely observe these substances? (look at them with a hand lens or microscope, touch them but do *not* taste them, etc.)

Arrange students into teams of four. Pass out a Properties of Matter data sheet, a Properties of Matter testing mat, a pair of goggles, and a hand lens to each student. Then, review the safety guidelines for observing and testing the substances in this activity. Tell students to use their best powers of observation!

SAFETY

- Wear your safety goggles at all times.
- Do not taste or sniff any of the substances.
- Do not pour any of the substances out of the containers. Use only the spoon or eyedropper that is assigned to each substance to avoid contamination.
- You will be touching the substances with your fingers. Do not put your fingers near your face after touching them. When the activity is over, you must wash your hands with soap and water.
- You will be using a hand lens to observe the substances. Do not let the hand lens touch the substance. Put your eye as close to the lens as possible, and lean over the cup until the substance comes into focus. Try closing the eye that is not close to the lens to get a better view.

Now, have one person from each team go to the materials table and carefully carry a tray back to his or her team. Tell students to wait until every team has its materials, and then you will go over the testing procedure together. Explain that their task is to be like Ada Twist, scientist, and ask questions and make observations while exploring the substances. Like Ada, they will also be following safety guidelines.

The first thing students should do is place a small plastic bath cup on each empty circle of their testing mat, which has circles labeled salt, cornstarch, sand, and baking soda. They should also place a craft stick next to each cup to use for stirring (stirring the water into the substance first, then stirring the vinegar into the substance and water). The purpose of the mat is to help the students identify the substance they are testing and allow for easy cleanup. After the activity, the plastic cups, substances, craft sticks, and mat can be tossed into the trash.

Next, practice the procedure for testing the substances by observing the salt together. Have students take turns putting 1 *level* teaspoon of the salt from the plastic cup labeled salt into their first cup. Remind them to keep the teaspoon *in* the original salt container; tell them not to use this spoon again in a different container to avoid contamination. Then, begin the testing as follows:

Test 1: Rub the substance between your fingers. How does it feel? Record the texture. *(Students may describe the salt as rough, hard, gritty, etc.)*

Test 2: Use a hand lens to look more closely at the substance. Can you see any crystals? Write yes or no. *(Explain that crystals can look like tiny cubes or other shapes with flat sides. Their flat surfaces reflect light, so they may look somewhat shiny. Students may write "yes," "no," or "can't tell," although the cubic shape of the salt grains should be obvious. The sand, depending on its mineral composition, may be a mixture of different-shaped crystals and more rounded grains.)*

Test 3: Use an eyedropper to add 3 full droppers of water *(3 teaspoons or 15 ml)* to the substance.

OBSERVING MATTER

Stir with a stick for 30 sec. What happens? *(Remind students to keep this eyedropper with the water container; tell them not to use this eyedropper with the vinegar to avoid contamination. Have them stir very well with the craft stick for about 30 sec. [counting to 30] and observe if the salt appears to disappear, bubble, get thick, or do something else. Most of the salt should eventually dissolve and disappear, but it is not important for students to use or understand the word dissolve at this point. They can also describe how the water appears [e.g., stays clear, turns cloudy, etc.].)*

Test 4: Use an eyedropper to add 10 drops of vinegar to the substance and water mixture. Stir with a stick for 30 sec. What happens? *(Remind students to keep this eyedropper with the vinegar container; tell them not to use this eyedropper with the water to avoid contamination. Have them stir very well with the craft stick for about 30 sec. [counting to 30] and observe if more of the salt appears to disappear, bubble, get thick, or do something else. A little more of the salt might eventually dissolve, but they should not observe bubbling. Students will most likely observe nothing happening.)*

After testing the salt, *ask*

? What else did you notice about the salt? (Answers will vary.)

? What questions do you have about the salt? (Questions will vary.)

Table 13.1. Sample Completed Data Table for Properties of Matter

Test	Salt	Cornstarch	Sand	Baking Soda
1. Texture (feel)	Rough and gritty	Slippery	Rough and gritty	Smooth
2. Crystals? (yes/no)	Yes	No	Yes	No
3. What happens with water?	Salt disappears, and water looks almost clear.	Water turns milky.	Sand does not disappear, and water looks cloudy.	Baking soda disappears, and water looks cloudy.
4. What happens with vinegar?	Nothing	Nothing	Nothing	Bubbles

Then, have students test the other three substances following the same procedure. Remind them of the safety guidelines as they work. A sample completed data table is shown in Table 13.1 (observations may vary).

explain

Our Results

Turn and Talk

After students have finished testing all four substances, have them turn and talk with a partner to compare the results of their tests. Then, *ask*

? What interesting observations did you make? (Answers will vary.)

? Were any of your results different from the other scientists' at your table? If so, why do you think so? (Answers will vary.)

? What do you think happened to the salt when you mixed it with the water? (Answers will vary.)

? What do you think happened to the cornstarch when you mixed it with the water? (Answers will vary.)

? What do you think happened to the sand when you mixed it with the water? (Answers will vary.)

? What did you notice when you added the vinegar to the baking soda? (It bubbled.)

? What else are you wondering about the substances? (Answers will vary.)

Explain that many of these questions will be answered through reading a nonfiction book during the next class period. Tell students to keep their Properties of Matter data sheets in a safe place because they will be referring to them later. Have students clean up by returning the tray of materials and stacking their cups. Then, have students fold up their mats with the craft sticks inside and dispose of them in the trash. Students should wash their hands after they clean up.

Properties of Matter Vocabulary

New Vocabulary List

Tell students that they will be learning some new vocabulary that will help them learn more about properties of matter. Give each student a set of five precut Vocabulary Cards (gas, solid, dissolve, matter, and liquid). Explain that all of these vocabulary words relate to the things the students observed in the Properties of Matter activity. They may be familiar with some of the words, but some may be new. Have students read each word aloud, then give them time to discuss with a partner what they think each word means.

Next, pass out the New Vocabulary List page to each student. A new vocabulary list is a "guess-and-check" type of visual representation. Students develop new vocabulary as they discuss or write their ideas about an unfamiliar word's meaning, read or hear the word in context, and then discuss or write their new understanding of the word. Read aloud each definition in the "What It Means" column, and then have students place each card where they think it belongs in the "Word" column. Tell them that at this point, it's OK to make a guess if they don't have much prior experience with the word. They will be able to find out if their prediction about each word's meaning is correct by reading the book *Matter.* During the read-aloud, they will be able to move their cards to the correct spot on the New Vocabulary List.

Matter Read-Aloud

 ### Using Features of Nonfiction

Connecting to the Common Core
Reading: Informational Text
Craft and Structure: K.4, 1.4, 2.4; K.5, 1.5, 2.5

Tell students you would like for them to signal (by touching one of their ears) when they hear a word on their vocabulary list as you read the book aloud. Introduce the author, Abbie Dunne, as you show them the cover of the book. Then, have them identify the table of contents, title page, glossary, index, and back cover as you flip through the book. *Ask*

? Is this book fiction or nonfiction? (nonfiction)

? How do you know? (It has photographs, a table of contents, glossary, index, etc.)

Read the book aloud, stopping at each page containing one of the new vocabulary words. After reading the word in context, read the glossary defi-

nition for the word as well. (The definitions on the New Vocabulary List are a combination of the in-text definitions and the glossary definitions.) Have students move their cards (if necessary) to the correct places on the New Vocabulary List. Then, have them write a few examples for each word from the text in the "Examples From the Text" column. Refer students to their Properties of Matter data sheet and write one or more examples for each word in the "Examples From the Activity" column. When you get to *gas,* students will likely not know what kind of gas is inside the bubbles they observed, so leave that "Examples From the Activity" space blank until after the *Matter* read-aloud. Repeat these steps for each word. Table 13.2 (p. 182) shows the answers.

Questioning

Connecting to the Common Core
Reading: Informational Text
Key Ideas and Details: K.1, 1.1, 2.1

Ask

? How did the book say you could tell if the salt is still in the water after it dissolves? (You could taste the water. The water would taste salty.)

Explain that when something dissolves, it seems to disappear. You can no longer see it, but it is still there. For example, if you stir salt into water and it dissolves completely, you would no longer be able to see the salt. The solution of salt and water would taste salty, although good scientists don't taste their experiments! If you stir sand into water, it would not dissolve. You would still be able to see the sand.

Then, *ask*

? What did you notice when you added the vinegar to the baking soda? (It bubbled.)

? What kind of matter do you think was inside the bubbles? (Answers will vary.)

Explain that bubbles are filled with gas. For example, when you blow a bubble with chewing

Table 13.2. Sample Completed Table for Matter Read-Aloud

Word	What It Means	Examples From the Text	Examples From the Activity
1. Matter	Anything that has weight and takes up space	Bed, books, me	Everything!
2. Solid	Matter that holds its size and shape	Rocks, ice cubes, metal	Salt, cornstarch, sand, baking soda
3. Liquid	Matter that is wet and takes the shape of its container	Milk, water, shampoo	Water, vinegar
4. Gas	Matter that has no shape and spreads out to fill a space	Air	?
5. Dissolve	To mix a substance into a liquid until you can no longer see it	Salt dissolves in water.	Salt and baking soda dissolve in water.

gum, you are filling it with a gas (your breath). When you blow a bubble with a bubble wand, you are filling it with a gas, too. Also, when you see bubbles inside boiling water, those are filled with gas (water vapor, which is an invisible form of water). In the activity, the students dripped vinegar onto baking soda and saw bubbles. Explain that when vinegar and baking soda are mixed together, they combine to form a new substance with new properties—a gas called carbon dioxide, or CO_2. This gas forms bubbles. However, if you could pop the bubbles, the invisible carbon dioxide gas inside would have no shape and would spread out into the room. Carbon dioxide is one of the gases that make up the air we breathe. Have students add carbon dioxide (or CO_2) as an example of a gas to the "Examples From the Activity" column of their New Vocabulary List. Finally, have students tape or glue the Vocabulary Cards to the proper spaces on the student page.

elaborate

Mystery Mixtures

Tell students that now that they have made observations of the properties of each substance, they can use that information to figure out the contents of

SAFETY

- Wear your safety goggles at all times.
- Do not taste or sniff any of the mixtures.
- Do not pour any of the mixtures or liquids out of the containers. Use only the spoon or eyedropper that is assigned to each substance to avoid contamination.
- You will be touching the mixtures with your fingers. Do not put your fingers near your face after touching them. When the activity is over, you must wash your hands with soap and water.
- You will be using a hand lens to observe the mixtures. Do not let the hand lens touch the mixture. Put your eye as close to the lens as possible, and lean over the cup until the mixture comes into focus. Try closing the eye that is not close to the lens to get a better view.

Mystery Mixture A and Mystery Mixture B! In other words, they can apply what they learned about the properties of the four different household substances to solve the mystery. They will be working with the same team they worked with for the Properties of Matter activity. Explain that they will need to refer to their Properties of Matter data sheet to compare the results of the tests on the known mixtures with those of the tests on these unknown mixtures. Then, pass out a Mystery Mixtures data sheet, a Mystery Mixtures testing mat, a pair of goggles, and a hand lens to each student. Review the safety guidelines for observing and testing the mystery mixtures in this activity. Tell students to use their best powers of observation!

Then, have one person from each team go to the materials table and carefully carry a tray back to their team. Tell students to wait until every team has its materials, and then you will go over the testing procedure together. Explain that their task is to be like Ada Twist, scientist, and ask questions and make observations to solve a science mystery! Like Ada, they will also be following safety guidelines.

The first thing students should do is place a small plastic bath cup on each circle of their testing mat, which has circles labeled Mystery Mixture A and Mystery Mixture B. They should also place a craft stick next to each cup to use for stirring (stirring the water into the mixture first, then stirring the vinegar into the mixture and water).

Next, review the procedure for testing the mystery mixtures by reading the directions at the top of the Mystery Mixtures data sheet together. Then, have students begin testing the mixtures as they

MYSTERY MIXTURES

did in the Properties of Matter activity. A sample completed data sheet is shown in Table 13.3 (observations may vary).

Table 13.3. Sample Completed Data Table for Mystery Mixtures

Test	Mystery Mixture A	Mystery Mixture B
1. Texture (feel)	Rough, gritty, and slippery	Rough, gritty, and smooth
2. Crystals? (yes/no)	Yes (some)	Yes (some)
3. What happens with water?	Water turns milky, but crystals/grains remain.	Water is a little cloudy, but crystals dissolve.
4. What happens with vinegar?	Nothing	Bubbles

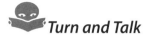

Turn and Talk

After students have finished testing both mystery mixtures, have them turn and talk with a partner to compare the results and observations of their tests. Be sure they refer to their Properties of Matter data sheets to come up with logical conclusions that are based on the properties of the known substances. Explain that good scientists always provide *evidence* when they make a claim. So, on their student page, they need to write more than just what they think the two substances in the mixture are. They must provide evidence to support their conclusions. Then, have students work together to fill out the conclusions and evidence statements at the bottom of the page. The best answers are as follows:

I think Mixture A contains cornstarch and sand because it turned milky, the crystals or grains didn't dissolve, and it did not bubble.

I think Mixture B contains baking soda and salt because both substances dissolved in water and it bubbled.

Synthesizing

Ask

? Which mystery mixture turned milky when mixed with water? (Mystery Mixture A)

? What do you think it must contain? (cornstarch)

? What is your evidence? (We observed the same thing happen with cornstarch in the Properties of Matter activity.)

? Which mixture had crystals that did not dissolve in water? (Mystery Mixture A)

? What do you think it must contain? (sand)

? What is your evidence? (We observed the same thing happen with sand in the Properties of Matter activity.)

? Which mixture had crystals that dissolved in water? (Mystery Mixture B)

? What do you think it must contain? (salt)

? What is your evidence? (We observed the same thing happen with salt in the Properties of Matter activity.)

? Which mixture bubbled when mixed with vinegar? (Mystery Mixture B)

? What do you think it must contain? (baking soda)

? What is your evidence? (We observed the same thing happen with baking soda in the Properties of Matter activity.)

? What are you still wondering? (Answers will vary.)

Congratulate students on being great scientists and using their observations, knowledge, and skills to solve a mystery, just like Ada Twist did!

evaluate

Matter Quiz

You may want to review the three states of matter by showing the short (1:39 min.) PBS Learning Media video called "What's the Matter?" (see "Website" section), by having students quiz each other on vocabulary using their New Vocabulary List pages, or by doing both. Then, pass out the Matter Quiz page. The answers are as follows:

1. Solid
2. Gas
3. Liquid
4. Liquid
5. Solid
6. C
7. D
8. E
9. B
10. A

Matter Mystery

As an additional evaluation activity, pass out the Matter Mystery student page, and have students work alone or with a partner to solve the mystery. The answers are as follows:

1. Cornstarch
2. Cornstarch does not have crystals. It turns water milky and does not bubble with vinegar.

Bonus: Students should draw a scientist on the back of their paper. Characteristics of a great scientist might include the following:

- Asks questions that lead to more questions
- Makes careful observations
- Uses tools
- Works safely
- Uses evidence to make claims
- Perseveres
- Communicates well

STEM at Home

Have students complete the "I learned that …" and "My favorite part of the lesson was …" portions of the STEM at Home student page as a reflection on their learning. They may choose to do the following at-home activity with an adult helper and share their results with the class. If students do not have access to the internet or have these materials at home, you may choose to have students complete this activity at school.

"At home, we can watch a short video together about how to make Oobleck, which is a substance that acts like both a solid and a liquid."

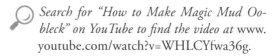 *Search for "How to Make Magic Mud Oobleck" on YouTube to find the video at* www.youtube.com/watch?v=WHLCYfwa36g.

"Then, we can make our own Oobleck by mixing 1 cup of water, 5 drops of food coloring, and 2 cups of cornstarch in a foil pie pan. Next, we can do a simple experiment by observing what will happen if we drop a marble from a distance of 2 feet into the pan of Oobleck."

For Further Exploration

This section is provided to help you encourage your students to use the science and engineering practices in a more student-directed format. This box lists questions and challenges related to the lesson that students may select to research, investigate, or innovate. Students may also use the questions as examples to help them generate their own questions. After selecting one of the questions in the box or formulating their own questions, students can individually or collaboratively make predictions, design investigations or surveys to test their predictions, collect evidence, devise explanations, design solutions, or examine related resources. They can communicate their findings through a science notebook, at a poster session or gallery walk, or by producing a media project.

Research

Have students brainstorm researchable questions:

? What kinds of scientists study matter?

? What kind of gas is in soda (or pop)?

? How do smells travel through the air?

Investigate

Have students brainstorm testable questions to be solved through science or math:

? Does salt dissolve faster in warm water or cold water?

? What combination of cornstarch and water makes the best Oobleck?

? Survey your friends: If you could be a scientist, what kind would you be? Graph the results, then analyze your graph. What can you conclude?

Innovate

Have students brainstorm problems to be solved through engineering:

? Can you design a toy rocket that works with vinegar and baking soda?

? Can you build a model of a volcano that uses vinegar and baking soda to represent lava?

? Can you design a way to prove that air is matter (has weight and takes up space)?

Website

"What's the Matter?" (video)

http://cet.pbslearningmedia.org/resource/evscps.sci. phys.matter/whats-the-matter

More Books to Read

Beaty, A. 2013. *Rosie Revere, engineer.* New York: Abrams.
Summary: Young Rosie dreams of being an engineer. Alone in her room at night, she constructs great inventions from odds and ends. Afraid of failure, Rosie hides her creations under her bed until a fateful visit from her great-great-aunt Rose, who shows her that a first flop isn't something to fear—it's something to celebrate.

Fries-Gaither, J. 2016. *Notable notebooks: Scientists and their writings.* Arlington, VA: NSTA Press.
Summary: Take a trip through time to discover the value of a special place to jot your thoughts, whether you're a famous scientist or a student. Engaging illustrations, photos, and lively rhyme bring to life the many ways in which scientists from Galileo to Jane Goodall have used a science notebook.

Griffin Burns, L. 2012. *Citizen scientists: Be a part of scientific discovery from your own backyard.* New York: Square Fish.
Summary: This book for older readers (grades 3–6) gives budding scientists ideas for gathering data for actual ongoing scientific studies such as the Audubon Bird Count and FrogWatch USA. Engaging photos and useful tips encourage children to try four different activities, one for each season.

Mason, A. 2005. *Touch it! Materials, matter, and you.* Tonawanda, NY: Kids Can Press.
Summary: This lively and easy-to-understand book explores materials—their color, shape, texture, size, mass, magnetism, and more.

Zoehfeld, K. 2015. *What is the world made of? All about solids, liquids, and gases.* New York: HarperCollins.
Summary: Part of the *Let's-Read-and-Find-Out Science* series, this book uses simple text and playful illustrations to explain the differences among the states of matter and includes a "Find Out More" section with experiments designed to encourage further exploration.

Name: _____

Properties of Matter

You can be like a scientist and explore the properties of matter!

Test 1: Rub the substance between your fingers. How does it feel? Record the texture.

Test 2: Use a hand lens to look more closely at the substance. Can you see any crystals? Write yes or no.

Test 3: Use an eyedropper to add 3 full droppers of water to the substance. Stir with a stick for 30 sec. What happens?

Test 4: Use an eyedropper to add 10 drops of vinegar to the substance and water mixture. Stir with a stick for 30 sec. What happens?

Test	Salt	Cornstarch	Sand	Baking Soda
1. Texture (feel)				
2. Crystals? (yes/no)				
3. What happens with water?				
4. What happens with vinegar?				

National Science Teachers Association

Properties of Matter

You can be like a scientist and explore the properties of matter!

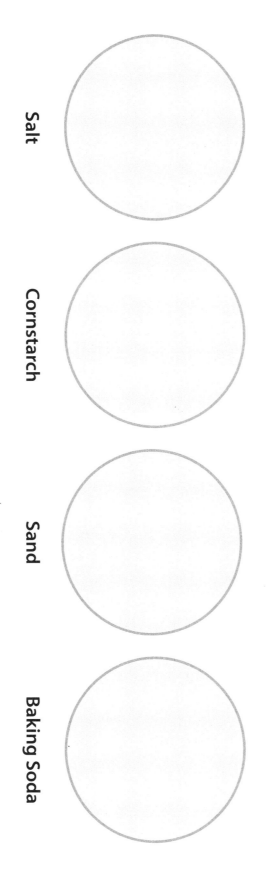

Salt

Cornstarch

Sand

Baking Soda

Vocabulary Cards

| Gas | Solid | Dissolve | Matter | Liquid |

| Gas | Solid | Dissolve | Matter | Liquid |

| Gas | Solid | Dissolve | Matter | Liquid |

| Gas | Solid | Dissolve | Matter | Liquid |

| Gas | Solid | Dissolve | Matter | Liquid |

| Gas | Solid | Dissolve | Matter | Liquid |

Name: _____

New Vocabulary List

Word	What It Means	Examples From the Text	Examples From the Activity
1.	Anything that has weight and takes up space		
2.	Matter that holds its size and shape		
3.	Matter that is wet and takes the shape of its container		
4.	Matter that has no shape and spreads out to fill a space		
5.	To mix a substance into a liquid until you can no longer see it		

Name: _____

Mystery Mixtures

You can be like a scientist and use your observations to solve a mystery!

Test 1: Rub the mystery mixture between your fingers. How does it feel? Record the texture.

Test 2: Use a hand lens to look more closely at the mystery mixture. Can you see any crystals? Write yes or no.

Test 3: Use an eyedropper to add 3 full droppers of water to the mystery mixture. Stir with a stick for 30 sec. What happens?

Test 4: Use an eyedropper to add 10 drops of vinegar to the mystery mixture and water. Stir with a stick for 30 sec. What happens?

Test	Mixture A	Mixture B
1. Texture (feel)		
2. Crystals? (yes/no)		
3. What happens with water?		
4. What happens with vinegar?		

I think Mixture A contains _____ and _____ because _____.

I think Mixture B contains _____ and _____ because _____.

National Science Teachers Association

Mystery Mixtures

You can be like a scientist and use your observations to solve a mystery!

Mystery Mixture A

Mystery Mixture B

Name: _____

Matter Quiz

Write *solid*, *liquid*, or *gas* on the lines below.

Block   Air   Water

1. _____   2. _____   3. _____

MILK

Shoe

4. _____   5. _____

Write the letter of the definition next to each word.

6. ____ Matter   A. To mix a substance into a liquid until you can no longer see it

7. ____ Solid   B. Matter that has no shape and spreads out to fill a space

8. ____ Liquid   C. Anything that has weight and takes up space

9. ____ Gas   D. Matter that holds its shape

10. ____ Dissolve   E. Matter that is wet and takes the shape of its container

National Science Teachers Association

Name: _____

Matter Mystery

Ada's teacher is filling jars with salt, cornstarch, sand, and baking soda, but she forgets to put labels on the jars! She asks Ada to help her identify what's inside one of the jars. Ada looks at the mystery substance with a hand lens and does not see any crystals. She takes a small sample of the substance and mixes it with water. The water turns a milky color. Then, she takes another sample, places 10 drops of vinegar in it, and observes that nothing happens. Use the chart below to help Ada solve the mystery!

Test	Salt	Cornstarch	Sand	Baking Soda
1. Texture (feel)	Rough and gritty	Slippery	Rough and gritty	Smooth
2. Crystals? (yes/no)	Yes	No	Yes	No
3. What happens with water?	Salt disappears, and water looks almost clear.	Water turns milky.	Sand does not disappear, and water looks cloudy	Baking soda disappears, and water looks cloudy
4. What happens with vinegar?	Nothing	Nothing	Nothing	Bubbles

1. Which substance do you think it is? _____

2. What is your evidence? _____

_____

_____

Bonus: Draw a picture of a scientist on the back of this page. Then, write some characteristics of a great scientist around your picture!

Name: _____

STEM at Home

Dear _____ ,

At school, we have been learning about the **properties of matter.**

I learned that: _____

_____

My favorite part of the lesson was: _____

_____

At home, we can watch a short video together about how to make Oobleck, which is a substance that acts like both a solid and a liquid.

Search for "How to Make Magic Mud Oobleck" on YouTube to find the video at *www.youtube.com/watch?v=WHLCYfwa36g.*

Then, we can make our own Oobleck by mixing 1 cup of water, 5 drops of food coloring, and 2 cups of cornstarch in a foil pie pan. Next, we can do a simple experiment by observing what will happen if we drop a marble from a distance of 2 feet into the pan of Oobleck.

What happens when a marble is dropped into Oobleck? Predict, then try it!

_____

_____

How is Oobleck like a solid?

_____

_____

How is Oobleck like a liquid?

_____

_____

Crayons

Description

Crayons provide a fun and familiar context for learning about science and engineering. Students observe their properties; explore how they can be changed by breaking, melting, and cooling; and learn the many steps involved in manufacturing crayons. After designing their own process for recycling broken crayons, they demonstrate their understanding through a creative writing activity.

Suggested Grade Levels: K–2

LESSON OBJECTIVES Connecting to the *Framework*		
Science and Engineering Practices	**Disciplinary Core Ideas**	**Crosscutting Concepts**
Asking Questions and Defining Problems Planning and Carrying Out Investigations Obtaining, Evaluating, and Communicating Information	**PS1.B:** Chemical Reactions **ETS1.A:** Defining and Delimiting Engineering Problems	Energy and Matter Cause and Effect

Featured Picture Books

TITLE: ***The Day the Crayons Came Home***
AUTHOR: **Drew Daywalt**
ILLUSTRATOR: **Oliver Jeffers**
PUBLISHER: **Philomel Books**
YEAR: **2015**
GENRE: **Story**
SUMMARY: *In this clever story of Duncan's crayons, a colorful bunch that have survived a series of misadventures, each color has a tale to tell and a plea to be brought home to the crayon box.*

TITLE: ***From Wax to Crayon***
AUTHOR: **Robin Nelson**
PUBLISHER: **Lerner Classroom**
YEAR: **2013**
GENRE: **Non-Narrative Information**
SUMMARY: *Simple text and full-color photographs describe each step in the production of crayons—from melting wax to coloring a picture.*

Time Needed

This lesson will take several class periods. Suggested scheduling is as follows:

Day 1: **Engage** with Mystery Object and *The Day the Crayons Came Home* Read-Aloud and **Explore** with Crayon Observations and Crayon Questions

Day 2: **Explain** with Card Sequencing, *From Wax to Crayon* Read-Aloud, and Melting Crayons Demonstration

Day 3: **Explain** with "How People Make Crayons" Video and Favorite Crayon Colors Graph

Day 4: **Elaborate** with Crayon Recycling Design Challenge

Day 5: **Evaluate** with Postcard From a Crayon

Materials

For Mystery Object

- Paper bag
- 1 crayon of any color

For Crayon Observations

- Crayons to be observed and broken (1 per student; to make wrapper removal easier, you can pre-score the wrappers with a knife before giving the crayons to students)
- Ruler (1 per student)
- Box of crayons, any size

For Crayon Recycling Design Challenge

- Ovenproof, nonstick or silicone candy-making or baking molds; silicone ice cube trays (interesting shapes are fun; you will need 1 cavity per student); or silicone muffin cups (1 per student)
- Cookie sheet
- Nonstick spray
- Oven or toaster oven (for teacher use only)

For Card Sequencing (per group of 2–4 students)

- Precut How Crayons Are Made Cards in plastic sandwich bags

For Melting Crayons Demonstration

- Blowdryer (for teacher use only)
- Cardstock
- Several colors of unwrapped crayons
- Hot glue gun (for teacher use only)

SAFETY

- Be careful when using hot appliances and hot or liquid wax in the classroom, and keep those items away from children.
- Melting crayons can produce irritating fumes. Before heating crayons, make sure the room has proper ventilation.

Student Pages

- Crayon Observations
- Postcard From a Crayon template
- STEM at Home

Background for Teachers

Crayons have been an important staple of the elementary classroom for many years. They were first invented to solve a problem voiced by many teachers in the late 19th century: the need for an affordable writing and drawing tool available in a wide variety of colors that was safe for classroom use. Artists' wax crayons were available, but many brands were expensive and often contained toxic pigments. The Binney & Smith chemical company of Pennsylvania came up with a solution. In 1903, it introduced the first box of Crayola brand crayons for children. The crayons, made of paraffin wax and colorful, nontoxic pigments, were individually wrapped in paper and labeled with their colors. Each box of eight crayons cost a nickel. Edwin Binney's wife, Alice Stead Binney, is credited with coming up with the name Crayola from the French words *craie,* meaning "chalk," and a shortened form of *oléagineux,* meaning "oily."

Although several crayon companies competed in the lucrative school market before Crayola did, the Crayola name is by far the most famous. The first box contained the colors red, orange, yellow, green, blue, violet, brown, and black. Now, there are 120 colors of Crayola crayons. Crayola has a team of chemists and chemical engineers who are in charge of developing new crayon colors. Their laboratory holds the secret formula to every crayon color! The engineers experiment with different color combinations to come up with new shades. When they discover a promising new color, they test it on hundreds of kids to see whether children like it. After extensive testing and further product development (including the invention of a catchy, descriptive name), a new crayon is ready for the box. Some of the improvements to the original 8-pack of Crayola crayons include a 48-color "stadium seating" box, a 64-color assortment with a built-in sharpener, washable and twistable versions, and crayons with glitter.

The invention, design, and manufacture of crayons demonstrate the intersection of science, technology, and engineering. This lesson also demonstrates how science and art intersect. Students are inspired by a picture book to think about all of the ways crayons can be changed. Then, they explore the properties of crayons and learn that by adding heat, crayons can be changed from solid to liquid. Students also learn that sometimes changes in matter are reversible, and sometimes they are not. Students observe how crayons are manufactured and design a process for creating crayons of mixed colors and different shapes out of crayon pieces. Finally, students creatively write about the changes their crayons experienced.

engage

Mystery Object

Inferring

In advance, hide a crayon in a mystery bag (a paper bag with a question mark on it will do just fine). Tell students that you have a mystery item in the bag, and give them some clues about the item: It is red, you can draw with it, and so on. Allow students to guess after each clue. When they have guessed correctly, pull out the crayon and show it to them. Say, "You may think this crayon is ordinary, but by the end of this lesson, you will think that crayons are extraordinary!"

The Day the Crayons Came Home Read-Aloud

Connecting to the Common Core
Reading: Literature
KEY IDEAS AND DETAILS: K.1, 1.1, 2.1

Determining Importance

Show students the cover of *The Day the Crayons Came Home.* Introduce the author, Drew Daywalt, and illustrator, Oliver Jeffers. Tell students that as you read the book, you would like them to notice all of the different things that happen to the crayons and the ways the crayons in the book are changed. Then, read the book aloud, using a different voice for each crayon (you will be discussing point of view later).

Questioning

After reading, *ask*

? Is this book fiction or nonfiction? (fiction)

? How can you tell? (It's a pretend story with characters, dialogue, setting, plot, etc. It doesn't

have any of the features of nonfiction, such as a table of contents, headings, bold print words, an index, etc.)

Connecting to the Common Core
Reading: Literature
CRAFT AND STRUCTURE: K.6, 1.6, 2.6

Ask

? Who's telling the story? (The story opens and closes with a narrator, but each page in between is told from the points of view of the crayons.)

? How does the text show the crayons' points of view? (The first page of each two-page spread is a postcard written by a different color of crayon. The postcard is written using words such as *I, we, my,* and *me,* which tells us that the crayon wrote it.)

? Why do you think the author, Drew Daywalt, wrote the book this way? (It's funny, it gives the reader a different perspective on crayons, etc.)

? How does the illustrator, Oliver Jeffers, help tell the story? (One page of each two-page spread features a handwritten postcard in the actual color of the crayon speaking. Each crayon has a different kind of handwriting to help show that a new character is being introduced. The other page is a drawing or collage illustrating the crayon's adventures.)

You may want to have students view the video "Oliver Jeffers: Picture Book Maker" to get a fascinating (and very funny!) behind-the-scenes view of how he writes and illustrates picture books (see "Websites" section).

Together, recount some of the ways the crayons were changed in the book: broken, melted by the Sun, chewed by a dog, sharpened, melted in the dryer, and so on. Tell students they are going to learn both science and engineering concepts by observing crayon properties, exploring how crayons can be changed, and learning how crayons are made.

Observing and measuring crayons

explore

Crayon Observations

Connecting to the Common Core
Mathematics
Measurement and Data: 2.MD.1

First, hold up a crayon and *ask*

? After reading the book *The Day the Crayons Came Home,* what are you wondering about crayons? (Answers will vary.)

? What properties of this crayon could we observe? (color, length, shape, etc.)

Then, give each student a crayon, a ruler, and a Crayon Observations student page. Using the

crayon, students should first draw a detailed picture of the crayon. Next, have them remove the wrapper from the crayon, and ask them to use all of their senses (except taste!) to make and record observations of the crayon. Observations should include the color, shape, odor (smell), and texture (feel) of the crayon. Review how to measure objects with a ruler, and have students measure and record the length of the crayon. Then, have them list some ways that they could change the crayon. *Ask*

? Do you think your crayon is a solid, a liquid, or a gas?" (solid) Why do you think so? (Answers will vary, but students may mention that a solid keeps its shape.)

? What are some ways you could change your crayon? (breaking, melting, sharpening, etc.)

Have students break the crayon into three or four smaller pieces. Then, *ask*

? How is your crayon different now? (more pieces, shorter lengths, different shapes, etc.)

? How it is the same? (still draws, same color, same odor, etc.)

? Is your crayon still a solid? (yes)

? Is it possible to change a crayon from a solid to a liquid? (Answers will vary.)

? How do you think you could change your crayon from a solid to a liquid? (Answers will vary.)

(*Note:* Each student should save his or her own crayon pieces, because students will be using the pieces in the elaborate activity.)

Crayon Questions

 Questioning

Next, show students a box of crayons. *Ask*

? Now, what are you wondering about crayons? (Answers will vary.)

 Turn and Talk

Have students share their wonderings with a partner, and then record some of their questions on a

"Crayon Questions" class chart. Ask students how each question could be answered (e.g., by doing research, asking an expert, or conducting an experiment). Then, add the following questions to the list (if they are not already on it):

? Where did this box of crayons come from?

? What are crayons made of?

? How do they get their shape?

? How do they get their wrappers?

? How did all of these colors end up in one box?

Discuss each question with your students, and allow them to share their ideas (responses will vary).

explain

Card Sequencing

Tell students that you have a book and a video that will answer many of their questions. But first, you would like them to try to put the steps of crayon-making in order.

Sequencing Before Reading

Give each group of two to four students a set of precut How Crayons Are Made Cards. Challenge them to put the cards in order to show the steps needed to manufacture, or make, crayons in a factory. Tell them that they will have an opportunity to reorder the cards as you read a book about the crayon-making process.

From Wax to Crayon Read-Aloud

Using Features of Nonfiction

Connecting to the Common Core
Reading: Informational Text
Craft and Structure: K.5, 1.5, 2.5

Have students compare their card sequences with those of other groups and explain their think-

ing. Then, show them the front cover of *From Wax to Crayon* and introduce the author, Robin Nelson. Share this brief biography of the author from the publisher's website (*www.lernerbooks.com/contacts/403/Robin-Nelson*): "Robin Nelson's jobs have always kept her surrounded by books—as an elementary teacher, working at a publishing company, and working in a library. But her favorite job is writing books for kids. She has written more than 140 nonfiction books for children. She lives with her family in Minneapolis."

Ask

? What are some clues that a book is nonfiction? (It has a table of contents, bold print words, a glossary, an index, etc.)

Flip through the book, pointing out that it does have many of the features of nonfiction (table of contents, photographs, bold print words, glossary, and index). Next, show students the back cover of the book. Explain that many books have a short summary on the back cover that can give the reader an idea of what the book is about. Read the description, and ask students if they think this book will be a good choice for answering some of their questions. Next, open to the table of contents, and explain that this feature also gives the reader an idea of what information a nonfiction book contains. By skimming the table of contents, they will see that the book begins with wax being melted and ends with a child using crayons to draw a picture, with many steps in between.

Connecting to the Common Core
Reading: Informational Text
Key Ideas and Details: K.1, 1.1, 2.1

Sequencing After Reading

Read the book aloud, giving students the opportunity to reorder their How Crayons Arc Made Cards as you read. The cards should be sequenced in the following order:

1. Wax melts.
2. A worker adds color.
3. The wax is shaped.
4. The wax gets hard.
5. A worker checks the crayons for chips or dents.
6. A machine wraps the crayons.
7. A machine sorts the crayons.
8. The crayons are boxed.
9. The crayons are sent to stores.
10. I draw pictures with many colors.

 Questioning

Then, revisit your class list of crayon questions and have the students use evidence from the text to answer the questions. Next, have students discuss the following questions, each time referring to the text for evidence to support their answers.

? How does the wax turn into a gooey liquid? (p. 4—it is heated in large tanks.)

? How is the wax made into the shape of a crayon? (p. 8—it is poured into a mold.)

? How does the wax become solid again? (p. 10—cold water flows under the mold.)

? When a worker finds a crayon with chips or dents, what does he or she do with it? (p. 12— melts it and molds it again.)

Tell students that melting wax is an example of a *reversible change*. Write "reversible change" on the board, and explain that many things can change from one state of matter to another and back again. For example, water can change from a solid (ice) to a liquid and then back to a solid. *Ask*

? What can you do to ice to change it to a liquid? (heat it or melt it)

? How can you reverse the change and make water become solid again? (cool it or freeze it)

? What can you do to solid wax to change it to a liquid? (heat it or melt it)

? How can you reverse the change and make wax become solid again? (cool it or freeze it)

Explain that liquid wax differs from water in that it becomes a solid at room temperature: You don't have to put it in a freezer to make it solid. In the book, cooling with water makes the wax harden into a solid.

MELTING CRAYONS DEMONSTRATION

Melting Crayons Demonstration

Tell students that you can show them how wax can change from a solid to a liquid and back again. Hot glue several colors of unwrapped crayons to a piece of cardstock. Have students watch and make observations as you use a blow-dryer on high heat to melt the crayons. After the wax has cooled and dried (wait about 30 sec.), have students feel the hardened wax.

Ask

? What changes did you observe? (The solid wax slowly started dripping down the paper as the crayons melted and turned into a liquid. Then, more and more of the wax melted and dripped down the paper. Finally, the wax hardened after the blow-dryer was taken away.)

? How does this demonstration show a reversible change? (Heat melted the solid wax into a liquid, but the change was reversible because the liquid wax hardened back into solid wax when it cooled.)

Challenge the students to work with a partner and think of a change that is *not* reversible. For example, when you boil a raw egg (which contains mostly liquid material), it becomes a solid. Cooling the egg will not reverse the change; it remains solid.

"How People Make Crayons" Video

Connecting to the Common Core
Reading: Informational Text
KEY IDEAS AND DETAILS: K.1, 1.1, 2.1

Making Connections: Text to World

Tell students that you have another resource to help them better understand how crayons are made. Show students the PBS Kids Daniel Tiger's Neighborhood video "How People Make Crayons" in which a young girl gives a tour of a crayon factory (see "Websites" section). As they listen and watch, have them think about the information from the video and how it relates to what they learned in the book *From Wax to Crayon.*

Connecting to the Common Core
Reading: Informational Text
INTEGRATION OF KNOWLEDGE AND IDEAS: K.9, 1.9, 2.9

After watching, discuss how the video compares with the book. *Ask*

? What is the same? (The video and the book feature many of the same steps in the crayon-making process, such as melting wax into a liquid, adding pigment, pouring wax into molds, hardening wax into a solid, wrapping crayons, boxing crayons, etc.)

? What is different? (The video ends in the factory, whereas the book shows a truck transporting the crayons to stores. In the video, we can see all the steps in action and get a better look at the machinery. The book is divided into sec-

tions, but the video is one continuous stream of information that is narrated and set to music.)

? Does the video provide any new information? (In the video, a "secret ingredient" [white powder] is stirred into the vat to help harden the wax before the pigment is added. We also see how all the different-colored crayons are brought in big boxes to one giant room in the factory, where they are placed into the machine that puts them into smaller boxes.)

Challenge the students to think about all of the science and engineering involved in making an ordinary crayon! *Ask*

? How do you think scientists and engineers might be involved in making crayons? (Answers will vary, but students may mention that scientists test different types of wax and pigments, and engineers use that information to figure out how to turn the raw materials into the best crayons possible. Engineers design every step of the crayon-manufacturing process, from the tanks that heat and melt the wax to the packing machines that put the crayons into boxes.)

? How do you think new crayon colors are invented? (Answers will vary, but explain that the first box of crayons sold by Crayola contained the colors red, orange, yellow, green, blue, violet, brown, and black. Now, there are 120 colors of Crayola crayons. Crayola has a team of chemists and chemical engineers who are in charge of developing new crayon colors. Their laboratory holds the unique, top-secret formula to every crayon color! The engineers experiment with different color combinations to come up with new shades. When they discover a promising new color, they test it on hundreds of kids to see how well the children like it. After a lot more testing and the invention of a catchy, descriptive name, a new crayon is ready for the box.)

? What is your favorite crayon color? (Answers will vary.)

Connecting to the Common Core
Mathematics
MEASUREMENT AND DATA: 2.MD.10

Favorite Crayon Colors Graph

Next, have students write their favorite crayon color on a sticky note or color a sticky note with their favorite color. Have them place their sticky notes on a whole-class bar graph with "Favorite Colors" on the *x*-axis and "Number of Votes" on the *y*-axis. Analyze the results together. Then, share with students that most kids around the world choose blue or red as their favorite crayon color. *Ask*

? How do our results compare with the favorite crayon colors of kids around the world? (Answers will vary.)

elaborate

Crayon Recycling Design Challenge

Connecting to the Common Core
Reading: Literature
KEY IDEAS AND DETAILS: K.1, 1.1, 2.1

Tell students that you have an exciting challenge for them, but first you want to revisit *The Day the Crayons Came Home.*

Questioning

Refer to the pages of *The Day the Crayons Came Home* where the crayons melted. Reread pages 27–28 about the turquoise crayon that melted in the dryer. *Ask*

? Why would a crayon melt in a dryer? (It is hot in the dryer.)

? How did the turquoise crayon get in the dryer?" (Duncan left it in his pocket.)

MELTING CRAYONS IN A MOLD

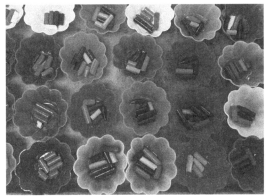

MELTING CRAYONS IN MUFFIN CUPS

? Why it is a bad thing if a crayon gets in the dryer? (It melts and gets stuck in the clothes.)

Next, revisit pages 13–14 about the orange and red crayons that melted together. *Ask*

? Why did the red and orange crayons melt? (They were left in the heat of the Sun.)

Students should realize that because crayons are made of wax, they will turn to liquid when heated and become solid again when they are cooled.

Next, have students look at the crayons they broke during the explore phase of the lesson. Tell them that broken crayons aren't very useful, which is why we often discard them. But perhaps there is a way to recycle the broken crayons! Tell students that you have a design challenge for them: Come up with a simple and safe way to recycle the crayons into new crayons. Remind students that engineers designed every component of the crayon-making process—from the tanks that heat and melt the wax

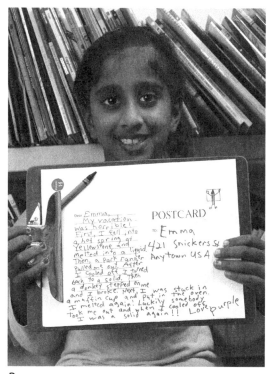

POSTCARD FROM A CRAYON

to the packing machines that put the crayons into boxes. Tell them students you would now like for them to think like engineers and brainstorm ways to turn their broken crayons into multicolored crayons of different shapes.

Turn and Talk

Once engineers understand a problem, they think about all of the possible solutions. There are often many different solutions to a problem. Brainstorming is a good way to share ideas with others. Have students turn and talk to share their initial ideas with each other. Remind students that at this point in the design process, all ideas are acceptable.

Next, explain that you have some tools to share that might give them some ideas for designing their process. Show students the nonstick or silicone baking or candy molds or muffin cups, and tell them that you will also be using an oven or toaster oven.

Then, let pairs or small groups of students discuss how they might design a step-by-step process for recycling the crayons into crayons with new shapes and colors. For example, students could exchange unwrapped crayon pieces with each other to mix up the colors, and then place their broken pieces into the molds (pretreated with nonstick spray). The molds can then be heated to melt the pieces together. After pairs or groups have discussed different design process possibilities, discuss the variations as a class and come up with one way to try together. Write each step on the board. Detailed instructions for recycling crayons can be found on the PBS Parents website Melted Crayon Art (see "Websites" section).

Take the trays home to melt the crayons if you do not have an oven or toaster oven at school. It is important that you use oven-safe, nonstick or silicone molds (placed on a cookie sheet) and low heat (250°F for about 20 min.) when melting the crayons. Use nonstick spray on the molds before adding the crayons so the recycled crayons will be easier to pop out once they have cooled and hardened (if they don't pop out easily, you can place them in the freezer for about 20 min. first). After cooling, give each student a new crayon. Have students compare the properties of the new crayon with those of the original crayon.

Ask

? How are the crayons the same as they were before being recycled? (They are solid and can be used to write and color.)

? How are they different after being recycled? (They have mixed colors and a different shape.)

? Do you think this change could be reversed? (yes, but not easily)

? How well did our recycling process work? (Answers will vary.)

? What would you change to make the process work better? (Answers will vary.)

You may want to have students test their recycled crayons by drawing a picture.

Recycled Crayons

evaluate

Postcard From a Crayon

 **Writing**

Give each student a template, copied on cardstock, for the postcard from a crayon activity. Tell them that they are going to be writing a friendly letter using the postcard template, written from the point of view of the crayon they observed at the beginning of the lesson. They will be using first person (*I, we, my,* and *me*) just as the author did in *The Day the Crayons Came Home.* Reread the first postcard in the book (from Maroon Crayon) as an example. Explain that, rather than describing an imaginative adventure the way Maroon Crayon did, they will be describing all of the things that happened to their

crayon during the recycling process. Students can, however, think of a creative way their crayon may have been broken and begin their postcard with that event. They should end with the crayon being recycled into a new crayon with a new color and shape, with all of the steps of the recycling process described in between.

Encourage students to use temporal words such as *first* and *next* to signal event order. They should also use words such as *solid, liquid, heated,* and *cooled* in their writing. In the margins or on the back of the postcard template, they can draw a scene showing one or more things that happened to the crayon during the recycling process.

Use the completed postcards to evaluate their understandings of the core idea that heating or cooling a substance may cause changes that can be observed, and sometimes these changes are reversible. You may also want to evaluate English Language Arts objectives such as writing a friendly letter, expressing point of view, or using temporal words.

STEM at Home

Have students complete the "I learned that …" and "My favorite part of the lesson was …" portions of the STEM at Home student page as a reflection on their learning. They may choose to do the following at-home activity with an adult helper and share their results with the class. If students do not have access to the internet at home, you may choose to have them complete this activity at school.

"At home, we can watch a video called 'The Life of an American Crayon' about how Crayola crayons are made."

🔍 *Search "Life of an American Crayon" to find the video at* www.crayola.com/videos/video-category/the-life-of-an-american-crayon.aspx.

"After we watch the video together, we can test different kinds of crayons to see how Crayola crayons compare with other brands!"

For Further Exploration

This section is provided to help you encourage your students to use the science and engineering practices in a more student-directed format. This box lists questions and challenges related to the lesson that students may select to research, investigate, or innovate. Students may also use the questions as examples to help them generate their own questions. After selecting one of the questions in the box or formulating their own questions, students can individually or collaboratively make predictions, design investigations or surveys to test their predictions, collect evidence, devise explanations, design solutions, or examine related resources. They can communicate their findings through a science notebook, at a poster session or gallery walk, or by producing a media project.

Research

Have students brainstorm researchable questions:

? Where do the raw materials for crayons come from?

? What improvements has the Crayola company made to the crayon?

? What does a chemical engineer do?

Investigate

Have students brainstorm testable questions to be solved through science or math:

? Find out the price of a box of Crayola crayons and the price of the same-sized box of another brand. Which brand is more expensive? How much more does it cost? Can you design a test to compare the brands?

? Survey your friends and family: What is your favorite crayon color? Graph the results, then analyze your graph. What can you conclude?

? When you mix salt and water, the salt seems to disappear. Is this a reversible change? How could you get the salt back to its original form? Try it!

Innovate

Have students brainstorm problems to be solved through engineering:

? Can you design a new crayon color by mixing different colors together? Can you come up with a catchy and descriptive name for your new color?

? What happens if you add glitter to the crayon pieces before melting? How well do the glitter crayons work after melting and cooling?

? Can you design a crayon-recycling program for your school?

Websites

"Oliver Jeffers: Picture Book Maker" (video)
www.youtube.com/watch?v=5KZu0X82l7k

PBS Kids, Daniel Tiger's Neighborhood: "How People Make Crayons"
http://cet.pbslearningmedia.org/resource/959d7d86-78fa-44e1-91a1-dcfa163ce7a0/how-people-make-crayons

PBS Parents: Melted Crayon Art
www.pbs.org/parents/crafts-for-kids/arts-and-crayons

"The Life of an American Crayon" (video)
www.crayola.com/videos/video-category/the-life-of-an-american-crayon.aspx

More Books to Read

Daywalt, D. 2013. *The day the crayons quit.* New York: Philomel Books.
Summary: Poor Duncan just wants to color. But when he opens his box of crayons, he finds only letters, all saying the same thing: His crayons have had enough. They quit! Beige Crayon is tired of playing second fiddle to Brown Crayon. Black Crayon wants to be used for more than just outlining. Blue Crayon needs a break from coloring all those bodies of water. Orange Crayon and Yellow Crayon are no longer speaking—each believes he is the true color of the Sun.

Hall, M. 2015. *Red: A crayon's story.* New York: Greenwillow Books.
Summary: A blue crayon mistakenly labeled as "red" suffers an identity crisis until a new friend offers a different perspective. Red discovers what readers have known all along … he's blue! This witty and heartwarming book is about finding the courage to be true to your inner self.

Hansen, A. S. 2012. *Melting matter.* Vero Beach, FL: Rourke Publishing.
Summary: Simple text and full-color illustrations help explain what happens when everyday items such as ice cream and candles melt. This brief introduction to melting also introduces the idea that something that changes its state by melting or freezing remains matter and compares melting with dissolving and burning.

Crayon Observations

1. Using your crayon, draw a picture of your crayon.

2. Write down observations about your crayon. Do not taste it!

Color	Shape	Odor	Texture	Length

3. List some ways you could change your crayon.

_____

_____

_____

How Crayons Are Made Cards

A worker adds color.	The crayons are sent to stores.
I draw pictures with many colors.	The crayons are boxed.
Wax melts.	A machine sorts the crayons.
A machine wraps the crayons.	The wax gets hard.
A worker checks the crayons for chips or dents.	The wax is shaped.

Name: _____

POSTCARD

To:

Dear _____

Name: _____

STEM at Home

Dear _____,

At school, we have been learning about **crayons**—how they are made and how they can be changed.

I learned that:

_____

_____

My favorite part of the lesson was:

_____

_____

At home, we can watch a video together called "The Life of an American Crayon" about how Crayola crayons are made.

Search "Life of an American Crayon" to find the video at ***www. crayola.com/videos/video-category/the-life-of-an-american-crayon.aspx.***

After we watch the video, we can test different kinds of crayons to see how Crayola crayons compare with other brands!

Brand	Crayon Observations
1. Crayola	
2.	
3.	

Our conclusion:

_____

_____

_____

Design a Habitat

Description

After reading a picture book about a boy who is begging his mom for a pet iguana, students learn about the needs of living things and the diverse habitats that provide those needs. Engineering design comes into play when students apply their knowledge about the needs of animals by designing and building a model habitat for an imaginary pet of their own.

Suggested Grade Levels: K–2

LESSON OBJECTIVES Connecting to the *Framework*		
Science and Engineering Practices	**Disciplinary Core Ideas**	**Crosscutting Concepts**
Engaging in Argument From Evidence Developing and Using Models	**LS1.C:** Organization for Matter and Energy Flow in Organisms **ETS1.B:** Developing Possible Solutions	Patterns Structure and Function

Featured Picture Books

TITLE: ***I Wanna Iguana***
AUTHOR: **Karen Kaufman Orloff**
ILLUSTRATOR: **David Catrow**
PUBLISHER: **Putnam**
YEAR: **2004**
GENRE: **Story**
SUMMARY: *Alex and his mother write notes back and forth in which Alex tries to persuade her to let him have a baby iguana for a pet.*

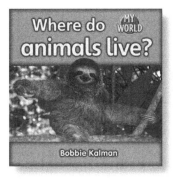

TITLE: ***Where Do Animals Live?***
AUTHOR: **Bobbie Kalman**
PUBLISHER: **Crabtree**
YEAR: **2010**
GENRE: **Non-Narrative Information**
SUMMARY: *Simple text and photographs describe the basic needs of living things and how different habitats meet the needs of different animals.*

Time Needed

This lesson will take several class periods. Suggested scheduling is as follows:

Day 1: Engage with *I Wanna Iguana* Read-Aloud and **Explore** with Observing Iguanas

Day 2: Explain with *Where Do Animals Live?* Read-Aloud and Animal Habitat Sort

Day 3: Elaborate with Design a Habitat Challenge and Animal Enrichment

Day 4: Evaluate with *I Wanna Iguana* Rereading and Write a Letter

Materials

For Animal Habitats Sort (per group of 2–3 students)

- Habitat Cards (precut)
- Plastic sandwich bag containing 1 animal figurine from each of the following 5 Safari Ltd TOOB sets:
  - 1 Safari Ltd Desert TOOB (Desert Habitat)
  - 1 Safari Ltd Ocean TOOB (Ocean Habitat)
  - 1 Safari Ltd Nature TOOB (Grassland Habitat)
  - 1 Safari Ltd Rainforest TOOB (Rainforest Habitat)
  - 1 Safari Ltd Arctic TOOB (Polar Habitat)

Note: You will need to omit or move some of the TOOB figurines to fit the habitats identified in this lesson (see Table 15.1). You will have enough animal figurines for up to 10 groups of 3 students.

For Design a Habitat (per student)

- Lunch-sized paper bag
- Animal figurines from Animal Habitat Sort
- Shoe box (1 per student)

> **SAFETY**
> Use caution when working with scissors to avoid cutting or puncturing skin or eyes.

Student Pages

- Design a Habitat Challenge and Animal Fact Card
- Write a Letter
- STEM at Home

Background for Teachers

Living things need food, water, and air to survive. Those are considered basic needs. Although living things have the same basic needs in common, they meet those needs in diverse ways. For example, animals fulfill their need for food by eating plants or other animals. Plants, however, make their own food using air, water, and sunlight through the process of *photosynthesis*. Plants obtain water and air through their roots and leaves. Animals have many different ways of meeting their needs for water and air. For example, some animals, such as fish, breathe air that is dissolved in water through their gills. Other animals, such as birds and mammals, breathe air through their lungs. Some desert animals, such as jackrabbits, can obtain water by eating plants that store water; some animals, such as deer, drink water from puddles, streams, and lakes. The way an animal meets its needs depends on the habitat in which it lives.

Table 15.1. TOOB Habitats Chart

Polar (sold as Arctic TOOB)	Desert	Ocean	Rainforest	Grassland (sold as Nature TOOB)
(Remove igloo and people.)	*(Remove person and cactus.)*	Dolphin	*(Remove person.)*	Bald eagle
		Beluga whale		Beaver
Arctic fox	Armadillo	Eagle ray	Anteater	Black bear
Arctic rabbit	Bobcat	Hammerhead shark	Caiman	Buffalo
Beluga whale	Coyote	Humpback whale	Emerald tree boa	Cardinal
Caribou	Desert bighorn ram	Killer whale	Iguana	Doe
Harp seal	Horned lizard	Moray eel	Jaguar	Fox
Husky	Mountain lion	Octopus	Poison dart frog	Gray wolf
Killer whale	Rattlesnake	Sea lion	Red-and-blue	Moose
Penguin*	Road runner	Sea turtle	macaw	Mountain lion
Polar bear	Scorpion	Sperm whale	Red-eyed tree frog	Prairie dog*
Walrus		Starfish	Spider monkey	Rabbit
		Tiger shark	Tapir	Raccoon
*Move here from Ocean TOOB.		*Polar is also an acceptable answer.	Toco toucan	*Move here from Desert TOOB.

A *habitat* is the immediate environment in which a living thing exists. It can be as large as a forest or as small as a tide pool or rotting log. Different animals are suited for different habitats. This lesson features five distinct habitats—desert, polar, rainforest, ocean, and grassland—but there are many more.

When an animal lives in a zoo, an artificial habitat must be designed to meet its needs. Designers of zoo habitats must research the animal's natural habitat and replicate it as authentically as possible given the constraints of the exhibit space at the zoo. The designer must not only consider the basic needs of food, water, and air but also research the animal's behaviors and create *animal enrichment* activities that enhance their well-being. Enrichment can include a place for an animal to climb, a challenge to capture its food, or even a toy to play with. Enrichment goes beyond the basic physical needs of animals and addresses their psychological needs. Many zoos have information on their websites about the enrichment they provide for their animals.

In this lesson, students learn about the needs of living things through a nonfiction read-aloud. They learn that animals and plants acquire food differently—plants make food with water, light, and air, whereas animals eat plants or other animals. Students learn that different animals are suited to live in different habitats that meet their basic needs. They then apply their knowledge to a design challenge where they design a habitat to meet the needs of a certain animal, making a physical model of the habitat using a shoe box and art supplies. Students then must explain how the habitat and enrichment activities meet the animal's basic needs.

engage

I Wanna Iguana Read-Aloud

> ### Connecting to the Common Core
> **Reading: Literature**
> KEY IDEAS AND DETAILS: K.1, 1.1, 2.1

 ### Inferring

Show students the cover of *I Wanna Iguana* and introduce the author and illustrator. *Ask*

? What do you think this book might be about? (Answers will vary.)

? What is an iguana? (Answers will vary.)

Then, read the book aloud.

 ### Questioning

After reading, share the back-cover information about author Karen Kaufman Orloff and how she was inspired to write this book after her son talked her into buying him a pet iguana. *Ask*

? How did Alex persuade his mom to let him have a pet iguana? (He wrote her letters and gave reasons the iguana would be a good pet to have.)

? Do you know anyone who has a pet iguana? (Answers will vary.)

? How do you take care of an iguana? (Answers will vary.)

? What do iguanas need to live? (Answers will vary.)

? Where do iguanas come from? (Answers will vary.)

explore

Observing Iguanas

> ### Connecting to the Common Core
> **Reading: Informational Text**
> KEY IDEAS AND DETAILS: K.1, 1.1, 2.1

Show students some of the Green Iguana resources from ARKive (*www.arkive.org*), including the Green Iguana Overview video (see "Websites" section). Have them listen and watch for information on where iguanas live and what they need to survive.

 ### Questioning

After the video, *ask*

? Where do green iguanas live? (jungle or rainforest)

? Is it cold or warm where iguanas live? (warm)

? What do iguanas eat? (leaves or plants)

? What do iguanas drink? (water)

? What do iguanas breathe? (air)

? Are iguanas awake during the day or at night? (day)

? Is there anything that surprised you about iguanas in the video? (Answers will vary.)

? What would Alex need to provide for his baby iguana to be healthy? (water, food, something to climb on, space to walk around, etc.)

explain

Where Do Animals Live? Read-Aloud

> ### Connecting to the Common Core
> **Reading: Informational Text**
> KEY IDEAS AND DETAILS: K.1, 1.1, 2.1

Determining Importance

Show students the cover of *Where Do Animals Live?* and introduce the author, Bobbie Kalman. Tell students that this book will help them understand the basic needs of iguanas and all other animals (air, food, and water). Have students signal (raise their hands) when they hear any of these basic needs as you read the book aloud. Students should signal when you get to page 6. Then, *ask*

? What do animals need to survive? (air, food, and water)

Tell students that plants also have basic needs. Like animals, plants need food to live and grow, but plants do not eat food—they make it! Plants make food using sunlight, air, and water. *Ask*

? What is the difference between what plants need and what animals need? (Animals eat their food; plants make their own food.)

Continue reading through page 11. Then, explain that the iguana pictured is different from the green iguana featured in *I Wanna Iguana*. This iguana lives in the desert and eats cacti. There is another kind of iguana called a *marine iguana* that lives near the ocean and spends a lot of its time underwater. These three types of iguanas live in different habitats to meet their needs.

Continue reading pages 11–12, and explain that these cold habitats are also called *polar habitats.*

 ### *Questioning*

Read the rest of the book aloud, noting the different animals that live in each habitat. After reading, check for understanding. *Ask*

? What is a habitat? (a place where certain types of animals live)

? What kinds of habitats were described in the book? (forest, desert, mountain, grassland, polar, wetland, and ocean)

Observing animal figurines

Explain that there are many other kinds of habitats, but for this lesson, you will focus on the desert, grassland, polar, rainforest, and ocean habitats.

Animal Habitat Sort

Give each group of two to three students a set of five animal figurines—one from each of the five habitats listed in the Materials section. Allow students time to make some observations of their five figurines. Then, *ask*

? What do all of your figurines have in common? (They are all animals.)

? How are they different? (They are different kinds of animals, and they are different colors and shapes. Some have legs, some have wings, some have fins, etc.)

? According to the book we just read, what do they all need to survive? (air, food, and water)

? Do you think all of these animals live in the same place in the wild? (no)

? Do you think they all eat the same kind of food? (no)

ANIMAL HABITAT SORT

Connecting to the Common Core
Reading: Informational Text
CRAFT AND STRUCTURE: 1.5, 2.5

 Using Features of Nonfiction

Remind students that all animals have the same basic needs: water, air, and food. However, different animals need different kinds of food, and animals get water in different ways. Some animals do best in very cold places, whereas others are healthiest in warm places. Some animals' needs are met underwater, and other animals' needs are met in very dry places. Give each group a set of the five Habitat Cards. Choose one of the habitats from the cards (polar, desert, ocean, rainforest, and grassland), and model how to use the table of contents to find the section of the book that discusses that habitat. Reread that section of the book. *Ask*

? Does anyone have a figurine of a type of animal that might live in that habitat? (Answers will vary.)

? What makes you think that animal might live there? (Answers will vary.)

Have students place the animal on the corresponding Habitat Card. Repeat the sorting procedure with the other Habitat Cards. Students should try to match one animal to each habitat. Keep in mind that the main goal of this activity is for students to learn that different animals are suited for different habitats. It is not essential that they get the "right" answer for each animal, because they are relying primarily on their schema to sort the animals (which will vary from student to student). However, the correct answers are shown in Table 15.2.

After students have sorted their animals into the different habitats, each group can trade animals with another group and sort those animals.

elaborate

Design a Habitat Challenge

Tell students that, as did the character Alex in *I Wanna Iguana,* they are going to try to persuade their parents to let them have a pet! This won't be just any pet, however—it will be one of the animals from the set of figurines they used. By designing a model of a habitat for the animal (using a shoe box and supplies from home), they will prove to their parents that they could meet all of the animal's needs. They will also be writing a letter to their parents to persuade them. Students should realize that most of the figurines are not of animals that would actually be kept as pets. Most of the animals would be somewhat ridiculous (and possibly even dangerous!) to keep as a pet. Remind students that wild animals should never be kept as pets. Explain that because the activity is just pretend, they can feel free to design a habitat that is huge and elaborate. The only limit is their imagination!

Table 15.2. Answer Key for Animal Habitat Sort

Polar	Desert	Ocean	Rainforest	Grassland
Arctic fox	Armadillo	Dolphin	Anteater	Bald eagle
Arctic rabbit	Bobcat*	Eagle ray	Caiman	Beaver
Beluga whale*	Coyote*	Hammerhead	Emerald tree boa	Black bear
Caribou	Desert bighorn	shark	Iguana	Buffalo
Harp seal	ram	Humpback whale	Jaguar	Cardinal
Husky	Horned lizard	Moray eel	Poison dart frog	Doe
Killer whale*	Mountain lion*	Octopus	Red-and-blue	Fox
Penguin	Rattlesnake*	Sea lion	macaw	Gray wolf
Polar bear	Road runner	Sea turtle	Red-eyed tree	Moose
Walrus	Scorpion	Sperm whale	frog	Mountain lion*
		Starfish	Spider monkey	Prairie dog*
*Ocean is also an	*Grassland is also	Tiger shark	Tapir	Rabbit*
acceptable answer.	an acceptable		Toco toucan	Raccoon
	answer.			
				*Desert is also
				an acceptable
				answer.

Animal Enrichment

Explain that although most of the animals from the figurine sets would not be appropriate pets for people to keep in their homes, some of them are kept in zoos. Tell students that zoos must not only make sure that an animal's basic needs (food, water, and air) are met but also provide things to keep the animal happy and healthy. Providing for needs beyond basic ones is called *animal enrichment*. Show students some examples of animal enrichment from zoos around the country, such as the first few minutes of the video "Animal Enrichment at the Oregon Zoo" (see "Recommended Websites for Animal Habitat Enrichment" section). Tell students that they will need to design at least one enrichment activity when they create their habitats.

Next, place all the figurines in a lunch-sized paper bag. Have students each pull an animal out of the bag. (The more outlandish the "pets" are, the more fun the activity.) Explain that the animal each students randomly selects is the animal for which he or she will be designing a "habitat in a box." Fill in the due date on the Design a Habitat

*P*OLAR HABITAT MODELS

Challenge student page, and give each student a copy of this and the Animal Fact Card student pages. Have each student write his or her name and the name of the animal on the Animal Fact Card, and then sketch the animal in the box at the bottom (students may want to trace the outline of the figurine). Explain that they will be doing research at home with an adult helper to find out more about the animal's needs and its habitat. You may want to send home a list of recommended websites for students to use with their parents for research (see "Recommended Websites for Animal Research" section). Review the directions together. Then, send the animal figurine and the assignment home to be completed as homework. Students will need to cut out and attach the completed Animal Fact Card to the shoe box and also place the animal in the habitat model for display in the classroom. Review the directions on the student page together.

Note: The name of the animal is printed on each model. You may need to help students find the name because it is in very small print. You need to decide whether the students will be expected to return the figurines to you after the assignment is turned in and displayed. It is best to let them know in advance!

evaluate

I Wanna Iguana Rereading

Connecting to the Common Core
Reading: Literature
Key Ideas and Details: K.1, 1.1, 2.1

📖 *Rereading*

Ask students to recall how the character Alex in *I Wanna Iguana* wrote a series of persuasive letters to his mom. Tell students that they will be writing similar letters to their parents or guardians to persuade them to let them keep the animals for which they built the model habitats. Explain that although it would be ridiculous and possibly even dangerous to keep their animal as a pet, thinking about what it would be like to have one is fun and a good way to show what they know about that animal and its needs. Reread some of the letters from *I Wanna Iguana,* including pages 24–25, showing the iguana on the diving board. Ask students to listen for the

reasons or arguments that Alex gives to persuade his mom to let him get an iguana. *Ask*

? How did Alex convince his mom that he could take care of the iguana's basic needs? (He told her that he would feed him every day, make sure the iguana had enough water, and clean the iguana's cage when it got messy.)

? Why do you think Alex's mom finally gave in? (He was persistent, he gave a lot of reasons for why he should have the iguana, he convinced her that he could take care of the iguana's basic needs, etc.)

Write a Letter

Connecting to the Common Core
Writing
Text Types and Purposes: K.1, 1.1, 2.1

✏️ *Writing*

Now, students can write a persuasive letter asking their parents or guardians to let them keep the animals in the habitats they designed. Give each student a copy of the Write a Letter student page. In their letters, they should explain the following:

- Where the animal comes from
- How they will meet all of its needs
- Why they should be allowed to keep it

STEM at Home

Have students complete the "I learned that …" and "My favorite part of the lesson was …" portions of the STEM at Home student page as a reflection on their learning. They may choose to do the following at-home activity with an adult helper and share their results with the class. If students do not have access to the internet or these materials at home, you may choose to have them complete this activity at school.

"At home, we can play a game from SwitchZoo called 'Build an Online Habitat.'"

Search "SwitchZoo Build an Online Habitat" to find the game, or go to http://switchzoo.com/games/habitatgame.htm.

1. "Choose your animal by clicking on a picture of an animal.

2. Click on the different features of the habitat to change them. (Check the percentage bar to see if your animal's needs are being met!)"

3. In the box below, sketch your animal in its habitat."

After completing the online activity, they will sketch their animals in their habitats.

For Further Exploration

This section is provided to help you encourage your students to use the science and engineering practices in a more student-directed format. This box lists questions and challenges related to the lesson that students may select to research, investigate, or innovate. Students may also use the questions as examples to help them generate their own questions. After selecting one of the questions in the box or formulating their own questions, students can individually or collaboratively make predictions, design investigations or surveys to test their predictions, collect evidence, devise explanations, design solutions, or examine related resources. They can communicate their findings through a science notebook, at a poster session or gallery walk, or by producing a media project.

Research

Have students brainstorm researchable questions:

? Who designs zoo habitats?

? What does your local zoo do for animal enrichment?

? What animals would make good classroom pets? What would they need to be happy and healthy?

Investigate

Have students brainstorm testable questions to be solved through science or math:

? Survey your friends and family: Would you rather live in a desert, rainforest, polar, grassland, or ocean habitat? Graph the results, and then analyze your graph. What can you conclude?

? Survey your friends and family: What kinds of pets do you have at home? Graph the results, and then analyze your graph. What can you conclude?

? Survey your friends and family: If you could keep any animal as a pet, which animal would you choose? Graph the results, and then analyze your graph. What can you conclude?

Innovate

Have students brainstorm problems to be solved through engineering:

? Can you design an enrichment activity for a favorite zoo animal? (Check out the videos in the "Recommended Websites for Animal Habitat Enrichment" section.)

? Can you design a model habitat for an animal at your local zoo?

? Can you design an enrichment toy or activity for your family or classroom pet?

Websites

ARKive Green Iguana Facts
www.arkive.org/green-iguana/iguana-iguana

ARKive Green Iguana Photos
www.arkive.org/green-iguana/iguana-iguana/ photos.html

ARKive Green Iguana Videos

www.arkive.org/green-iguana/iguana-iguana/ videos.html

Recommended Websites for Animal Habitat Enrichment

Oregon Zoo Animal Enrichment Video

www.oregonzoo.org/gallery/videos/oregon-zoos- internationally-recognized-enrichment-program- helps-zoos-animals-thrive

Phoenix Zoo Animal Enrichment

http://phoenixzoo.org/animals/enrichment

St. Louis Zoo Animal Enrichment (includes videos)

www.stlzoo.org/animals/enrichmenttraining/ani- malenrichment

Recommended Websites for Animal Research

ARKive: Animal Facts, Photographs, and Videos
www.arkive.org

SwitchZoo Animal List and Profiles
www.switchzoo.com/animallist.htm

National Geographic Kids
http://kids.nationalgeographic.com/animals

More Books to Read

Jenkins, S., and R. Page. 2005. *I see a kookaburra.* New York: Houghton Mifflin.
Summary: Jenkins' trademark paper-collage art- work depicts six different habitats and the animals that live in each.

Na, I. S. 2015. *Welcome home bear: A book of animal habitats.* New York: Knopf Books for Young Readers. Summary: Bear begins to look for a new place to live. He visits several habitats and discovers that his own habitat is the perfect place for him to live after all.

Nun, D. 2012. *Why living things need … Food.* Chicago: Heinemann.
Summary: From the *Why Living Things Need …* series, this book uses simple text and photographs to explain that living things need food; plants make their own food using water, air, and sunlight; and animals eat plants or other animals. Other titles in this series include *Air, Homes, Light,* and *Water.*

Pattison, D. 2014. *I want a dog: My opinion essay.* Little Rock, AR: Mims House.
Summary: Dennis writes an opinion essay for his teacher. But will his essay persuade his parents to get the dog of his dreams? The book includes information on dog breeds and responsible dog ownership.

Pattison, D. 2015. *I want a cat: My opinion essay.* Little Rock, AR: Mims House.
Summary: Mellie writes an opinion essay for her teacher. But will her essay persuade her parents to get the cat of her dreams? The book includes information on cat breeds and responsible cat ownership.

Seuss, Dr. 2015. *What pet should I get?* New York: Ran- dom House.
Summary: This recently discovered Dr. Seuss book follows the signature style of illustration and rhyme as a brother and sister go to a pet store and can't decide which pet to buy. The "Editor's Note" at the end of the book contains information on Dr. Seuss (Theodor Geisel) and his love for animals (with photos of him and some of his pets), his writing process, and how the manuscript was discovered.

Habitat Cards

Directions:
Cut out the cards and match the animal figurines to the correct habitat.

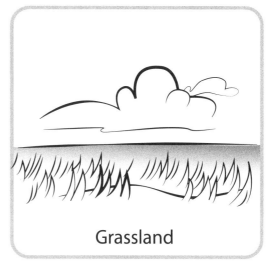

Grassland

Desert

Rainforest

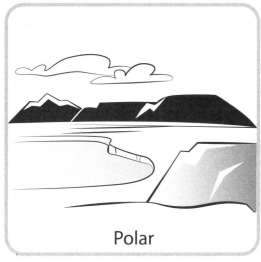

Polar

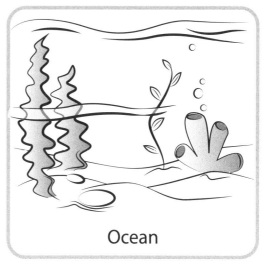

Ocean

Name: _____

Design a Habitat Challenge

Challenge: Design and build a habitat model for your animal! Work with an adult helper to do the following:

1. Find out about your animal's needs.

2. Find out what your animal's natural habitat looks like.

3. Fill out the Animal Fact Card.

4. Design and build your model using a shoe box and other materials. Your model should include the figurine.

5. Cut out the Animal Fact Card and attach it to your shoe box.

Check (✓) that your habitat model meets your animal's needs:

☐ **Food to eat**

☐ **Water to drink**

☐ **Air to breathe**

☐ **Activity or toy for enrichment**

Habitat model is due on _____.

Animal Fact Card

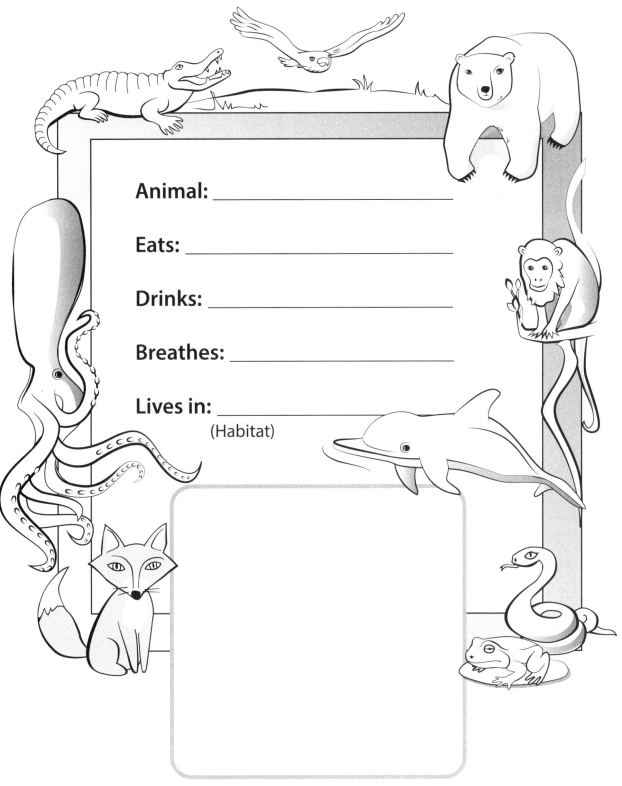

Animal: _____

Eats: _____

Drinks: _____

Breathes: _____

Lives in: _____
(Habitat)

Name: _____

Write a Letter

Pretend that you want to persuade your parent(s) to let you keep your animal as a pet. (Remember, wild animals should never be kept as pets in real life!) Write a letter to him or her and include the following information:

- Where the animal comes from

- How you will meet all of its needs

- Why you should be allowed to keep it

Dear _____,

_____

_____

_____

_____

_____

_____

_____

_____

_____

Sincerely,

_____

Name: _____

STEM at Home

Dear _____,

At school, we have been learning that animals live in **habitats** that meet their basic needs.

I learned that: _____

_____

_____

My favorite part of the lesson was: _____

_____

_____

At home, we can play a game called "Build an Online Habitat."

Search "SwitchZoo Build an Online Habitat" to find the game, or go to *http://switchzoo.com/games/habitatgame.htm.*

1. Choose your animal by clicking on a picture of an animal.

2. Click on the different features of the habitat to change them. (Check the percentage bar to see if your animal's needs are being met!)

3. In the box below, sketch your animal in its habitat.

Plant a Tree

Description

Students hear the inspiring true story of Wangari Maathai, a Kenyan environmentalist and Nobel Peace Prize winner whose vision and determination led to the planting of 30 million trees in Africa. They learn about the many benefits we receive from trees and then plant a tree of their own.

Suggested Grade Levels: K–2

LESSON OBJECTIVES Connecting to the *Framework*		
Science and Engineering Practices	**Disciplinary Core Ideas**	**Crosscutting Concept**
Asking Questions and Defining Problems Obtaining, Evaluating, and Communicating Information	**ESS3.C:** Human Impacts on Earth Systems **ETS1.A:** Defining and Delimiting Engineering Problems **ETS2.B:** Influence of Engineering, Technology, and Science on Society and the Natural World	Systems and System Models

Featured Picture Books

TITLE: ***Wangari's Trees of Peace: A True Story From Africa***
AUTHOR: **Jeanette Winter**
ILLUSTRATOR: **Jeanette Winter**
PUBLISHER: **Harcourt Children's Books**
YEAR: **2008**
GENRE: **Story**
SUMMARY: *This true story of Wangari Maathai, environmentalist and winner of the Nobel Peace Prize, shows how one woman's passion, vision, and determination can inspire great change.*

TITLE: *We Planted a Tree*
AUTHOR: **Diane Muldrow**
ILLUSTRATOR: **Bob Staake**
PUBLISHER: **Golden Books**
YEAR: **2010**
GENRE: **Narrative Information**
SUMMARY: *Simple text and cartoon-style illustrations reveal the benefits of planting a single tree, both for those who see it grow and for the world as a whole.*

Time Needed

This lesson will take several class periods. Suggested scheduling is as follows:

Day 1: **Engage** with *Wangari's Trees of Peace* Read-Aloud and Google Earth Field Trip to Mount Kenya

Day 2: **Explore** with Observe a Tree and **Explain** with *We Planted a Tree* Read-Aloud

Day 3: **Elaborate** with "Plant for the Planet" Video and Research a Planting Location and Type of Tree

Day 4: **Elaborate** with Plant a Tree

Day 5: **Evaluate** with We Planted a Tree

Materials

For Wangari's Trees of Peace *Read-Aloud*

- Globe or world map

For Google Earth Field Trip to Mount Kenya

- Google Earth app
- Projector or interactive whiteboard
- Internet connection

For Observe a Tree

- Clipboard (1 per student)
- Pencil (1 per student)
- Tape measure or string and yardstick to measure the circumference of the trunk

For Plant a Tree

- Tree to plant (Trees can be donated by a local nursery, home improvement store, the Arbor Day Foundation [10 free trees with membership], parents, or your school's Parent Teacher Organization. Consult with a local arborist to find a tree that is best suited for your school's plant hardiness zone and for the specific site your students select.)
- Tape measure or string and yardstick to measure the circumference of the trunk
- Ruler or meter stick
- Shovels
- Small hand shovels (optional)

For We Planted a Tree booklet

- Crayons or colored pencils
- Video-recording device (optional)

SAFETY

- Wear safety glasses or goggles when planting trees.
- Encourage students to wear sun-protective clothing.
- Have students wash their hands with soap and water after completing the activity.

Student Pages

- Observe a Tree
- We Planted a Tree booklet
- STEM at Home

Background for Teachers

Wangari Maathai was born in 1940 in a small village in Kenya. She was a brilliant student, and with her teacher's help, she won a Kennedy scholarship to study biology at Mount St. Scholastica College in Kansas. After that, she earned an MS at the University of Pittsburgh, and then pursued doctoral studies in Germany and at the University of Nairobi, where she earned her PhD and became a professor.

When Maathai returned to Kenya from the United States, she was devastated by the deforestation of her homeland and the changes in daily life it brought, especially for women living in rural areas. She started the Green Belt Movement in Kenya in 1977 by planting nine seedlings in her backyard. She began working with local women to plant trees and would pay them if the trees they planted were still living after three months. For most of these women, Maathai's planting project provided them with their first earnings ever. Soon, women all over Kenya were planting seedlings.

Maathai was met with opposition from the Kenyan government and businesses that were cutting down trees for timber and clearing land for coffee plantations. She was even arrested and jailed. News of her arrest spread in Kenya and other countries, and people from around the world began to unite and demand her release. After Maathai was released from jail, she began traveling the world telling her story, speaking out for the environment and for women's rights.

MAP OF KENYA

By 2004, 30 million trees had been planted as part of Maathai's Green Belt Movement. Consequently, the incomes of 80 thousand people had increased. As a result of her efforts, Wangari was awarded the Nobel Peace Prize that year. In its citation, the Norwegian Nobel Committee noted Maathai's contribution to "sustainable development, democracy and peace." Maathai died in 2011 at age 71, but her trees and her message of hope live on.

Maathai's story is an engaging, real-world context in which students can learn about human impacts on Earth systems. In a version of her story written specifically for young children, students learn that cutting down trees in Maathai's village to make room for buildings and crops negatively affected the people and the environment. Students then learn about the benefits of trees during another read-aloud and apply their knowledge by planting a tree in an area the class researches and selects together. These activities provide students an experience with the scientific practice of obtaining, evaluating, and communicating information as they use grade-appropriate texts (picture books) and media (videos and websites) to obtain information about the natural world.

Deforestation, the removal of trees transforming a forest into cleared land, is a global problem. Forests cover about 30% of the Earth's surface and provide homes for about 70% of Earth's land animals. A study published in *Science* in 2013 revealed that the Earth is losing the equivalent of 50 soccer fields of forest every day (Hansen et al. 2013)! The biggest cause of deforestation is farming. Forests are cleared to grow crops and create grazing areas for livestock. In addition, loggers cut down forests for create wood and paper products. Forests are also cut down to make space for buildings such as homes and shopping centers. Deforestation is a complicated problem because the reason behind it usually comes down to people's need to make money and provide for their families. Trees are one of Earth's most important natural resources. They play an important role in *ecosystems*, communities of living and nonliving components of an environment interacting as a system. We depend on trees for providing food and wood products, conserving water and soil, removing carbon dioxide from the air, and adding oxygen to the air. Animals and other plants depend on trees as well. Students must understand the importance of trees to humans and all life on Earth and realize their actions have an impact on trees. Nurturing a sense of wonder about trees will encourage students to do more to protect and conserve this vital resource.

engage

Wangari's Trees of Peace Read-Aloud

Connecting to the Common Core
Reading: Literature
KEY IDEAS AND DETAILS: K.1, 1.1, 2.1

 Questioning

Show students the cover of *Wangari's Trees of Peace: A True Story From Africa*. Introduce the author and illustrator, Jeanette Winter. *Ask*

? From looking at the cover, what do you think this book might be about? (Answers will vary.)

? Where is Africa? (Answers will vary.)

After students respond, show them Africa on a globe or world map. Then, read through page 21, where Wangari says, "We need a park more than we need an office tower." *Ask*

? Why do you think Wangari says that? Why would a park be more needed than an office tower? (Answers will vary, but many students will realize that a park benefits people as a place to play and enjoy nature and is also a home for many animals.)

Before reading page 22, where Wangari is hit by the "government men," you will need to consider the maturity of your students and then decide whether to show the illustration of Wangari with blood on her face.

 Visualizing

Continue reading, but stop before reading pages 30–31, which begin, "And if you were to climb to the very top of Mount Kenya today, you would see …" Here, have students close their eyes and visualize what the millions of trees Wangari planted would look like from the top of Mount Kenya. Discuss what the students are visualizing in their minds, then reveal the illustrations. *Ask*

? How did your mental picture compare with the illustrator's interpretation of the scene? (Answers will vary.)

After reading, *ask*

? How do you think Wangari felt when she came home to Kenya to find the trees gone? (She was sad.) What makes you think so? (She was crying, and she looks sad in the illustration.)

? Why were people cutting the trees down? (to make room for buildings)

The book says that the trees were cut down to make room for buildings, but it is important to explain the two other major reasons people cut down trees: to create fields for crops and livestock and to use the trees for wood and paper products. *Ask*

? What did Wangari do right away to help solve the problem? (She planted trees in her own backyard.)

? On page 25, the book says there were "30 million trees where there were none." Did Wangari plant all 30 million trees? (No, she had the help of many women.)

Explain that because of Wangari's work planting trees in Kenya and helping women, she received one of the most prestigious prizes in the world, the Nobel Peace Prize. She was the first African woman to ever receive the prize.

Google Earth Field Trip to Mount Kenya

Reread pages 30–31, "And if you were to climb to the very top of Mount Kenya today, you would see the millions of trees growing below you, and the green Wangari brought back to Africa." *Ask*

? Would you like to stand at the very top of Mount Kenya to see the trees that Wangari planted? (Most students will likely say, "Yes!")

Tell students that Mount Kenya is the second-highest mountain on the continent of Africa and that you are going to take them there on a "virtual" field trip! Open the Google Earth app and project the program on a screen. Tell students that this app allows you to see Earth from space, "fly" around the globe, land on the ground, and look around. Follow the instructions below to take a Google Earth field trip to Mount Kenya.

1. Begin at your school by entering the address of your school in the search box.

2. Type *Africa* in the search box to fly across the ocean to the continent of Africa.

3. Type *Kenya* in the search box to zoom in on the country of Kenya.

4. Type *Mount Kenya* in the search box to zoom in on Mount Kenya.

5. Zoom out to show the green ring around

Using Google Earth

the bottom of the mountain. Tell students that this map is made from photographs taken from a satellite orbiting the planet. The green ring around the mountain shows the millions of trees that Wangari and the women that worked with her planted.

6. Zoom back in on the top of the mountain, and drag the "Street View" icon (🧍) to the top of the mountain.

7. Use the controls at the top, right-hand corner to turn around and look at the views from the top of Mount Kenya.

Tell students that, next, they are going to learn about why trees are so important, which will help them understand why planting trees was so important to Wangari.

explore

Observe a Tree

Connecting to the Common Core
Mathematics
MEASUREMENT AND DATA: K.MD.1

Choose a tree in your school-yard or nearby for the students to observe. Any tree will do, but a more mature tree might be best for this activity. In advance, use a tree identification app or the Arbor Day Foundation's website to determine the species of the tree (*www.arborday.org/trees*).

Give each student a copy of the Observe a Tree student page, a clipboard, and a pencil. Tell students that they are going outside to observe a tree. Be sure to bring a tape measure. Invite students to sit quietly in the shade of the tree. You may want to bring towels or blankets for students to sit on. Have students begin by drawing the general shape of the tree on their student page. Then, *ask*

? How could we find out how big around the tree trunk is? (Answers will vary.)

Show students the tape measure. Model how to measure around the trunk of the tree with the tape measure, and have students record that measurement on the student page. Explain that the distance around a circular object is known as the *circumference*.

Next, show students a leaf from the tree and discuss its shape. Have students draw the shape of the leaf on the student page. Tell students that the shape of a leaf is one way to figure out the kind of tree. Tell students what kind of tree it is and how you figured that out.

Finally, share a reason that you think this tree is important (e.g., it provides homes for animals), and ask students to think of some other reasons it is important (e.g., it provides shade). Then, have students complete the sentence "This tree is important because …" on the. student page, listing some reasons this tree is important. Refer to *Wangari's Trees of Peace* and remind students that Wangari thought trees were important—so important that she dedicated a lot of time and energy to planting trees in her country. *Ask*

? Why are trees important? (Answers will vary.)

? What things do people get from trees? (Answers will vary.)

? Can you think of any other living things that benefit from trees? (Answers will vary.)

? What questions do you have about trees? (Answers will vary.)

Then, tell students that you have a book that can help them learn more about why trees are important. You may want to read the book outside near the tree you have been observing.

explain

We Planted a Tree Read-Aloud

Connecting to the Common Core
Reading: Informational Text
INTEGRATION OF KNOWLEDGE AND IDEAS: K.8, 1.8, 2.8

Show students the cover of *We Planted a Tree* and introduce the author, Diane Muldrow, and illustrator, Bob Staake. Open to the dedication and copyright page, and tell students that the author included a quote from Wangari Maathai. Read the quote aloud: "When we plant trees, we plant the seeds of peace and seeds of hope." Tell students that the author of this book, Diane Muldrow, was inspired by Wangari's work, so she included a quote from Wangari on the dedication page of the book.

Determining Importance

Tell students that as you read the book aloud, you would like them to listen for how trees make the world better. Have them signal by wiggling their fingers in the air (to represent branches) when they hear an example of how trees make the world better. Read the book aloud, stopping to discuss the benefits of trees each time they are mentioned.

After reading, remind students that the book said, "We planted a tree, and that one tree made the world better." *Ask*

? What evidence does the author give that trees make the world better? (The tree in the story provided shade, clean air, sap for syrup, fruit, and food for animals. It also held the soil in place and made the soil better for growing a garden.)

Explain to students that trees are cut down every day all around the world. Forests are cleared to make room for planting crops. Trees are cut down to make paper, wood products, and building materials. Things that we use from nature, such as trees, water, and land, are called *natural resources*. Explain that although we benefit from natural resources, we have to be aware of how using them affects other living things. Trees are important parts of ecosystems. An *ecosystem* is all the living things, such as animals and plants, that share an environment. Everything in an ecosystem has an important role, or job. Removing one thing from an ecosystem can harm the other living things in the ecosystem. So it is important to think about the whole ecosystem when using natural resources such as trees. *Ask*

? How could removing trees harm other living things in an ecosystem? (Animals would lose their homes, food, or both; the soil might wash away, which would harm the other plants; people would lose shade; etc.)

? What are some things that we can do to reduce the harmful effects of cutting down trees? (Answers will vary but may include using less wood or paper, recycling paper products, planting trees, etc.)

Tell students that one thing they can do to help is replace some of the trees that are cut down by planting new trees.

elaborate

"Plant for the Planet" Video

 Making Connections: Text to Text

Tell students that Wangari Maathai once said, "It's the little things that citizens do. That's what will make the difference. My little thing is planting trees." Tell students that you have a video to share about a child who was so inspired by Wangari's story

that he began a tree-planting project of his own. Show the first 1:37 min. of "Plant for the Planet" (see "Websites" section), which features 11-year-old Felix Finkbeiner from Germany, who was inspired to plant millions of trees. After the video, *ask*

? Would you like to plant a tree in our schoolyard or community so that you can make a difference like Wangari and Felix did? (Answers will vary, but most students will likely say, "Yes!")

? Where do you think would be a good place to plant a tree? (Answers will vary.)

Research a Planting Location and Type of Tree

Tell students that they can use the Google Earth app again to see the area surrounding the school. Enter your school address in the Google Earth app. Zoom in and out to look around, and drag the "Street View" icon ( ), which allows you to "walk around" the school grounds. Locate a few places that might be good for a tree to grow (e.g., a place with plenty of sunlight, with room to grow, and away from places with a lot of foot or vehicular traffic). Next, take a walk around the school grounds, noting the trees that are already there, and visit the places you selected on Google Earth. Choose the location where your class thinks the tree would grow best. Be sure to get the planting location approved by your school or district administration ahead of time. (You may also want to talk to your neighborhood planning department to find planting areas in your community if there is not an appropriate area on your school grounds.)

Tell students that it is important to choose a tree that will thrive in your area. For example, if you live in a cold area, a palm tree might not survive because it is a tree that typically grows in tropical areas. Demonstrate for students how to use the Arbor Day Foundation's Best Tree Finder: Tree Wizard (see "Websites" section) to generate a list of trees that will thrive in your school's plant hardiness zone. Project the website on your screen. Go through each step until a list of appropriate trees is generated for you. Read about the trees, look at

PLANTING A TREE

the pictures, and then select a tree to plant. You may want to contact a local arborist to help make your decision. (See Materials lists for suggested resources for acquiring donated trees.) Research the tree you selected so that students know what kind of fruit or nut it will produce, what its shape will be when it grows and the leaves have filled out, what the tree might be used for, how big it will grow, and so on.

Plant a Tree

Plan a day when you will plant the tree as a class. The specific instructions for planting a tree depend on whether the tree's roots are exposed, potted, or bound. For detailed instructions on planting your tree, see the Arbor Day Foundation's step-by-step instructions and videos. Allow all students to be involved by letting them each place a scoop of dirt around the tree, with either a small shovel or their hands. You may want to invite parents to help plant or the local newspaper to document the planting. Take a class picture and celebrate your newly planted tree!

Tell students that Wangari said, "Anybody can dig a hole and plant a tree. But make sure it survives. You have to nurture it, you have to water it, you have to keep at it until it becomes rooted so it can take care of itself." Brainstorm ways that you will nurture your newly planted tree. For example, you can do the following:

● Water it regularly.

● Keep mulch around it.

● Put a small fence around it to keep animals from eating it.

 evaluate

We Planted a Tree

Connecting to the Common Core
Writing
TEXT TYPES AND PURPOSES: K.3, 1.3, 2.3

Writing

Give each student a copy of the We Planted a Tree student pages, along with a crayon or colorerd pencil. Tell them that in this booklet, they are going to write or draw the steps they followed the day they planted the tree. Students might write the following:

● First, we dug a hole.

● Next, we put the tree in the hole.

● Then, we put dirt around the tree.

● Last, we watered the tree.

The last page of the booklet refers to the book *We Planted a Tree* with the line "We planted a tree, and that one tree makes the world better because … ." Students can use crayons or colored pencils to draw or write any of the reasons previously discussed about how trees make the world better, such as by providing shade, clean air, sap for syrup, fruit, and food for animals; holding the soil in place; and making the soil better for growing a garden.

Optional activity: Create a video as a class to share your tree-planting experience. Begin with the line "We planted a tree, and that one tree makes the world better because …," and have each student, or pair of students, give one of the reasons he or she listed on the last page of his or her booklet. End with a shot of the whole class with the tree they planted. You may want to watch the student-made video titled "What Are Trees?" (see "Websites" section) for some ideas on how to format the video. This video features kindergarteners sharing information about trees.

STEM at Home

Have students complete the "I learned that …" and "My favorite part of the lesson was …" portions of the STEM at Home student page as a reflection on their learning. They may choose to do the following at-home activity with an adult helper and share their results with the class. If students do not have access to the internet or these materials at home, you may choose to have them view the Arbor Day Foundation's website at school.

"At home, we can choose a favorite tree nearby. We can draw its shape, use crayons to make a leaf rubbing, and measure the trunk …

For Further Exploration

This section is provided to help you encourage your students to use the science and engineering practices in a more student-directed format. This box lists questions and challenges related to the lesson that students may select to research, investigate, or innovate. Students may also use the questions as examples to help them generate their own questions. After selecting one of the questions in the box or formulating their own questions, students can individually or collaboratively make predictions, design investigations or surveys to test their predictions, collect evidence, devise explanations, design solutions, or examine related resources. They can communicate their findings through a science notebook, at a poster session or gallery walk, or by producing a media project.

Research

Have students brainstorm researchable questions:

? What is the largest tree in the world?

? What is the oldest tree in the world?

? What is Arbor Day?

Investigate

Have students brainstorm testable questions to be solved through science or math:

? What kinds of trees do we have in our school-yard, backyard, or local park?

? Compare the leaves of trees in your school-yard. Can you sort them into different groups?

? Compare the sizes of tree trunks in your schoolyard. Which one is the thickest?

For Further Exploration (*continued*)

Innovate

Have students brainstorm problems to be solved through engineering:

? Can you design a procedure for collecting apple seeds and sprouting them in your classroom?

? Can you design a structure to protect a newly planted tree?

? Can you design a poster to teach others about the importance of trees?

Optional activity: Next, we can use a tree identification app or the Arbor Day Foundation's website (*www.arborday.org/trees/index-identification.cfm*) to try to find out what kind of tree it is."

Reference

Hansen, M. C., P. V. Potapov, R. Moore, M. Hancher, S. A. Turubanova, A. Tyukavina, D. Thau, S. V. Stehman, S. J. Goetz, T. R. Loveland, A. Kommareddy, A. Egorov, L. Chini, C. O. Justice, and J. R. G. Townshend. 2013. High-resolution global maps of 21st-century forest cover change. *Science* 342 (6160): 850–853.

Websites

Arbor Day Foundation's Best Tree Finder: Tree Wizard
www.arborday.org/trees/planting

"Plant for the Planet" (video)
www.pbslearningmedia.org/resource/yvcc-sci-plantplanet/plant-for-the-planet

"What Are Trees?" (kindergarten video)
www.youtube.com/watch?v=VFHUEkzohjl&feature=youtu.be

More Books to Read

Bulla, D. R. 2001. *A tree is a plant.* New York: Harper-Trophy.
Summary: The life cycle of an apple tree is followed through the seasons.

Hopkins, H. J. 2013. *The tree lady: The true story of how one tree-loving woman changed a city forever.* New York: Beach Lane Books.
Summary: Kate Sessions's passion for trees transformed the city of San Diego. This is her story.

Johnson, J. C. 2010. *Seeds of change: Planting a path to peace.* New York: Lee & Low Books.
Summary: Sonia Lynn Sadler's vivid scratchboard-and-oil illustrations make this more-detailed biography of Wangari Maathai come alive.

Lauber, P. 1994. *Be a friend to trees.* New York: Harper-Trophy.
Summary: This book discusses the importance of trees as sources of food, oxygen, and other essential things. It also gives helpful tips for conserving this important natural resource.

Name: _____

Observe a Tree

1. Drawing:

[ ]

2. Trunk circumference (distance around the trunk): _____

3. Leaf shape:

[ ]

4. Kind of tree: _____

5. This tree is important because _____

_____

_____

_____

We Planted a Tree

By: _____

We planted a tree, and that one tree made the world better because . . .

_____

_____

_____

_____

National Science Teachers Association

Next, we

First, we

Last, we

Then, we

STEM at Home

Dear _____,

At school, we have been learning about **how trees help the Earth.**

I learned that: _____

_____

My favorite part of the lesson was: _____

_____

_____

At home, we can choose a favorite tree nearby. We can draw its shape, use crayons to make a leaf rubbing, and measure the trunk.

Shape of Tree (Draw the shape of your tree.)	Leaf Rubbing (Place a leaf under this paper, and rub a crayon over top.)	Circumference of Trunk (Measure the distance around the trunk.)

This is our favorite tree because _____

_____

 Optional activity: Next, we can use a tree identification app or the Arbor Day Foundation's website *(www.arborday.org/trees/index-identification.cfm)* to try to find out what kind of tree it is.

Pillbots

Description

After making observations of pill bugs, students are challenged to solve a human problem through biomimicry, the design of technologies that are modeled on living things. They read about some pill bug–inspired technologies as well as some other examples of biomimicry, and then design a device that mimics a pill bug's structures and behaviors.

Suggested Grade Levels: K–2

LESSON OBJECTIVES Connecting to the *Framework*		
Science and Engineering Practices	**Disciplinary Core Ideas**	**Crosscutting Concept**
Developing and Using Models Constructing Explanations and Designing Solutions	**LS1.A:** Structure and Function **ETS1.B:** Developing Possible Solutions **ETS2.B:** Influence of Engineering, Technology, and Science on Society and the Natural World	Structure and Function

Featured Picture Books

TITLE: ***Next Time You See a Pill Bug***
AUTHOR: **Emily Morgan**
PUBLISHER: **NSTA Kids**
YEAR: **2013**
GENRE: **Non-Narrative Information**
SUMMARY: *This book invites children and adults to interact with these fascinating animals and learn about their extraordinary features.*

TITLE: ***National Geographic Kids: Robots***
AUTHOR: **Melissa Stewart**
PUBLISHER: **National Geographic Children's Books**
YEAR: **2014**
GENRE: **Non-Narrative Information**
SUMMARY: *Young readers will learn about the most fascinating robots of today and tomorrow in this colorful, photo-packed book.*

Time Needed

This lesson will take several class periods. Suggested scheduling is as follows:

Day 1: Engage with *Next Time You See a Pill Bug* Introduction **Explore** with Pill Bug Observations, and **Explain** with *Next Time You See a Pill Bug* Read-Aloud

Day 2: Explain with Biomimicry: Pillbot Video and *Robots* Read-Aloud

Day 3: Elaborate with Pillbot Designs and **Evaluate** with My Pillbot

Materials

For Pill Bug Observations (per student)

- Pill bugs
- Clear plastic container (with sides high enough to contain the pill bugs, or use a lid with tiny air holes punched through it)
- Piece of paper towel small enough to cover ½ of container bottom, dampened with water from a clean spray bottle
- Hand lens

SAFETY
- Wash hands with soap and water after completing this activity.
- Ensure that pill bugs do not become dehydrated, are not too hot or cold, and are not handled roughly.
- Remind students that all living things should be handled gently.

Student Pages

- Let's Learn About Pill Bugs
- Pill Bug Observations
- My Pillbot
- STEM at Home

Background for Teachers

Turn over a rock or rotting log nearly anywhere in the United States, and (if it is above freezing) you are likely to find a pill bug! Pill bugs, also called *roly-polies,* are small terrestrial isopods abundant in temperate areas throughout the world. Because they are engaging, harmless, and easily collected, they provide an excellent opportunity for children to learn about invertebrate body parts and behaviors. In this lesson, students also learn how studying common pill bugs has led roboticists to some exciting technologies that mimic their structures and functions.

Although many students might think of pill bugs as bugs or insects, they are neither. Pill bugs are actually crustaceans, like lobsters, shrimp, and crabs. But pill bugs are unusual crustaceans because they live their entire lives on land. Like all crustaceans, pill bugs breathe through gills. Their gills must be moist for them to breathe. However, pill bugs are not able to breathe underwater like their crustacean relatives, so it is important to store them in a place that is damp, but not too wet. A small aquarium or plastic container with moist soil is all you need to store them safely in the classroom. Pill bugs have 14 legs, 2 antennae, and 2 eyes, and their exoskeletons are divided into many segments. The most notable behavior of the pill bug is its ability to roll into a ball when it feels threatened.

Researchers in South Korea and Germany have developed technologies that mimic the structures and behaviors of pill bugs to solve human problems. German researchers have created a prototype for the OLE (pronounced "oh-luh") pill bug to detect and fight forest fires. They have scaled up the pill bug's form to the size of a St. Bernard. But instead of having 14 legs like a pill bug, OLE only has 6. These enormous, 200 lb. robots scuttle around the forest floor at speeds of 6–12 miles per hour and use infrared "biosensors" to detect fire sources. To protect itself, the OLE has a segmented shell that allows it to curl into a ball just like a real pill bug. This ceramic-fiber compound shell can withstand temperatures of more than 2300°F! According to researchers, 30 OLEs could protect a forest as large as 2,700 square miles.

A PILL BUG

Roboticists in South Korea have designed a robot called the Pillbot that mimics a pill bug. This robot is about the size of a softball, and it has two modes: protection and locomotion. In protection mode, the Pillbot rolls into a ball and can be "bowled" into a location that is too dangerous for humans. Once it reaches the target, it unrolls into locomotion mode and can then move around and collect information in this dangerous area. See the "Websites" section at the end of this lesson for more information about these pill bug–inspired robots.

OLE and the Pillbot are examples of *biomimicry*, which is the design and production of materials, structures, and systems modeled on living things. This field of science is known as *biomimetics*. Scientists and engineers study nature and use its solutions to solve human problems. One of the most well-known examples of biomimicry is the invention of Velcro (see Biomimicry Photo Gallery in "Websites" section). Swiss inventor George de Mestral noticed how strongly cockleburs stuck to his pants after a walk through the woods, so he decided to look closely at them under a microscope. He observed that the burs were covered in small hooks and that the hooks caught the loops in the fabric of his pants. This observation inspired him to design a loop-and-hook fastening system, which we now know as Velcro. Olympians wear swimsuits that mimic sharkskin, underwater communication devices mimic the sounds that dolphins send through the water, NASA has suggested the development of aircraft that are modeled on the shape of twirling maple seeds, and the list goes on and on.

In this lesson, students begin by observing the structures and behaviors of a familiar animal, the pill bug. They read about some pill bug–inspired technologies as well as some other examples of biomimicry. Then, they are challenged to design a pillbot to solve a human problem. Students share their designs through sketches and drawings. These activities allow students to experience the science and engineering practice of developing models, while addressing the crosscutting concept of structure and function.

engage

Next Time You See a Pill Bug
Introduction

Making Connections:
Text to Self

Show students the cover of *Next Time You See a Pill Bug* and introduce the author, Emily Morgan. Tell

them that as a child, the author enjoyed exploring the outdoors, looking under rocks and logs to see what was living there. Now, she and her young son like to explore the woods in their backyard together, collecting pill bugs and other living things to observe. Ask students if they have ever collected pill bugs or played with them. If so, where did they find them? What did they do with them? Read aloud only pages 6–7, which encourage students to pick up a pill bug and let it crawl around on their hands, observe it closely, and describe it.

OBSERVING A PILL BUG

Tell students that, later, they are going to have an opportunity to do just that!

Anticipation Guide

Project a copy of the Let's Learn About Pill Bugs student page. Preassess the students' understandings about pill bugs by having them signal (thumbs-up or thumbs-down) to indicate whether they agree or disagree with each of the following statements (they should also write *T* or *F* in the left-hand column of the student page):

1. Pill bugs have 14 legs.
2. Pill bugs are insects.
3. Pill bugs hatch from eggs.
4. Pill bugs roll into a ball when they feel threatened or scared.
5. Pill bugs prefer very dry places.

Tell them that after observing pill bugs and reading the rest of the book, they will be revisiting the student page to see if their guesses were correct.

explore

Pill Bug Observations

In advance, collect some live pill bugs from the local environment (one per student), and keep them in a temporary habitat containing some damp paper towels or damp leaf litter. Make sure the sides of the container are high enough that the pill bugs cannot escape (or use a lid with tiny air holes punched through). You can also have your students collect the pill bugs for homework and bring them to class for this activity.

Give each student a Pill Bug Observations student page and a hand lens. Tell them that they will be closely observing pill bugs to learn more about their body parts and behaviors. Remind them to treat the pill bugs gently, then give each student a pill bug in a clear plastic container with half of the bottom covered with a piece of damp paper towel. (Students will be observing whether the pill bugs seem to prefer damp or dry places, so it is important not to cover the entire container bottom with the damp paper towel.) Review how to use a magnifier properly: Put your eye close to the lens, shut the other eye, and move the hand lens close to the pill bug until it comes into focus. Students will observe the pill bug; make a detailed, labeled sketch of it on the student page; and describe its body parts and behaviors. Next, they will observe and record the pill bug's reactions to different stimuli in a chart.

explain

Next Time You See a Pill Bug Read-Aloud

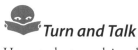 Turn and Talk

Have students explain what they have observed by sharing their drawings and observations with a partner. Then, *ask*

? What did you notice about your pill bug's body parts? Did you see segments, feet, or antennae? (Answers will vary.)

? What did you notice about your pill bug's behavior in response to your actions? Did it move away from touch, flip itself back over, roll into a ball, and move back to the damp paper towel? (Answers will vary.)

? Why do you think your pill bug reacted that way? (Answers will vary.)

As a class, discuss whether students have evidence that any of the statements on the Let's Learn About Pill Bug's student page are true or false. They will most likely have evidence to show that statement 1 is true ("Pill bugs have 14 legs"), statement 4 is true ("Pill bugs roll into a ball when they feel threatened or scared"), and statement 5 is false ("Pill bugs prefer very dry places").

Connecting to the Common Core
Reading: Informational Text
KEY IDEAS AND DETAILS: K.1, 1.1, 2.1

 Determining Importance

Now, tell students that you are going to share the rest of the book *Next Time You See a Pill Bug* and that this book will provide more evidence about the statements on the anticipation guide. It might also help them understand some of the pill bug behaviors they observed earlier. Have students signal when they hear evidence from the text for or against any of the five statements. Stop and discuss each one as you read the book aloud. Students should record the correct answers in the right-hand column of the student page. The correct answers are as follows:

1. Pill bugs have 14 legs. (true, p. 9)
2. Pill bugs are insects. (false, pp. 9–11; they are crustaceans)
3. Pill bugs hatch from eggs. (true, p. 13)
4. Pill bugs roll into a ball when they feel threatened or scared. (true, p. 15)
5. Pill bugs prefer very dry places. (false, pp. 23–25; pill bugs need moisture)

After reading, *ask*

? If your pill bug moved back to the damp paper towel when you moved it to a dry place, why do you think it did so? (Pill bugs need to stay in damp or moist areas so they can breathe through their gills.)

? If your pill bug rolled up when you touched it or turned it over, why do you think it did so? (It felt threatened or scared.)

? What body parts help the pill bug roll up? (its segments or its segmented exoskeleton)

Revisit page 15 of the book, which shows a pill bug flattened out and then rolled up into a ball to protect itself. Students should be able to see from the pictures how the exoskeleton protects the inner, softer part of its body. Explain that this defense mechanism is so unique and special that *roboticists,* or engineers who design robots, have actually tried to copy it!

Biomimicry: Pillbot Video

 Making Connections: Text to World

Tell students that a team of roboticists in South Korea have created a working robot called the Pillbot. The Pillbot is based on many of the structures and abilities of real pill bugs. Show students the video of the Pillbot (see "Websites" section), and *ask*

? How does the Pillbot compare to a real pill bug? (It crawls over obstacles, it rolls into a ball, it has a hard exoskeleton, etc.)

? What do you think a robotic pill bug might be used for? (Answers will vary.)

Explain that this little robot is about the size of a softball and can be rolled up and "bowled" into a location that is too dangerous for humans. Once it reaches the target point, it unrolls and then crawls around and collects information. Roboticists in Germany are working on another type of pillbot—the OLE (pronounced "oh-luh") pill bug, which could someday be used to fight forest fires. It carries water and fire extinguishers and has a fireproof exoskeleton. Explain that engineers often look to nature for ideas. Imitating living things to solve a human problem is called *biomimicry.* Explain that the prefix *bio* means "life" and the word *mimic* means "to

imitate." So the invention of robotic pillbots is an example of biomimicry—"imitating life."

Robots Read-Aloud

 **Chunking**

Show students the cover of the book *National Geographic Kids: Robots,* and ask if they know what a robot is. You will likely get a wide variety of responses. In fact, engineers themselves don't always agree on the definition of *robot.* Explain that because the book is nonfiction, you can enter the text at any point. You don't have to read the book from cover to cover if you are looking for specific information. Tell students that you will be reading the parts of the book that explain how engineers sometimes look to nature for inspiration. Read and discuss pages 4–7, which describe these characteristics of a robot:

- Has movable parts
- Can make decisions
- Is designed by people to do a job by itself
- Collects information from its surroundings
- Processes the information and figures out what to do next
- Does only things it is programmed to do

 **Questioning**

Then, *ask*

? What makes a Pillbot a robot? (It has movable parts, it is designed to do a job by itself, it collects information, etc.)

Tell students to listen carefully as you read another section of the book. This section gives more examples of biomimicry—robots inspired by nature. Have students listen for the different kinds of animals that roboticists study as they design robots. Read aloud pages 16–21 of *Robots,* making sure to share the photographs and insets as you read. Then, share another example of biomimicry by reading about the Robotuna pictured on page 13.

After reading, *ask*

? What is the branch of science called that uses *biomimicry* (borrowing ideas from nature)? (biomimetics)

? What kinds of animals did roboticists study to design the robots you learned about? (ladybugs, geckos, dogs, jellyfish, snakes, fish)

? Why do roboticists study animals? (to get ideas for solving design problems)

? Can you guess what animal roboticists have studied more than any other animal in the world? (humans!)

Then, read pages 32–33, about humanlike robots. Explain that studying how humans move and behave is also an example of biomimicry. For more examples of biomimicry, see the "Websites" section for a photo gallery.

elaborate

Pillbot Designs

Tell students they are going to have the opportunity to design their very own robot! They will be using biomimicry by studying the body parts and movements of pill bugs to invent a pillbot. The purpose of designing a pillbot is to solve a human problem or need. You may want to have students observe live pill bugs again to get inspiration for their pillbot designs. Alternately, you can view a video segment that gives a close-up view of the pill bug's body parts and behaviors, such as the one at *www.youtube.com/watch?v=DWW8Caur8Co.*

Begin the brainstorming process by discussing questions such as the following:

? What are some unique body parts you noticed when observing your pill bug? (14 legs, antennae, hard exoskeleton, segments, etc.)

? What are some unique movements or behaviors you noticed when observing your pill bugs? (They roll up when threatened, they crawl over things, they flip over when turned on their backs, etc.)

? What are some human problems that a pillbot might be able to solve? (Answers will vary.)

? Are there places that are unsafe for humans that a pillbot might be able to explore? (Answers will vary.)

? Are there jobs that a robotic pill bug could do that humans could not? (Answers will vary.)

? Are there toys or devices that could be inspired by a pill bug's movements or body parts? (Answers will vary.)

Then, brainstorm some pillbot ideas together. Examples might include an expandable backpack that automatically rolls up for storage when it is empty, a device that transports something by rolling up into a ball and then unrolling when it reaches its destination, a modified soccer ball that rolls up when it is kicked and then unrolls and moves by itself to make the game more fun and interesting, and so on.

MY PILLBOT

human problem the pillbot solves; and explain how the pillbot is an example of biomimicry.

evaluate

My Pillbot

Connecting to the Common Core
Writing
TEXT TYPES AND PURPOSES: K.3, 1.3, 2.3

 *Writing*

Have each student select an idea from your brainstorming session or come up with an idea of his or her own. Give each student a copy of the My Pillbot student page, and have them begin designing their pillbots. Students should be able to make a simple, labeled sketch to illustrate how the features of the pillbot help it solve a human problem; describe the

STEM at Home

Have students complete the "I learned that …" and "My favorite part of the lesson was …" portions of the STEM at Home student page as a reflection on their learning. They may choose to do the following at-home activity with an adult helper and share their results with the class. If students do not have access to the internet or these materials at home, you may choose to have them complete this activity at school.

"At home, we can watch a video together called 'RoboSnail' about how roboticists, or engineers who design robots, are studying the movements of snails and slugs to invent a new kind of robot."

Search "RoboSnail" on pbslearningmedia.org *to find the video at* www.pbslearningmedia.org/resource/eng06.sci.engin.systems.robosnail/robosnail.

"After we watch the video, we can design our own robot based on a different animal!"

For Further Exploration

This section is provided to help you encourage your students to use the science and engineering practices in a more student-directed format. This box lists questions and challenges related to the lesson that students may select to research, investigate, or innovate. Students may also use the questions as examples to help them generate their own questions. After selecting one of the questions in the box or formulating their own questions, students can individually or collaboratively make predictions, design investigations or surveys to test their predictions, collect evidence, devise explanations, design solutions, or examine related resources. They can communicate their findings through a science notebook, at a poster session or gallery walk, or by producing a media project.

Research

Have students brainstorm researchable questions:

? Where do pill bugs live?

? What are some other types of isopods, and where do they live?

? What are some other examples of biomimicry?

Investigate

Have students brainstorm testable questions to be solved through science or math:

? Do pill bugs prefer bright places or dark places?

? What types of food do pill bugs prefer?

? Can a pill bug find its way through a maze?

Innovate

Have students brainstorm problems to be solved through engineering:

? How could you use biomimicry to invent something that is based on how an elephant uses its trunk?

? How could you use biomimicry to invent something that is based on how a snake moves?

? How could you use biomimicry to invent something that is based on how a maple seed spins through the air?

Websites

Biomimicry Photo Gallery
http://inhabitat.com/finding-design-inspiration-in-nature-biomimicry-for-a-better-planet

"Pill Bug" (video)
www.youtube.com/watch?v=DWW8Caur8Co

"Firefighting Robot" (article)
Note: The pill bug is inaccurately referred to as an insect. *www.popsci.com/scitech/article/2008-03/firefighting-robot*

"OLE Pill Bug Robot" (article)
www.engadget.com/2007/08/12/ole-pill-bug-robot-concept-could-fight-forest-fires

"Pillbot" (video)

www.youtube.com/watch?v=-vi-5PisiDY

"RoboSnail" (video)

www.pbslearningmedia.org/resource/eng06.sci.
engin.systems.robosnail/robosnail

More Books to Read

Becker, H. 2014. *Zoobots: Wild robots inspired by real animals.* Toronto: Kids Can Press.
Summary: This book for older readers (grades 3–6) explores the world of robo-animals, or zoobots. Twelve double-page spreads reveal vivid, Photoshop-rendered illustrations of robot prototypes such as the bacteria-inspired Nanobot, which can move through human blood vessels, and the OLE pill bug, which can fight fires. Each spread shows a smaller illustration of the animal on which the zoobot is based.

Hughes, M. 2004. *Pill bugs.* Chicago: Raintree.
Summary: Simple text and full-color, up-close photographs in this book for young readers describe pill bug anatomy, feeding, growth, reproduction, and hibernation.

Lee, D. 2011. *Biomimicry: Inventions inspired by nature.* Toronto: Kids Can Press.
Summary: This book for older readers (grades 3–6) examines the extraordinary innovations of the natural world and the human inventions they have inspired.

Name: _____

Let's Learn About Pill Bugs

Before Reading True or False		**After Reading** True or False
_____	1. Pill bugs have 14 legs.	_____
_____	2. Pill bugs are insects.	_____
_____	3. Pill bugs hatch from eggs.	_____
_____	4. Pill bugs roll into a ball when they feel threatened or scared.	_____
_____	5. Pill bugs prefer very dry places.	_____

Name: _____

Pill Bug Observations

Make a labeled sketch of your pill bug in the box below.

How many legs does your pill bug have? _____

Observe your pill bug's body parts. What do you notice?_____

_____

_____

Observe your pill bug's reactions to different stimuli. What do you notice?

What I Do	What My Pill Bug Does
Gently touch it	
Gently turn it over	
Move it to a dry place in the container	

Name: _____

My Pillbot

Name of my pillbot: _____

Labeled sketch of my pillbot:

```


```

1. The problem my pillbot solves is _____

_____

_____

2. My pillbot solves the problem by _____

_____

_____

3. My pillbot is an example of **biomimicry** because _____

_____

_____

_____

Name: _____

STEM at Home

Dear _____,

At school, we have been learning about **pill bugs**—how they move, breathe, and defend themselves. We have also been learning about **biomimicry**—how engineers try to mimic, or copy, living things to design robots.

I learned that: _____

_____

My favorite part of the lesson was: _____

_____

_____

At home, we can watch a video together called "RoboSnail" about how roboticists, or engineers who design robots, are studying the movements of snails and slugs to invent a new kind of robot.

 Search "RoboSnail" on *pbslearningmedia.org* to find the video at ***www.pbslearningmedia.org/resource/eng06.sci.engin. systems.robosnail/robosnail.***

After we watch the video, we can design our own robot based on a different animal!

Sketch of Real Animal	Sketch of Robot

Flight of the Pollinators

Description

Students learn about the process of pollination, the variety of pollinators involved, and the way both plants and pollinators benefit from the system of pollination. Then, students develop a simple model that mimics a pollinator and use it to demonstrate plant pollination.

Suggested Grade Levels: K–2

LESSON OBJECTIVES Connecting to the *Framework*		
Science and Engineering Practices	**Disciplinary Core Ideas**	**Crosscutting Concepts**
Developing and Using Models Obtaining, Evaluating, and Communicating Information	**LS2.A:** Interdependent Relationships in Ecosystems **ETS1.B:** Developing Possible Solutions	Structure and Function Systems and System Models

Featured Picture Books

TITLE: *Flowers Are Calling*
AUTHOR: **Rita Gray**
ILLUSTRATOR: **Kenard Pak**
PUBLISHER: **HMH Books for Young Readers**
YEAR: **2015**
GENRE: **Narrative Information**
SUMMARY: *Beautiful artwork and poetry come together to introduce children to the wonders of pollination and the variety of pollinators.*

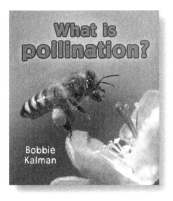

TITLE: *What Is Pollination?*
AUTHOR: **Bobbie Kalman**
PUBLISHER: **Crabtree**
YEAR: **2011**
GENRE: **Non-Narrative Information**
SUMMARY: *Photographs, diagrams, and straightforward text introduce a variety of pollinators and explain the importance of pollination for both the plants and the pollinators.*

Chapter
18

Time Needed

This lesson will take several class periods. Suggested scheduling is as follows:

Day 1: **Engage** with *Flowers Are Calling* Read-Aloud and **Explore** with Look at a Flower—What Do You See?

Day 2: **Explain** with *What Is Pollination?* Read-Aloud

Day 3: **Elaborate** with Pollinator Model Design Challenge

Day 4: **Evaluate** with Pollination Presentations

Materials

For Look at a Flower—What Do You See? (per student or pair)

- Flower (Check with a local florist to get flowers he or she is ready to discard. A diverse selection is recommended so that students can see and smell a variety of flowers. Lilies, irises, daffodils, alstroemeria, tulips, or others with obvious pistils and stamens are best for this activity. Make sure that the flowers are mature so that the pistils and stamens are visible.)
- Hand lens
- Cotton swab
- Piece of clear tape

For Pollinator Model Design Challenge (per student)

- 1 acrylic glove (Magic brand works well)
- 5 Velcro dots (3/8 in. or 0.9 cm; just hooks, not loops)
- 5 multicolor acrylic pom-poms (0.19 in. or 5.0 mm size)
- 2 small paper cups
- A variety of supplies to build and decorate models, such as construction paper, pipe cleaners, googly eyes, coffee filters, scissors, tape, and glue

Student Pages

- Look at a Flower—What Do You See?
- What Is Pollination?
- Pollinator Model Design Challenge
- 4-3-2-1 Pollination Presentation Rubric
- STEM at Home

Background for Teachers

The Natural Resources Conservation Service estimates that 75% of the world's plants and about 35% of the world's crops depend on animals for pollination (NRCS 2016). Some scientists estimate that animal pollinators are responsible for one in every three bites of food we eat! *Pollination* is critical to the sexual reproduction of flowering plants. Most flowers have male and female parts. The *stamen* (male part) makes a powder called *pollen*. The *pistil* (female part) must receive pollen to make seeds. The pistil

260

National Science Teachers Association

has three parts: the *stigma, style,* and *ovary.* When pollen from a stamen reaches a stigma, the flower has been *pollinated.* The pollen travels down the style to the ovary. Inside the ovary are *ovules.* After pollination, the flower's petals fall off, the ovaries become fruit, and the ovules become seeds.

There are different ways flowering plants are pollinated. Some flowers can *self-pollinate,* which means pollen from the stamen moves to the pistil of the same flower. Flowers that self-pollinate have male and female parts close together. Sunflowers are an example of a flower that can self-pollinate. *Wind pollination* occurs when the wind carries pollen from one flower to another. Flowers that are pollinated by the wind produce large amounts of tiny pollen grains, and much of the pollen does not make it to another flower. Wind-pollinated flowers are usually not fragrant and do not produce nectar, because they do not need to attract pollinators. Many trees and grasses are pollinated

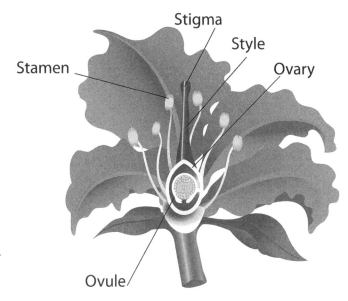

FLOWER DIAGRAM

by wind. *Cross-pollination* occurs when an animal moves pollen from one flower to another flower of the same species. Animals that move the pollen, such as insects, birds, and bats, are called *pollinators.* Pollinators visit flowers to find food. Many of them eat the nectar produced by flowers, and some pollinators, such as bees, even eat the pollen. In their quest for nectar, these animals get pollen stuck on their bodies. When the animals visit other flowers of the same species, some of the pollen falls off. Thus, the animals unknowingly become pollinators.

Scientists have discovered that many pollinators are in danger. Strong evidence shows a decline in both the numbers and the diversity of some pollinators, including bees, butterflies, bats, and hummingbirds. Pesticides, disease, habitat loss, invasive plants, and climate change are thought to be the primary reasons these vital organisms are disappearing. One of the most important pollinators, the honeybee, is experiencing colony collapse disorder (CCD). CCD is a syndrome characterized by a nearly abandoned colony that includes dead bee bodies and lacks adult worker bees but still has a live queen and, usually, immature bees and honey. No cause for CCD has been scientifically proven, but some evidence points to a combination of factors, including parasitic mites and the overuse of a certain type of pesticide.

Pollination is a key concept in understanding the interdependent relationships in ecosystems. In this lesson, students learn that plants depend on animals for pollination. This understanding is crucial to comprehending the impact of pollinators on our ecosystems. Students create a model to demonstrate their understanding of the process of pollination and the structures and functions of plants and animals that are part of the pollination system.

engage

Flowers Are Calling Read-Aloud

Connecting to the Common Core
Reading: Informational Text
CRAFT AND STRUCTURE: K.5, 1.5, 2.5

 **Inferring**

Show students the cover of *Flowers Are Calling* and introduce the author, Rita Gray, and the illustrator, Kenard Pak. *Ask*

❓ What do you think the title *Flowers Are Calling* means? Whom or what do you think the flowers are calling? (Answers will vary.)

❓ Do you notice any animals on the cover? (Students will likely notice the bee, butterfly, and hummingbird on the cover.)

❓ What do you notice about the colors and shapes of the flowers on the cover? (The flowers are different colors and shapes.)

❓ Why do you think flowers are different colors and shapes? (Answers will vary.)

 **Synthesizing**

Tell students that, as you read, you would like them think about what the title *Flowers Are Calling* means. Read the book aloud, stopping after the page that says, "They're calling some children to look again." Then, *ask*

❓ Have your ideas changed about what the title *Flowers Are Calling* means? (Students should realize that the flowers are attracting different animals in different ways.)

❓ What animals were the flowers "calling" in the book? (butterfly, bumblebee, hummingbird, honeybee, beetle, bee fly, pollen wasp, moth, and bat)

OBSERVING FLOWER STRUCTURES IN OUR CLASSROOM

❓ What do all of these animals have in common? (They all fly, they are attracted to flowers, they eat nectar, etc.)

❓ Have you ever seen any of the animals in the book in the wild? (Answers will vary.)

❓ Why do animals visit flowers? (Animals eat the flowers' nectar.)

❓ Why would flowers need to attract animals? (Answers will vary.)

explore

Look at a Flower—What Do You See?

Connecting to the Common Core
Reading: Informational Text
INTEGRATION OF KNOWLEDGE AND IDEAS: K.7, 1.7, 2.7

OBSERVING FLOWER STRUCTURES IN OUR SCHOOL-YARD

COLLECTING POLLEN

Give each student or pair of students a flower, a hand lens, and the Look at a Flower—What Do You See? student page. Have students draw a detailed sketch of the flower. (Students do not necessarily need to know the vocabulary associated with the different flower parts at this time.) Turn to pages 28–30, which are titled "Look at a Flower—What Do You See?" As you read the sections aloud, have students listen for what each characteristic has to do with "calling" animals to visit the flower. Point out the illustrations that accompany each section, and explain that the illustrator provided this art to help the reader better understand each characteristic. After reading each section, have students observe the colors, patterns, shape, and smell of their own flowers and fill in their observations in the table. (*Note:* Time of opening is not on the student page because that characteristic cannot be observed during class time. However, read the paragraph and discuss so that students know that time of open-

ing is also an important factor in attracting certain animals.) Later, you may want to take students outside to observe flower structures on flowering plants found in your school-yard. In this way, they can compare how the same flower structures may look different on different plants.

Tell students that the reason that the flowers were "calling" to the animals has to do with a special powdery substance inside of the flower. Tell students to look carefully to find the powder. When they find it, they should rub some off with a cotton swab and smear it in the box on the paper. Then, have students place a piece of clear tape over the powder to hold it in place. Tell students that, in the next part of the lesson, they will find out what this mysterious powder is and why it is so important. (Some students may know that the powder is called *pollen*, but assure them that there is much to learn about why it is there and what it does.)

explain

What Is Pollination? Read-Aloud

Connecting to the Common Core
Language
VOCABULARY ACQUISITION AND USE: K.6, 1.6, 2.6

Connecting to the Common Core
Reading: Informational Text
CRAFT AND STRUCTURE: K.5, 1.5, 2.5

Cloze

Show students the cover of *What Is Pollination?* by Bobbie Kalman. Tell them this book can help them discover what that mysterious powder is and what it has to do with the flowers and the animals in *Flowers Are Calling*. Give students the What Is Pollination? student page. Directions for students are as follows:

1. Cut out the cards in the boxes.
2. Read the cloze paragraph, and fill in each blank with the card you think belongs there.
3. Listen carefully while your teacher reads the book *What Is Pollination?*
4. After reviewing the paragraph as a class, move the cards if necessary. Then, glue or tape them on the page.
5. On the back, draw a picture of what *pollination* means.

The paragraph should read as follows:

pollen is the fine powder at the center of most flowers. When it moves from one flower to another flower of the same kind, **pollination** takes place. Flowers must be pollinated to make **fruits** and **seeds**. Animals that carry pollen from one flower to another are called **pollinators**. They are not pollinating flowers on purpose. Most animals visit flowers because they are looking for **nectar**!

Questioning

Ask

? Do pollinators *know* that they are helping the plants? (no)

? Why do pollinators visit flowers? (to get nectar or food for themselves)

? How do both the plants and pollinators benefit from pollination? (The plants get their pollen moved to other flowers, which allows them to make new plants, and the pollinators get food.)

Explain that pollinators and plants work together as a system. Systems in the natural world have parts that work together. For example, on page 11 of *What Is Pollination?*, students can see how the shape of a hummingbird's beak works with the shape of tubular flowers. On page 17, they can see how the furry body of a bumblebee works to carry sticky pollen produced by the plant.

On page 31, the author writes, "Each time you bite into an apple, pear, or vegetable, say a silent 'Thank you' to the pollinators that made it possible."

? Why should we thank pollinators? (If plants were not pollinated, fruits and vegetables would not grow.)

? Why are pollinators in danger? (People are building in wilderness areas, which causes animals, including pollinators, to lose their homes and food. Pesticides and diseases are killing many pollinating insects.)

? What can we do to help pollinators? (Tell people why pollinators are important. Grow native flowers at home or school. Plant a vegetable or other garden.)

elaborate

Pollinator Model Design Challenge

Tell students that you have a challenge for each of them—to design and build a model that helps demonstrate how pollinators move pollen from one place to another. They will be using the following materials to build their models:

- 5 small pom-poms to represent pollen (0.19 in. or 5 mm size)

- 2 small paper cups to represent two of the same type of flower

- 1 acrylic glove on which they can tape or glue the following materials to make their models (see photo):

    - 5 small Velcro dots to represent the structures on the pollinator that pollen sticks to

    - Other materials to add more structures and details to their model: construction paper, pipe cleaners, googly eyes, coffee filters, tape, and glue

Their models will need to transfer pom-poms (pollen) from one cup (flower) to the other cup (flower). They may decorate the cups (e.g., add petals) if they would like to make them look more like flowers.

Tell students that before they begin, you want to give them the opportunity to see some pollinators in action. Explain that you have a clip from a movie called *Wings of Life* that a filmmaker named Louis Schwartzberg made to teach people about pollination. Tell them that as they watch, you would like them to look for different types of pollinators, observe their different body parts, and watch how the pollinators interact with flowers. Show students the 4 min. clip from *Wings of Life* (see "Websites" section).

MODEL OF A POLLINATOR

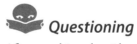

Connecting to the Common Core
Reading: Informational Text
KEY IDEAS AND DETAILS: K.1, 1.1, 2.1

Questioning

After watching the video, *ask*

? What pollinators were featured in the video? (hummingbirds, bees, butterflies, and bats)

? How did they get from flower to flower? (by flying)

? Why were these animals visiting the flowers? (to get nectar)

? What body parts help them get to the nectar (Wings help them fly to the flowers, hummingbirds' long beaks can go deep inside flowers, bats and butterflies have long tongues to slurp nectar, bees' bodies are small enough to go inside many flowers, etc.)

Then, give each student the Pollinator Model Design Challenge student page. Some suggestions for pollinators to model are a bee, wasp, butterfly, moth, fly, beetle, hummingbird, or bat. Have each student choose a pollinator to model and record it

on the paper, find a photograph of that pollinator online, print it out, and attach it to the page. (See "Websites" section for suggested pollinator photo galleries.) The photos will be used for reference as students make their models.

Next, they will describe how the real pollinator gets food from the flower and how the model pollinator will show this. They will also describe the parts of the real pollinator's body that the pollen sticks to and how the model pollinator will show this. Finally, they will explain how both plants and pollinators benefit from their interaction and how humans benefit from pollination. Students will use the photo and this information to help them design and build their models.

evaluate

Pollination Presentations

Connecting to the Common Core
Speaking and Listening
PRESENTATION OF KNOWLEDGE AND IDEAS: K.4, 1.4, 2.4

 *Synthesizing*

After students have completed their models, pass out the 4-3-2-1 Pollination Presentation Rubric. Students should use the information from the Pollinator Model Design Challenge student page to help them with their presentations. You may consider having students present their models to an outside audience, such as a local park official or nature expert.

After giving students sufficient time to practice, you can have them take turns giving their presentations live or have them record videos of

their presentations. They must include the following information:

- A demonstration of how the pollinator moves pollen from one flower to another
- A description of the body parts that the pollinator uses to get food from the flower and the body parts that the pollen sticks to
- An explanation of how both plants and pollinators benefit from pollination
- An explanation of how humans benefit from pollination

They can also share what they might do to improve their models. Use the rubric to evaluate their presentations.

STEM at Home

Have students complete the "I learned that …" and "My favorite part of the lesson was …" portions of the STEM at Home student page as a reflection on their learning. They may choose to do the following at-home activity with an adult helper and share their results with the class. If students do not have access to the internet or these materials at home, you may choose to have them complete this activity at school.

"At home, we can watch a video together called 'RoboBees to the Rescue' about how **roboticists**, or engineers who design robots, at Harvard University are designing a robotic bee to pollinate plants."

Search "RoboBees to the Rescue" on pbslearningmedia.org *to find the video at* www.pbslearningmedia.org/resource/arct14. sci.nvrobobee/robobees-to-the-rescue.

"After we watch the video, we can design our own robot that is based on a different pollinator, such as a butterfly, hummingbird, beetle, moth, or bat."

For Further Exploration

This section is provided to help you encourage your students to use the science and engineering practices in a more student-directed format. This box lists questions and challenges related to the lesson that students may select to research, investigate, or innovate. Students may also use the questions as examples to help them generate their own questions. After selecting one of the questions in the box or formulating their own questions, students can individually or collaboratively make predictions, design investigations or surveys to test their predictions, collect evidence, devise explanations, design solutions, or examine related resources. They can communicate their findings through a science notebook, at a poster session or gallery walk, or by producing a media project.

Research

Have students brainstorm researchable questions:

? What kinds of plants would attract pollinators to your yard or school-yard?

? Which crops in our area depend on pollinators?

? Which pollinators are in danger, and what can we do to help?

Investigate

Have students brainstorm testable questions to be solved through science or math:

? What are some common pollinators that visit our school-yard?

? How many of the foods that I eat in a day require animal pollinators? (Keep a tally of how many times you eat vegetables, fruits, or nuts—or foods made using those products—in a day.)

? Which plants seem to attract the most pollinators in our school-yard?

Innovate

Have students brainstorm problems to be solved through engineering:

? Can we build a feeder to attract hummingbirds to our school-yard?

? Can we design a flower garden (either on a plot of land or in pots) to attract butterflies?

? Can we design a vegetable garden (either on a plot of land or in pots) to help pollinators?

Reference

NRCS (Natural Resources Conservation Service). 2016. Insects and pollinators. U.S. Department of Agriculture. *www.nrcs.usda.gov/wps/portal/nrcs/main/ national/plantsanimals/pollinate.*

Websites

National Geographic "Gold Dusters" Pollinator Photo Gallery
http://ngm.nationalgeographic.com/2011/03/ pollinators/moffett-photography

Penn State University Entomology Department: Pollinator Image Gallery
http://ento.psu.edu/pollinators/image-galleries

U.S. Department of Agriculture: "Be a Friend to Pollinators" (brochure)
www.nrcs.usda.gov/wps/portal/nrcs/detail/national/ plantsanimals/pollinate/?cid=stelprdb1142431

Wings of Life (Video Clip: The Beauty of Pollination)
http://video.disney.com/watch/the-beauty-of- pollination-wings-of-life-4da84833e06fd54fff590f49

More Books to Read

Bersani, S. 2015. *Achoo! Why pollen counts.* Mount Pleasant, SC: Arbordale Publishing.

Summary: A cute storyline about a baby black bear that is allergic to pollen not only teaches readers about pollen allergies but also explains how vital this fine powder is to the animals and plants in the forest.

Konicek-Moran, R., and K. Konicek-Moran. 2016. *From flower to fruit.* Arlington, VA: NSTA Press.

Summary: Rich illustrations and an engaging narrative draw the reader into the world of botany. The book introduces the parts of a flower, the process of pollination, and the production of fruit. It includes activities and background information for parents and teachers.

Rich, S. 2014. *Mrs. Carter's butterfly garden.* Arlington, VA: NSTA Press.

Summary: In this story of how former First Lady Rosalynn Carter started a front-yard project that grew into a butterfly-friendly trail through her hometown of Plains, Georgia, students will learn why having welcoming spaces for butterflies is good for people and how to create their own butterfly gardens at home or school.

Slade, S. 2011. *What if there were no bees? A book about the grassland ecosystem.* North Mankato, MN: Picture Window Books.

Summary: Part of the *Food Chain Reactions* series, this book highlights the importance of bees to the ecosystem. By addressing the question "What if there were no bees?," the reader learns these insects are a keystone species because many other species would likely become extinct without them.

Look at a Flower—
What Do You See?

1. Observe the flower carefully. Draw a picture that shows its shape, colors, patterns, and parts.

[ ]

2. Listen as your teacher reads about each characteristic of a flower, then record the observations for your flower.

Characteristic	Observation
Color	
Pattern	
Shape	
Smell	

3. Look for the powdery substance in the center of your flower. Use a cotton swab to smear some in the box below and tape it in place.

Name: _____

What Is Pollination?

_____ is the fine powder at the center of most flowers. When it moves from one

flower to another flower of the same kind, _____ takes place. Flowers must be

pollinated to make _____ and _____. Animals that carry pollen

from one flower to another are called _____. They are not pollinating flowers on

purpose. Most animals visit flowers because they are looking for _____!

Directions: Cut out the cards below and place them in the paragraph above. Then, listen as
your teacher reads the book *What Is Pollination?*

fruits	**pollen**	**nectar**
pollination	**seeds**	**pollinators**

Name: _____

Pollinator Model Design Challenge

Challenge: Design a model of a pollinator that can be used to demonstrate how it moves pollen from one flower to another while getting food.

Directions: Choose a real pollinator as an inspiration for your model. Then, design your model using the materials provided.

Real Pollinator	Model Pollinator
Name and photo	Labeled sketch
How does the pollinator get food from the flower?	How will your model show this?
What parts of the pollinator's body does the pollen stick to?	How will your model show this?

1. How do both plants and pollinators benefit from pollination?

    Plants get _____

    Pollinators get _____

2. How do humans benefit from pollination?

_____

Name: _____

4~3~2~1
Pollination Presentation Rubric

Demonstrate the model of a pollinator that you designed. Your presentation should include the following:

4 Points: A demonstration of how your model pollinator moves pollen from one flower to another .

4   3   2   1   0

3 Points: A description of the body parts that your model pollinator uses to get food from the flower and the body parts that the pollen sticks to

3   2   1   0

2 Points: An explanation of how both plants and pollinators benefit from pollination

2   1   0

1 Point: An explanation of how humans benefit from pollination

1   0

Score: _____/10

Name: _____

STEM at Home

Dear _____,

At school, we have been learning about **pollinators**, or animals that move pollen from one flower to another.

I learned that: _____

_____

_____

My favorite part of the lesson was: _____

_____

_____

At home, we can watch a video together called "RoboBees to the Rescue" about how **roboticists,** or engineers who design robots, at Harvard University are designing a robotic bee to pollinate plants.

 Search "RoboBees to the Rescue" on *pbslearningmedia.org* to find the video at *www.pbslearningmedia.org/resource/arct14.sci.nvrobobee/robobees-to-the-rescue.*

After we watch the video, we can design our own robot that is based on a different pollinator, such as a butterfly, hummingbird, beetle, moth, or bat.

Sketch of Real Pollinator	Sketch of Robot Pollinator

A Birthday Is No Ordinary Day

Description

Every trip around the Sun brings us to another one—birthday, that is! There aren't many events in a child's life quite as exciting as his or her own birthday. Through an engaging picture book, students are invited to consider each birthday as a celebration of one more trip around the Sun. They investigate how many hours of daylight there will be on their next birthday and compare this number with those of other students, leading them to conclude that the hours of daylight are greater in the summer months and fewer in the winter months. Then, students design a birthday card for a family member or friend that teaches the recipient how truly remarkable a birthday is!

Suggested Grade Levels: K–2

LESSON OBJECTIVES Connecting to the *Framework*		
Science and Engineering Practices	**Disciplinary Core Ideas**	**Crosscutting Concepts**
Analyzing and Interpreting Data Using Mathematics and Computational Thinking	**ESS1.B:** Earth and the Solar System	Patterns Cause and Effect

Featured Picture Books

TITLE: *A Birthday Cake Is No Ordinary Cake*
AUTHOR: **Debra Frasier**
ILLUSTRATOR: **Debra Frasier**
PUBLISHER: **Harcourt Children's Books**
YEAR: **2006**
GENRE: **Story**
SUMMARY: *A lyrical recipe uses the changes in the natural world to explain the time that passes between one birthday and the next.*

TITLE: *Jump Into Science: Sun*
AUTHOR: **Steve Tomecek**
ILLUSTRATOR: **Carla Golembe**
PUBLISHER: **National Geographic**
YEAR: **2016**
GENRE: **Non-Narrative Information**
SUMMARY: *Part of the* Jump Into Science *series, this book introduces the Sun as a star and explains the daily and yearly phenomena that are results of the position of the Earth relative to the Sun.*

Time Needed

This lesson will take several class periods. Suggested scheduling is as follows:

Day 1: Engage with *A Birthday Cake Is No Ordinary Cake* Read-Aloud and **Explore** with My Birthday Cake

Day 2: Explain with Birthday Seasons and *Jump Into Science: Sun* Read-Aloud

Day 3: Elaborate with Birthday Celebrations (ongoing) and **Evaluate** with Design a Birthday Card

Materials

- Crayons
- List of student birthdays
- Computer or tablet
- App or website providing sunrise time, sunset time, and hours of daylight information
- 4 pieces of poster board
- Desktop globe
- Pushpin or small sticker
- Lamp with the shade removed

SAFETY

- Remind students not to not touch electric light bulbs.
- Be sure never to use the lamp near a water source.
- Tell students to be careful when handling pushpins because they are sharp and can puncture skin.

Student Pages

- My Birthday Cake
- Happy Birthday template
- STEM at Home

Background for Teachers

As our planet rotates, we experience day and night. Most days of the year, however, the hours of daylight and nighttime are not equally divided. When we are experiencing summer, there are more hours of daylight. When we are experiencing winter, there are fewer. In the Northern Hemisphere, the longest day of the year (the *summer solstice*) falls between June 20 and June 22, and the shortest day of the year (the *winter solstice*) falls between December 20 and December 23. The changes in length of day are caused by the tilt of Earth on its axis and the orbit of Earth around the Sun. As Earth orbits the Sun, one hemisphere is always tilted more toward the Sun than the other (except on two days—the *vernal equinox* and the *autumnal equinox*). The hemisphere that is tilted toward the Sun experiences longer periods of daylight. At the same time, the opposite hemisphere experiences the opposite season and shorter periods of daylight.

The *Framework* suggests that students in elementary school develop an understanding of Earth and the Solar System, specifically the observable patterns caused by the movements of the Sun, Earth, Moon, and planets. One of these patterns is the seasonal changes in the hours of daylight throughout the year. In the primary grades, students should understand that this pattern can be observed, described, and predicted. They should have opportunities to make observations of how the hours of daylight change throughout the year and recognize a pattern. This task can be challenging to do on a long-term basis in the early elementary classroom, so this lesson puts the concept in the context of most children's favorite day of the year—their birthday! Students learn that each candle on their birthday cake represents one trip around the Sun. Using a website or app, the teacher provides each student the times of sunrise and sunset and the hours and minutes of daylight on his or her birthday. The class then compares the day lengths for all of the students' birthdays throughout the year. Students learn the basic concept that the longest days of the year are in the summer and the shortest in the winter. It should be noted that the emphasis in this lesson is on relative comparisons of the amount of daylight in different seasons and that students are not assessed on measuring or calculating the hours of daylight. Likewise, although the cause of seasons is introduced in one of the featured picture books, students should not be assessed on this concept because it is more appropriately assessed in middle school.

engage

A Birthday Cake Is No Ordinary Cake Read-Aloud

 Making Connections: Text to Self

Note: Before beginning the read-aloud, have a list of student birthdays available for any student who cannot recall the date of his or her birthday.

Show students the cover of *A Birthday Cake Is No Ordinary Cake* and introduce the author and illustrator, Debra Frasier. Then, *ask*

? What makes a birthday cake so special? (It is given on a birthday, often during a party. It has colorful decorations, it usually has a name written on it, it has candles on top, etc.)

? Do you have any special birthday traditions? (Answers will vary.)

? Do you eat cake, go out to dinner, or open presents? (Answers will vary.)

 Turn and Talk

Have students turn and talk to a partner about their family's birthday traditions. Share some of your own birthday traditions or a story about a special birthday you had.

 Determining Importance

Next, point out to students the picture of the Sun on the cover of the book. *Ask*

? What do you think the Sun has to do with birthdays? (Answers will vary.)

Tell students that as you read, you would like them to listen for how the book connects the Sun to birthdays.

> Connecting to the Common Core
> **Reading: Literature**
> INTEGRATION OF KNOWLEDGE AND IDEAS: K.7, 1.7, 2.7

Read the book aloud, stopping to discuss what the Sun has to do with birthdays each time the Sun appears. For example, you could say the following:

- Page 7: "The Earth spins eastward toward the Sun to make morning, then spins away to make night. No spinning, no cake."
- Pages 8–9: "The Earth spins in a circle around the Sun from your birthday to your next birthday."
- Pages 12–13: "Collect the first sunrise after your birthday. You will need 364 more sunrises until your next birthday."
- Pages 26–27: "After collecting your 365th sunrise …"

• Pages 30–31: "Light a candle for each time you've circled the Sun. … And remember— we're traveling a circle. This recipe is a circle. It's all coming round again."

Questioning

After reading, *ask*

? So what does the Sun have to do with birthdays? (Students should realize that each birthday represents another trip they have taken around the Sun during their life.)

? Can you recall some of the ingredients in the birthday cake in the book? (365 sunrises, bright spring flowers, at least 12 full moons, the shade of two trees on the longest day of the year, the first cool fall morning, the sound of snowflakes falling, etc.)

? What message do you think the author is trying to communicate through this book? (To have a birthday, you must experience a whole year of seasons. The author came up with a creative way to express the idea that a birthday equals one more trip around the Sun.)

explore

My Birthday Cake

Connecting to the Common Core
Reading: Literature
KEY IDEAS AND DETAILS: K.1, 1.1, 2.1

Reread page 30 of the book that says, "At last, your cake is done. Let's light a candle for each time you've circled the Sun." Give each student the My Birthday Cake student page. *Ask*

? How many candles should your cake have? (The same number of candles as their age.)

? How many times have you circled the Sun? (The same number of times as their age.)

Have students draw candles on top of the cake to represent each time they have circled the Sun in their lifetime. They should write their name beneath the words *Happy Birthday,* write their birth date on top of the cake, and then write in the number of trips around the Sun for their *next* birthday. *Ask*

? What other information needs to be written on your birthday cake? (sunrise, sunset, hours, and minutes of daylight)

? Where do you think you could find that information? (Answers will vary.)

Connecting to the Common Core
Mathematics
MEASUREMENT AND DATA: 1.MD.3, 2.MD.7

Ask

? Do sunrises and sunsets occur at the same time every day? (Answers will vary.)

? What have you observed in your daily life about sunrises and sunsets? In other words, what evidence makes you think so? (Students may have noticed that sometimes when they wake up in the morning, it is dark outside, and other times, it is light outside. They may have also noticed that it gets dark earlier in the winter, and the days seem longer in the summer.)

Tell students that scientists are able to predict the *exact time* sunrise and sunset occur for each day. In fact, many websites and apps can tell the exact time sunrise and sunset will occur on their birthdays (see "Websites" section for such an app). Model how to use one of these apps to find the time of sunrise and sunset on your next birthday. If you do not have tablets for classroom use, you can get this information from the Time and Date Sun Calculator (see "Websites" section).

Have students watch as you enter your location and the month. Model where to find the sunrise time, sunset time, and total hours of daylight. Remind students that *a.m.* refers to the time before noon and *p.m.* refers to the time after noon. Then,

FINDING HOURS OF DAYLIGHT

OUR BIRTHDAYS

if tablets are available for student use, have students enter their next birthday and look up the sunrise time, sunset time, and hours of daylight data for that day. If tablets aren't available, you will need to look up the data for each student. (You can have students work on cutting out their cakes and decorating them with crayons while they are waiting for you to look up the information.)

Once students have the data for their own birthdays, they can record the sunrise time, sunset time, and hours of daylight (in hours and minutes) on the My Birthday Cake student page. Make sure they write the hours and minutes of daylight large enough that others can read it from a distance. Then, have students cut out the cakes, if they haven't already. They will be using their cake cutouts for the next activity.

explain

Birthday Seasons

In advance, place four posters evenly spaced around the room, with the words *Spring, Summer, Fall,* and *Winter* written on them. Then, *ask*

? During what season is your birthday: spring, summer, fall, or winter? (Answers will vary.)

Tell students that they will be using the posters of the four seasons to help them line up in order by birthday. Have students hold their completed

paper cakes in front of them and line up to form a large circle in chronological order of their birthdays.

You may need to help them figure out where to stand relative to the poster of their birthday season and each other's birthdays. Once they have formed a semblance of a circle and are standing in approximately the right place relative to each other, help them analyze data from their "human graph."

Connecting to the Common Core
Mathematics
MEASUREMENT AND DATA: 1.MD.4, 2.MD.10

 **Questioning**

Ask

? Is the length of day the same on everyone's birthday? (No, they are different.)

? Why are they different? (The sunrise and sunset times are different every day.)

? Which student's birthday has the most hours and minutes of daylight? (Answer will vary, depending on your students' birth dates.)

? In what season is that person's birthday? (summer)

? Which student's birthday has the fewest hours and minutes of daylight? (Answer will vary, depending on your students' birth dates.)

DAY AND NIGHT DEMONSTRATION

? In what season is that person's birthday? (winter)

? How do the hours of daylight in the summer compare with the hours of daylight in the winter? (There are more hours of daylight in the summer than in the winter.)

? What patterns do you notice? (Students should notice that the most hours of daylight, or the longest days, occur in the summer months, and the fewest hours of daylight, or the shortest days, occur in the winter months. They may notice that the hours of daylight are similar in spring and fall.)

Jump Into Science: Sun Read-Aloud

Tell students that you have a nonfiction book called *Jump Into Science: Sun* that can help explain why the length of day changes as the seasons change. You will need the four seasons posters spaced out evenly around the room for the read-aloud. Also, have a desktop globe (tilted on its axis) handy to refer to as you read. Tell students that you will be using the globe as a model of the Earth to demonstrate some of the events in the book as you read. Have a volunteer help you locate and mark your school's general location on the globe, using a pushpin or sticker to represent your place on Earth. This can help students visualize some of the phenomena described in the book.

Show them the cover of *Jump Into Science: Sun* and introduce the author and illustrator, Steve Tomecek and Carla Golembe, respectively. Tell them that as you read the book aloud, you will be stopping to demonstrate some of the ideas in the book.

 **Stop and Try It**

Earth's Axis Demonstration

Begin reading *Sun* aloud, skipping pages 10–15 (these pages are not relevant to the concept being taught). Stop after reading page 17, and point out Earth's tilted axis on your desktop globe. Spin the globe counterclockwise to show that "Earth is always spinning, just like a basketball on a player's finger. The line that Earth spins around is called an axis" (p. 17). Point out that the axis is imaginary; you can't really see it from space!

Day and Night Demonstration

Then, read pages 18–19, about day and night. After reading, place the lamp in the center of the room to represent the Sun, and turn it on. Turn off the classroom lights. Using the globe to represent Earth, model how day changes to night in your location by slowly spinning the globe and having students observe the pushpin or sticker move from the lighted part of the globe to the shaded part of the globe. Turn the classroom lights back on and turn off the lamp. (*Note:* Although the reason for the seasons is introduced here, students should not be assessed on this concept because it is more appropriately assessed in middle school.)

Connecting to the Common Core
Reading: Informational Text
KEY IDEAS AND DETAILS: K.1, 1.1, 2.1

 Questioning

Next, read page 22, which is about the summer. Ask students to examine the illustration carefully. *Ask*

? What time is it on the clock? (9:00 p.m.)

? Is that morning or evening? (evening)

? What is the girl doing? (sleeping)

? What is it like outside her window? (It is daylight.)

? What time of year is it? (summer)

? Have you ever had to go to bed when it is still light outside in the summer?

Then, reread the text on page 22, which explains that there are more hours of daylight in the summer than any other season. Next, read page 23, which is about the winter. Ask students to examine the illustration carefully. *Ask*

? What time is it on the clock? (7:00 a.m.)

? Is that morning or evening? (morning)

? What is the boy doing? (eating a bowl of cereal)

? What is it like outside his window? (snowing and dark)

? What time of year is it? (winter)

? Have you noticed that it is dark in the morning when you leave for school on some winter days? (Answers will vary.)

Then, reread the text on page 23, which explains that there are fewer hours of daylight in the winter than any other season.

 Synthesizing

Finally, finish reading the book aloud. After reading, ask students to think about some of the "big ideas" that they learned from the books *A Birthday*

Cake Is No Ordinary Cake and *Sun*, as well as from the activities. *Ask*

? What causes day and night? (Earth spinning on its axis.)

? What causes the hours of daylight, or the length of day, to be longer in the summer? (Our place on Earth is tilted toward the Sun in the summer.)

? What causes the hours of daylight, or the length of day, to be shorter in the winter? (Our place on Earth is tilted away from the Sun in the winter.)

? How long does it take Earth to travel, or orbit, all the way around the Sun? (365 days, or one year.)

? So how many orbits old are you? (same number as their age)

 Turn and Talk

Have students turn and talk to a partner about the season their birthday falls in and the observations they have made about the hours of daylight (length of day) on their birthday.

elaborate

Birthday Celebrations

Create a large version of the graphic on the back inside cover of *A Birthday Cake Is No Ordinary Cake* and display it in your classroom (see "Websites" section for a printable called "How Many Days to *Your* Birthday?" from author Debra Frasier's website). Have students each write his or her name and birthdate on a small cake- or cupcake-shaped cutout or sticky note and place it in the appropriate spot around the graphic.

On or near each child's actual birthday, use an app or website to look up sunrise time, susnset time, and hours of daylight for that day. Share the data with the class, noting the changes in day length as you do this throughout the year. You can mark the occasion of summer birthdays, too, by celebrating "half birthdays" for students whose birthdays fall

A BIRTHDAY CELEBRATION

during summer break (e.g., an August 16 birthday would be celebrated on February 16). Compare the hours of daylight on each summer birthday with the hours of daylight on the "half birthday," which falls in the opposite season.

You can also give each birthday boy or girl a special bookmark that says, "Congratulations! You've circled the Sun ___ times!" (printable from the author's website; see "Websites" section), reinforcing the idea that a birthday represents a trip around the Sun. To further reinforce the concept, celebrate birthdays throughout the year by having the birthday boy or girl walk in a circle around the room (holding a globe, if you would like) to model the Earth's orbit around the Sun. The student who has the next birthday can stand in the center of the room to represent the Sun (holding a picture or cutout of the Sun if you like). Sing this variation of the "Happy Birthday" song as the birthday boy

or girl walks around the "Sun" one time for each year of his or her life:

Happy birthday to you

____ trips around the Sun (fill in the blank with the student's age)

You're another year older

And we hope you've had fun!

evaluate

Design a Birthday Card

Connecting to the Common Core
Writing
RESEARCH TO BUILD AND PRESENT KNOWLEDGE: K.8, 1.8, 2.8

Writing

Ask students to think of a friend or family member who has a birthday coming up. Tell them that they are going to have the opportunity to design a birthday card for that person, but this will not be an ordinary birthday card! This card will use science, technology, and math to teach the recipient about what a birthday actually represents—another trip around the Sun.

Students can use the birthday card template provided in the student pages or make their own cards. They will need to use an app or website to look up the sunrise time, sunset time, and hours of daylight data for the recipient's birthday. After writing the recipient's name on the cover and coloring in the Sun, students should fill out the following information on the inside of the card for full credit:

1. The month and day of the recipient's birthday

2. Sunrise time on the recipient's birthday

3. Sunset time on the recipient's birthday

4. The hours and minutes of daylight on the recipient's birthday

5. A comparison with the hours of daylight

on the student's own birthday (more/less/the same)

6. A suggestion of what the recipient could do outside on his or her birthday (considering the season and the length of day)

7. A response to "A birthday is no ordinary day. A birthday is another trip around the _____!" (Sun)

8. A labeled sketch showing that a birthday represents a trip around the Sun

Students' labeled drawings for item 8 will give you an opportunity to assess their understanding of the key concepts in this lesson. Visit students as they work, and ask them to use their drawings to explain their thinking.

Finally, have the students sign their cards and decorate or personalize them as they wish.

STEM at Home

Have students complete the "I learned that …" and "My favorite part of the lesson was …" portions of the STEM at Home student page as a reflection on their learning. They may choose to do the following at-home activity with an adult helper and share their results with the class. If students do not have access to the internet or these materials at home, you may choose to have them complete this activity at school.

"At home, we can find out what time the Sun will rise and set on our birthdays. We can also find out who in our household has the most hours of daylight on his or her birthday and who has the fewest!"

 Search "Sunrise Sunset HD" in your web browser to find the app at https://itunes.apple.com/us/app/Sunrise-Sunset-hd/id650453412?mt=8. *Or search "Time and Date Sun Calculator" to find the website at* www.timeanddate.com/sun.

Websites

Debra Frasier's Website: How Many Days to *Your* Birthday?
www.debrafrasier.com/docs/bdaycake/yearmap.pdf

Debra Frasier's Website: Printable Bookmarks
www.debrafrasier.com/docs/bdaycake/bookmarks.pdf

Sunrise Sunset HD App
https://itunes.apple.com/us/app/Sunrise-Sunset-hd/id650453412?mt=8

For Further Exploration

This section is provided to help you encourage your students to use the science and engineering practices in a more student-directed format. This box lists questions and challenges related to the lesson that students may select to research, investigate, or innovate. Students may also use the questions as examples to help them generate their own questions. After selecting one of the questions in the box or formulating their own questions, students can individually or collaboratively make predictions, design investigations or surveys to test their predictions, collect evidence, devise explanations, design solutions, or examine related resources. They can communicate their findings through a science notebook, at a poster session or gallery walk, or by producing a media project.

Research

Have students brainstorm researchable questions:

? What do the abbreviations *a.m.* and *p.m.* mean, and where did they come from?

? What is a solstice? What is an equinox?

? What is Daylight Saving Time? Who first came up with the idea?

For Further Exploration (*continued*)

Investigate

Have students brainstorm testable questions to be solved through science or math:

? How does the length of your shadow change throughout the day? Measure it!

? How many hours of daylight are there on the summer solstice in your area? At the North Pole? At the South Pole?

? How many hours of daylight are there on the winter solstice in your area? At the North Pole? At the South Pole?

Innovate

Have students brainstorm problems to be solved through engineering:

? Can you build a working sundial?

? Can you build a model that shows how Earth is tilted on its axis as it orbits the Sun?

? What problems does Daylight Saving Time solve, and what problems does it cause for people?

Time and Date Sun Calculator
www.timeanddate.com/worldclock/Sunrise.html

More Books to Read

Branley, F. M. 1986. *What makes day and night?* New York: HarperCollins.
Summary: This book provides a simple explanation of how the rotation of Earth causes day and night.

Branley, F. M. 2002. *The Sun: Our nearest star.* New York: HarperCollins.
Summary: This book describes the Sun and how it provides light and energy, which allows plant and animal life to exist on Earth.

Morgan, E. 2013. *Next time you see a sunset.* Arlington, VA: NSTA Press.
Summary: Beautiful photographs and simple explanations describe what is really happening during a sunset—Earth is turning! The book provides other observable evidence of Earth's turn, such as changes in length and direction of shadows and the position of the Sun, Moon, and stars in the sky.

Name: _____

My Birthday Cake

1. Write your name and birthday on top of the cake.
2. Draw a candle on top for each year of your age.
3. Cut out and decorate the cake.
4. Your teacher will help you fill in the rest.

Happy Birthday

_____ _____
Month   Day

On My Next Birthday

Trips around the Sun: _____

Sunrise: _____a.m.   Sunset: _____p.m.

Hours and minutes of daylight:

_____h _____m

Happy Birthday
to

7. A birthday is no ordinary day. A birthday is another trip around the _____ !

8. Labeled sketch showing the above

Signed,

_____

1. Your birthday is on: _____

2. The Sun will rise at _____ a.m.

3. The Sun will set at _____ p.m.

4. You will have _____ hours and _____ min. of daylight on your birthday.

5. Your birthday has (more/less/the same) hours of daylight compared with mine.

6. Here's what you could do outside on your birthday!

_____

_____

_____

_____

_____

_____

STEM at Home

Dear _____,

At school, we have been learning about **patterns of the Earth and Sun**: how the hours of daylight change throughout the year and how every birthday represents another trip around the Sun.

I learned that: _____

_____

My favorite part of the lesson was: _____

_____

At home, we can find out what time the Sun will rise and set on our birthdays. We can also find out who in our household has the most hours of daylight on his or her birthday and who has the fewest!

Search "Sunrise Sunset HD" in your web browser to find the app at *https://itunes.apple.com/us/app/Sunrise-Sunset-hd/id650453412?mt=8.* Or search "Time and Date Sun Calculator" to find the website at *www.timeanddate.com/sun.*

Name	Birthday	Sunrise	Sunset	Hours and Minutes of Daylight
		a.m.	p.m.	
		a.m.	p.m.	
		a.m.	p.m.	
		a.m.	p.m.	

Conclusion: On their birthdays, _____ has the

most hours of daylight and _____ has the fewest

hours of daylight.

Our Blue Planet

Description

This lesson focuses on where water is found on Earth and how technology can help us map the shapes and kinds of water in an area. By exploring with maps, globes, and satellite images of Earth and reading a book that describes bodies of water, students identify where both liquid and solid water (ice) are found on Earth. Students also use the Google Earth app to take virtual field trips to different places on the planet and to locate the bodies of water closest to their school.

Suggested Grade Levels: K–2

LESSON OBJECTIVES Connecting to the *Framework*		
Science and Engineering Practices	**Disciplinary Core Ideas**	**Crosscutting Concept**
Developing and Using Models Obtaining, Evaluating, and Communicating Information	**ESS2.B:** Plate Tectonics and Large-Scale System Interactions **ESS2.C:** The Roles of Water in Earth's Surface Processes **ETS2.A:** Interdependence of Science, Engineering, and Technology	Scale, Proportion, and Quantity

Featured Picture Books

TITLE: **All the Water in the World**
AUTHOR: **George Ella Lyon**
ILLUSTRATOR: **Katherine Tillotson**
PUBLISHER: **Atheneum Books for Young Readers**
YEAR: **2011**
GENRE: **Narrative Information**
SUMMARY: *Rhythmic language and vibrant artwork describe why "all the water in the world is all the water in the world," which keeps cycling through various forms and places.*

TITLE: **Earth's Landforms and Bodies of Water**
AUTHOR: **Natalie Hyde**
PUBLISHER: **Crabtree**
YEAR: **2015**
GENRE: **Non-Narrative information**
SUMMARY: *Vivid photography and simple text introduce children to the different landforms and bodies of water that are found on Earth. The book includes ways that maps and globes are used to model Earth's features.*

Time Needed

This lesson will take several class periods. Suggested scheduling is as follows:

Day 1: **Engage** with *All the Water in the World* Read-Aloud and **Explore** with "The Blue Marble" and Google Earth Virtual Field Trip

Day 2: **Explain** with Comparing Bodies of Water and *Earth's Landforms and Bodies of Water* Read-Aloud

Day 3: **Elaborate** with Where's Our Water? and **Evaluate** with Our Blue Planet Place Map

Materials

- "The Blue Marble" photograph from *Apollo 17* (see "Websites" section)
- Google Earth and Google Maps apps
- Projector or interactive whiteboard
- Internet connection
- Globe and world map (*Note:* Keep a globe and a world map handy throughout the lesson. If possible, provide extras for groups or pairs of students to use.)
- Student computers or handheld devices
- Crayons or markers
- Scissors
- Bodies of Water Cards (uncut)
- Cutout strips of Ocean Cards (1 per student)
- 9 × 12 in. white cardstock or construction paper (1 piece per student)
- Glue

SAFETY
Use caution when handling scissors to avoid puncturing skin.

Student Pages

- Google Earth Virtual Field Trip
- Bodies of Water
- Our Blue Planet Place Map
- STEM at Home

Background for Teachers

In 1972, NASA took a photograph that changed the way we see our world. In fact, it is one of the most widely distributed photographs of all time. This photo of Earth, taken as the *Apollo 17* astronauts were heading to the Moon, gave us a new perspective on our planet. It reminded the astronauts of a swirly blue glass marble, so the photograph was aptly titled "The Blue Marble."

The blue color of our planet is due to the abundance of water, which gives off blue light upon reflection. Nearly three-fourths (about 71%) of the surface of Earth is covered in water, and most of that water (about 96.5%) is contained within the ocean as *saltwater*. The greatest volume of *freshwater* on Earth is not located in rivers or lakes; it is located underground or frozen in *glaciers* and *polar ice caps*. In fact, only about 1% of all the water on Earth is accessible freshwater. Our water is precious—all that's

here is all we have. Thus, understanding Earth's water is a key concept in K–12 science education.

An *ocean* is a large, deep body of saltwater. There is really just *one* ocean that covers our planet, but explorers and oceanographers have divided the world ocean into five named regions: Atlantic, Pacific, Indian, Arctic, and Southern. All these ocean regions flow into each other, which means there is only one ocean. There used to be only four named oceans, but since 2000, most countries recognize the Southern Ocean as the fifth ocean. (Note that older classroom maps and globes may not have the Southern Ocean labeled.). Also, many people use the words *ocean* and *sea* to mean the same thing, but geographically, a *sea* is a large body of saltwater that is completely or partly surrounded by land (often part of an ocean).

This lesson also addresses several bodies of freshwater: lakes, ponds, rivers, streams, canals, and glaciers. A *lake* is a large body of (usually) freshwater surrounded on all sides by land, whereas a *pond* is a smaller body of still water. A *river* is a long, narrow body of water that flows into a lake or the ocean. A *stream* is a general term for a small body of moving water. Depending on its location or certain characteristics, a stream may be referred to as a *river, branch, brook, creek,* or other term. A *canal* is a humanmade waterway that connects two bodies of water. Canals can be either freshwater or salt-

"THE BLUE MARBLE" (NASA PHOTOGRAPH)

OCEAN REGIONS

water depending on the bodies of water they connect. A *glacier* is a dense layer of slow-flowing ice that forms over many years, sometimes centuries. A glacier differs from an *iceberg*, which is a huge body of ice that floats on water. Understanding how bodies of water are named can be tricky. For example, the Dead Sea is actually a saltwater lake, the Sea of Galilee is actually a freshwater lake, and there are many more exceptions to the naming conventions that people have used throughout history. For students, learning the names of bodies of water is not as important as their understanding that (1) water can be found as a liquid and a solid in a wide variety of bodies, (2) these bodies can be located on maps, and (3) technology can help us map our planet.

Since "The Blue Planet" photo was taken, there have been great advances in photographing and mapping our planet. Satellites orbiting Earth can take pictures, and global positioning systems can locate us (or at least, our smartphones) on maps. In this lesson, students will use the Google Earth application to locate and compare different bodies of water on Earth. The composite images on Google Earth are made using photographs taken by satellites orbiting our planet, airplanes that fly over the Earth, and even Google cars that drive around and take footage of the "street view." This technology allows us to explore our planet from the comfort of our classrooms. In this lesson, students use the satellite images from Google Earth to "fly" to various bodies of water, and then use the map view to locate and name

various bodies of water near them. To evaluate their understanding, you will have students make their own "place-map" model of our blue planet, showing the locations of the five named ocean regions.

engage

All the Water in the World Read-Aloud

 *Inferring*

> Connecting to the Common Core
> **Reading: Literature**
> KEY IDEAS AND DETAILS: K.2, 1.2, 2.2

Show students the cover of *All the Water in the World* and introduce the author, George Ella Lyon, and the illustrator, Katherine Tillotson. Read the first line, which says, "All the water in the world is all the water in the world." *Ask*

? What do you think the author means by this? (Answers will vary.)

Continue reading the book aloud and stop after reading page 11, which says, "Water doesn't come. It goes. Around." *Ask*

? What do you think the author means by those lines? (Answers will vary.)

Have students listen for the answers to the two questions you've asked as you continue reading the book to the end. From the reading, they should recognize that all the water in the world has been here before in different places and different forms. There is no other supply of water—all the water in the world is all the water we have. After reading the book, *ask*

? Where is water found on Earth? (Answers will vary.)

Tell students that they will be learning all about all the water in the world!

explore

"The Blue Marble"

Project the famous NASA photograph titled "The Blue Marble" (see "Websites" section).

 *Inferring*

Ask

? What do you observe about this picture? (Answers will vary.)

? How do you think it was made? (Answers will vary.)

Explain that this photograph of Earth was taken in 1972 by the *Apollo 17* astronauts as they were traveling to the Moon. This photograph is famous because it was the first to show an almost fully illuminated Earth from the view of a spacecraft, because the astronauts had the Sun behind them when they took the image. It is also the first time the south polar ice cap was photographed from space. An interesting fact is that nobody knows for sure which astronaut actually took the picture! What we do know for sure is that the photograph had a powerful effect on people and changed the way they thought about the Earth.

 *Questioning*

Ask

? What are you wondering about the photograph? (Answers will vary.)

? What makes the blue color on Earth? (water—oceans, seas, etc.)

? What makes the brown and green colors on Earth? (land)

? What makes the white colors on Earth? (clouds and ice)

? Why do you think the photograph was titled "The Blue Marble?" (The Earth's shape is similar to a marble, the Earth is mostly blue, and the swirls of clouds look like the swirls on some marbles.)

? From looking at this photo, can you tell whether Earth is mostly land or mostly water? (Answers will vary, but students should realize that the photo shows only one side of Earth, so it is impossible to tell by looking at it.)

To find out whether Earth is mostly land or mostly water, students will need to see the whole Earth, not just one side. Use a globe to show students a three-dimensional view of Earth. Tell students that a globe is a *model* of Earth. *Ask*

? How is a globe like the real Earth? (It is round, it spins, etc.)

? How is it different? (It is much smaller, it is on a stand, etc.)

Point out that some globes have an arrow somewhere that shows the direction Earth spins on its axis. If you are looking down on the North Pole, a globe should turn counterclockwise to represent how the Earth spins in space. Spin the globe slowly in a counterclockwise direction, and *ask*

? How does this model of Earth compare with "The Blue Marble" photograph we saw? (The globe is round, but the photo is flat; the globe is not a real picture, but the photo is a real picture; the globe does not show clouds, but the photo does show clouds; both the globe and the photo show that the Earth has a round shape; etc.)

? On the globe, does it look like Earth is mostly land or mostly water? (Answers will vary, but by looking at a globe, it is more evident that Earth is mostly water.)

? Is it possible to travel by water all the way around the globe without crossing any land? (Yes. Have a volunteer demonstrate this by placing one finger on an ocean region and moving it completely around the globe without crossing any landforms.)

USING GOOGLE EARTH

Students should notice by observing the map and a globe that the amount of water on Earth greatly exceeds the amount of land. (They will learn from the reading in the explain phase of the lesson that water covers three-quarters of the Earth's surface and that most of the water is in Earth's ocean.)

Google Earth Virtual Field Trip

(*Note:* Depending on the availability of technology, this activity could be done as a whole group with the application projected on a screen or in pairs on computers or handheld devices.)

Tell students that they are going on a field trip! This is not a real field trip; it is a "virtual" field trip to explore Earth's water using a computer application called Google Earth. Explain that the images on the Google Earth app are made with *satellite* cameras that orbit Earth, airplanes that fly above Earth, and even cars that drive around to take photographs. Engineers at Google put these photographs together so that we can "fly" around our planet and see what different places actually look like.

If students have not had previous experience with this app, you can show them the Google Earth tutorial on the Searching for Places page (see "Websites" section). The search feature on Google Earth allows students to enter the name of a place and fly there. Point out that sometimes the red placemark icon that shows up is not located

exactly on the body of water they have entered in the search box, so they will need to zoom out or zoom in (using a two-finger pinch) to get a better view. Students will need to enter the country or city (found in parentheses) for rivers and ponds to more accurately locate those bodies of water.

Give each student a copy of the Google Earth Virtual Field Trip student pages. In pairs, groups, or as a whole class, use the Google Earth app to "fly" to all of the different bodies of water listed on the student pages. There are ocean regions, seas, lakes, rivers, canals, ponds, and glaciers to visit. Have students make observations of each type of body of water and note similarities and differences. Then, have pairs of students develop a definition for each body of water based on the evidence they collected from the virtual field trip and write it in the "Our Definition" column. For example, "An ocean is … a large body of water that connects to other bodies of water around the Earth."

explain

Comparing Bodies of Water

After students have had a chance to locate the various bodies of water and develop working definitions for them, ask the following questions:

Ocean Regions and Seas

? Based on the evidence from the virtual field trip, how did you define *ocean*? (Answers will vary.)

? How did you define *sea*? (Answers will vary.)

? Which is larger, an ocean or a sea? (An ocean is larger than a sea.)

? What is your evidence from the virtual field trip? (Answers will vary.)

? Have you been to an ocean or sea? (Answers will vary.) Could you see to the other side? (no) Why not? (It is too far, they are too big, and the Earth's surface is curved.)

? How many oceans do you think there are on Earth? (Answers will vary, but in the reading that follows, they will learn that the Earth has one ocean with five named regions.)

Lakes, Rivers, Canals, and Ponds

? How did you define *lake*? (Answers will vary.)

? How did you define *river*? (Answers will vary.)

? How is a river different from a lake? (A river is longer and thinner than most lakes. Rivers are connected to other bodies of water.)

? What is your evidence from the virtual field trip? (Answers will vary.)

? How did you define *canal*? (Answers will vary.)

? How is a canal different from a river? (A canal usually has straighter sides and goes in more of a straight line.)

? What is your evidence from the virtual field trip? (Answers will vary.)

? How did you define *pond*? (Answers will vary.)

? How is a pond different from a lake? (It is smaller.)

? What is your evidence from the virtual field trip? (Answers will vary.)

Glaciers

? How did you define *glacier*? (Answers will vary.)

? Why do you think a glacier is considered a body of water? (It is made of frozen water.)

? Does a glacier flow like a river? (Answers will vary, but students may have observed the grooves formed by the flowing ice. In the reading that follows, students will learn that glaciers are thick layers of slowly moving ice.)

Earth's Landforms and Bodies of Water Read-Aloud

Connecting to the Common Core
Language
VOCABULARY ACQUISITION AND USE: K.4, 1.4, 2.4

Next, show students the cover of *Earth's Landforms and Bodies of Water*, and tell them that this book will help them learn more about some of the different bodies of water on Earth. Read pages 4–5 aloud. Point out the map of the world at the top of page 5.

Ask

? How do you think this map was made? (using photographs taken by satellites)

Skip pages 6–13, which are about rocks, soil, and landforms (you may want to revisit these pages later). Then, explain that the rest of the book describes several bodies of water, but before you continue reading, you would like the class to try to match these different bodies of water to their descriptions.

 ### Card Sort (Before Reading)

Give each student a copy of the Bodies of Water student page and the Bodies of Water Cards. Have them cut out the cards and place each one next to the description they think matches. Encourage students to think of how some of these bodies of water looked on the virtual field trip. If they are not sure, they can guess at this point. Let students know that they will have a chance to move their cards after you read the book aloud.

After students have placed their cards, read aloud page 14 of *Earth's Landforms and Bodies of Water*, which defines an ocean as a large, deep body of saltwater and explains that most of the water in the world is located in the five ocean regions on Earth. Stop and look at a large map of the world. Have students locate all five ocean regions. Use a globe to show the same bodies of water, and point out that older globes and maps may not have the Southern Ocean labeled because that region wasn't named until the year 2000. Then, have students observe how the Pacific Ocean appears on the globe versus on the map. Explain that it is hard to show on a map that the Pacific Ocean is actually in between Asia and the American continents. Then, remind students that, although the names all include *ocean,* there is really only *one* ocean on Earth because all ocean water can flow freely around the globe and

mix with other ocean water (which you demonstrated in the explore phase).

Ask

? If there is really only one "world ocean," why do you think five oceans have been named? (It is convenient to separate the "world ocean" geographically by naming different parts of it; having only one named ocean would make it confusing for sailors, map makers, and people in general.)

Then, continue reading to the end of the book. After reading, *ask*

? Which two bodies of water on the Bodies of Water Cards were not described in the book? (seas and canals)

? Which description do you think goes with *sea*? (description 6)

Explain that sometimes people use the terms *ocean* and *sea* interchangeably, but there is a difference. Seas are smaller than oceans and are usually located where the land and the ocean meet. Seas are partly or totally enclosed by land. The terms can get tricky, though; some bodies of water, such as the Dead Sea, are actually saltwater lakes!

? Which description do you think goes with *canal*? (description 7)

? Can you think of other bodies of water that were not described in the book? (bays, gulfs, straits, wetlands, puddles, etc.)

 ### Card Sort (After Reading)

After reading the book, go through the answers together and have students move their cards, if necessary. When students have all of the cards correctly placed, they can glue or tape them into the appropriate boxes. The answer key is in Table 20.1 (p. 296).

Table 20.1. Answer Key for Bodies of Water

Description	Card
1. A large, deep body of saltwater	Ocean
2. A long, narrow body of moving water that flows into a lake or the ocean	River
3. A large body of (usually) freshwater surrounded by land on all sides	Lake
4. A small body of still water	Pond
5. A thick layer of moving ice	Glacier
6. A large body of saltwater that is completely or partly surrounded by land; often part of the ocean	Sea
7. An artificial waterway that connects two bodies of water	Canal

Questioning

Then, *ask*

? Which bodies of water are saltwater? (oceans and seas)

? Which bodies of water do you think are freshwater? (streams, rivers, lakes, ponds, and glaciers)

? There are actually some saltwater rivers and lakes on Earth. Do you know of any lakes that are saltwater? (Some students may be familiar with Utah's Great Salt Lake or other saline lakes around the world.)

? Are canals made of saltwater or freshwater? (It depends on the bodies of water they connect.)

? Do you think most of the water on Earth is saltwater or freshwater? (saltwater, because most of the Earth's water is in the oceans)

? Do we drink freshwater or saltwater? (freshwater)

Explain that it is important to conserve and protect our freshwater sources, because although the Earth is three-fourths water, only a tiny fraction of it is drinkable! Our water is precious; all that's here is all we have. *Ask*

? What are some ways we can conserve, or save, our water? (Answers will vary but may include turning off the faucet when we brush our teeth, not leaving water running, being careful not to litter or pollute water, using less water on lawns by planting drought-resistant plants, etc.)

elaborate

Where's Our Water?

Students can apply their knowledge of different bodies of water by locating and identifying the nearest bodies of water to their school using the Google Earth app. For this activity, you will be switching the display from the images taken by satellites to the maps that have been made from these images. The bodies of water will be easier to see in the map view than in the satellite view. Demonstrate how to switch from Google Earth satellite view to map view following these steps:

1. Enter the school's address in the "search" field of Google Earth.

2. Click on "Map View" (; the last icon in the tool bar).

3. Explain that this view is a map that has been made with the satellite and fly-over pictures.

4. Explain that, on this map, blue represents water and brown and green represent land.

The following activity could be done as a class or with partners: Slowly zoom out and stop when you see a body of water. Determine what kind of body of water it is by its size, shape, and name. Keep zooming out, pausing to take note of all the bodies of water on the map. Together, see if you can locate which ocean, sea, stream, river, lake, pond, canal, and glacier is closest to the school.

evaluate

Our Blue Planet Place Map

 **Synthesizing**

Give each student a copy of the Our Blue Planet Place Map student page and a strip of Ocean Cards to cut out. Have them refer to a classroom globe, map, or Google Earth to correctly place the names of all five of Earth's ocean regions. (Point out that Pacific Ocean will be used twice, and remind students that some maps and globes may not have the Southern Ocean labeled.) Then, have students color the water blue, the land a different color, and the ice white. They can then fill in the map key showing the colors they used for areas of land, water, and ice. Finally, have them answer the question at the bottom, which asks, "Why does Earth have the nickname 'The Blue Planet'?" When students have completed their place maps, they can glue them onto a 9 × 12 in. piece of white cardstock or construction paper. If possible, laminate the maps and then send them home with students to act as

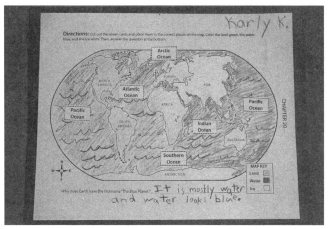

OUR BLUE PLANET PLACE MAP

a daily visual reminder that "all the water in the world is all the water in the world!"

STEM at Home

Have students complete the "I learned that …" and "My favorite part of the lesson was …" portions of the STEM at Home student page as a reflection on their learning. They may choose to do the following at-home activity with an adult helper and share their results with the class. If students do not have access to the internet at home, you may choose to have them complete this activity at school.

"At home, we can read about how Google Street View technology works. First, read the passage below with an adult helper. Then, we can begin exploring together by following the directions."

For Further Exploration

This section is provided to help you encourage your students to use the science and engineering practices in a more student-directed format. This box lists questions and challenges related to the lesson that students may select to research, investigate, or innovate. Students may also use the questions as examples to help them generate their own questions. After selecting one of the questions in the box or formulating their own questions, students can individually or collaboratively make predictions, design investigations or surveys to test their predictions, collect evidence, devise explanations, design solutions, or examine related resources. They can communicate their findings through a science notebook, at a poster session or gallery walk, or by producing a media project.

For Further Exploration (*continued*)

Research

Have students brainstorm researchable questions:

? How much of Earth's water is frozen?

? What was the first satellite in space? How many human-made satellites are now orbiting Earth?

? What is the longest river in the world? Largest lake? Largest ocean?

Investigate

Have students brainstorm testable questions to be solved through science or math:

? Which is longer, the Nile River or the Amazon River? What is the difference in length?

? Locate the nearest ocean on a map. Find a city or town on the coast that might be fun to visit. Type your home address into Google Maps or another map program, and use the "Directions" feature. Type in the name of your coastal destination. How many miles away is it? How long would it take to get there by car? How much longer would it take to get there if you walked?

? Survey your friends and family: Would you rather live on the shore of a river, a lake, or an ocean? What would be the benefits and risks of your choice? Graph the results, then analyze your graph. What can you conclude?

Innovate

Have students brainstorm problems to be solved through engineering:

? Can you use Google Earth to plan a vacation?

? Can you design a model to show the shapes and kinds of land and bodies of water in your state or country?

? Can you design a way to keep a beach from eroding into the ocean?

Websites

"The Blue Marble" From *Apollo 17* (1972)
http://earthobservatory.nasa.gov/IOTD/view.php?id=1133

Google Earth
www.google.com/earth

Google Earth Tutorial: Searching for Places
www.google.com/earth/learn/beginner.html#tab=searching-for-places

Google Maps
www.google.com/maps

More Books to Read

Dorros, A. 1991. *Follow the water from brook to ocean*. New York: HarperCollins.
Summary: This *Let's-Read-and-Find-Out Science* book explains how water flows from brooks, to streams, to rivers, over waterfalls, and through canyons and dams to eventually reach the ocean.

Olien, R. 2016. *Water sources*. Mankato, MN: Capstone Press.
Summary: This fact-filled book will introduce young readers to rivers, oceans, lakes, groundwater, and other bodies of water. Water on Earth in the form of ice is also covered.

Name: _____

Google Earth Virtual Field Trip

Directions: Use the Google Earth search feature to "fly" to the following bodies of water on Earth. Zoom in or zoom out with a two-finger pinch to get a good look! Put a check (✓)in the box after you have seen each one. Next, write a definition for each body of water that is based on your observations.

Body of Water	Our Definition
1. **Ocean Regions** ☐ Atlantic Ocean ☐ Pacific Ocean ☐ Arctic Ocean ☐ Indian Ocean ☐ Southern Ocean	**An *ocean* is …**
2. **Seas** ☐ Caribbean Sea ☐ Mediterranean Sea	**A *sea* is …**
3. **Lakes** ☐ Lake Superior ☐ Lake Victoria	**A *lake* is …**

Body of Water	Our Definition
4. **Rivers** ☐ Nile River (Cairo) ☐ Yangtze River (Wuhan)	**A *river* is …**
5. **Canals** ☐ Panama Canal ☐ Suez Canal	**A *canal* is …**
6. **Ponds** ☐ Walden Pond (Massachusetts) ☐ Antonelli Pond (California)	**A *pond* is …**
7. **Glaciers** ☐ Pine Island Glacier ☐ Bering Glacier	**A *glacier* is …**

Name: _____

Bodies of Water

Directions: Cut out the Bodies of Water Cards and match them to the correct description.

Description	Picture
1. A large, deep body of saltwater	
2. A long, narrow body of moving water that flows into a lake or the ocean	
3. A large body of (usually) freshwater surrounded by land on all sides	

Description	Picture
4. A small body of still water	
5. A thick layer of moving ice	
6. A large body of saltwater that is completely or partly surrounded by land; often part of the ocean	
7. An artificial waterway that connects two bodies of water	

Bodies of Water Cards

Sea

Pond

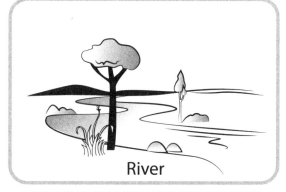

River

Lake

Ocean

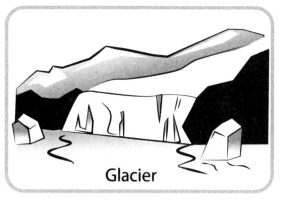

Glacier

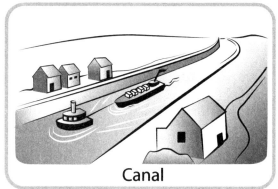

Canal

Ocean Cards

Arctic Ocean	Atlantic Ocean	Indian Ocean	Pacific Ocean	Pacific Ocean	Southern Ocean
Arctic Ocean	Atlantic Ocean	Indian Ocean	Pacific Ocean	Pacific Ocean	Southern Ocean
Arctic Ocean	Atlantic Ocean	Indian Ocean	Pacific Ocean	Pacific Ocean	Southern Ocean
Arctic Ocean	Atlantic Ocean	Indian Ocean	Pacific Ocean	Pacific Ocean	Southern Ocean
Arctic Ocean	Atlantic Ocean	Indian Ocean	Pacific Ocean	Pacific Ocean	Southern Ocean
Arctic Ocean	Atlantic Ocean	Indian Ocean	Pacific Ocean	Pacific Ocean	Southern Ocean
Arctic Ocean	Atlantic Ocean	Indian Ocean	Pacific Ocean	Pacific Ocean	Southern Ocean
Arctic Ocean	Atlantic Ocean	Indian Ocean	Pacific Ocean	Pacific Ocean	Southern Ocean

National Science Teachers Association

Our Blue Planet Place Map

Directions: Cut out the Ocean Cards and glue them in the correct places on the map. Color the water blue, the land a different color, and the ice white. Then, answer the question at the bottom of the page.

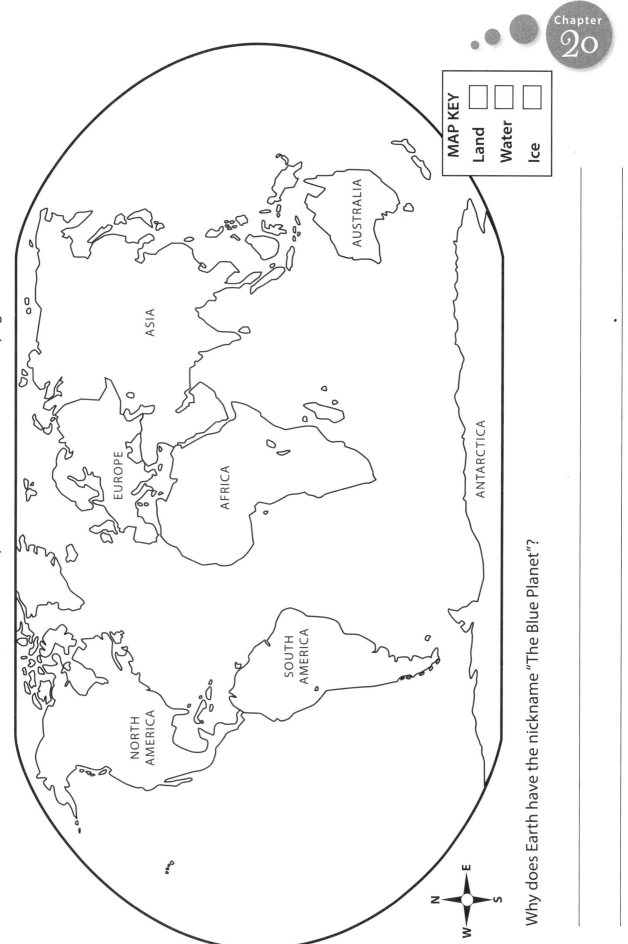

MAP KEY

Land ☐

Water ☐

Ice ☐

ASIA

EUROPE

AFRICA

AUSTRALIA

ANTARCTICA

SOUTH AMERICA

NORTH AMERICA

N E S W

Why does Earth have the nickname "The Blue Planet"?

Name: _____

STEM at Home

Dear _____,

At school, we have been learning about **maps, bodies of water** on Earth, and how **satellites** collect information about Earth.

I learned that: _____

_____

_____

My favorite part of the lesson was: _____

_____

_____

At home, we can read about how Google Street View technology works. First, read the passage below with an adult helper. Then, begin exploring together by following the directions.

About Google Street View

Do you like to look at maps? One new kind of map is the Google Street View map, which allows you to view places as if you were standing right there! The photographs you see on these maps are often taken by cameras mounted to the tops of special green and white Google Maps camera cars. But cars can't go everywhere, so sometimes the photos are taken by cameras mounted on bikes, backpacks, boats, or even snowmobiles! The photos are then joined together to make the full 360° pictures you see.

Using this technology, you can relax in the comfort of your own home while you take a virtual walk through your neighborhood. Street View even offers views of national parks and other famous places. Let's take a look!

Using Google Street View

1. Go to *www.google.com/maps*.

2. Type your address into the box at the top that says, "Search Google Maps," and hit "enter."

3. Does a picture of your home appear below the search box? If so, click on the picture.

4. The picture will expand to full view. Click and drag the picture to explore the 360° view, if possible. What do you observe?

5. At the top of the screen, locate the date that the picture was taken. Does your home look any different now?

6. Click the arrow in the gray box to bring back the search box. Then, try typing a famous place into the search bar, such as Niagara Falls, Old Faithful, the Grand Canyon, or anywhere else you would like to visit! Click on the picture, then click on the pictures that may appear at the bottom of the screen. The pictures marked with a circular arrow will give you 360° views.

7. Draw a picture of something you observed in the box below.

Appendix

Alignment With the *Next Generation Science Standards*

Chapter 6: The Handiest Things

Performance Expectations
K-2-ETS1-1: Ask questions, make observations, and gather information about a situation people want to change to define a simple problem that can be solved through the development of a new or improved object or tool.
K-2-ETS1-2: Develop a simple sketch, drawing, or physical model to illustrate how the shape of an object helps it function as needed to solve a given problem.

Science and Engineering Practices	Disciplinary Core Ideas	Crosscutting Concept
Asking Questions and Defining Problems Define a simple problem that can be solved through the development of a new or improved object or tool. **Constructing Explanations and Designing Solutions** Use tools and/or materials to design and/or build a device that solves a specific problem or a solution to a specific problem.	**ETS1.A: Defining and Delimiting Engineering Problems** A situation that people want to change or create can be approached as a problem to be solved through engineering. **ETS1.B: Developing Possible Solutions** Designs can be conveyed through sketches, drawings, or physical models. These representations are useful in communicating ideas for a problem's solutions to other people. **ETS2.B: Influence of Engineering, Technology, and Science on Society and the Natural World** People depend on various technologies in their lives; human life would be very different without technology.	**Structure and Function** The shape and stability of structures of natural and designed objects are related to their function(s).

Note: The activities in this lesson will help students move toward the performance expectations listed, which is the goal after multiple activities. However, the activities will not by themselves be sufficient to reach the performance expectations.

Chapter 7: Build It!

Performance Expectations

K-2-ETS1-2: Develop a simple sketch, drawing, or physical model to illustrate how the shape of an object helps it function as needed to solve a given problem.

2-PS1-3: Make observations to construct an evidence-based account of how an object made of a small set of pieces can be disassembled and made into a new object.

Science and Engineering Practices	Disciplinary Core Ideas	Crosscutting Concept
Asking Questions and Defining Problems Define a simple problem that can be solved through the development of a new or improved object or tool. **Developing and Using Models** Develop a simple model based on evidence to represent a proposed object or tool.	**PS1.A: Structure and Properties of Matter** A great variety of objects can be built up from a small set of pieces. **ETS1.B: Developing Possible Solutions** Designs can be conveyed through sketches, drawings, or physical models. **ETS2.B: Influence of Engineering, Technology, and Science on Society and the Natural World** People depend on various technologies in their lives; human life would be very different without technology.	**Structure and Function** The shape and stability of structures of natural and designed objects are related to their function(s).

Note: The activities in this lesson will help students move toward the performance expectations listed, which is the goal after multiple activities. However, the activities will not by themselves be sufficient to reach the performance expectations.

Chapter 8: Robots Everywhere

Performance Expectations

K-2-ETS1-2: Develop a simple sketch, drawing, or physical model to illustrate how the shape of an object helps it function as needed to solve a given problem.

K-2-ETS1-3: Analyze data from tests of two objects designed to solve the same problem to compare the strengths and weaknesses of how each performs.

Science and Engineering Practices	Disciplinary Core Ideas	Crosscutting Concept
Developing and Using Models Develop a simple model based on evidence to represent a proposed object or tool. **Constructing Explanations and Designing Solutions** Use tools and/or materials to design and/or build a device that solves a specific problem or a solution to a specific problem.	**ETS1.B: Developing Possible Solutions** Designs can be conveyed through sketches, drawings, or physical models. These representations are useful in communicating ideas for a problem's solutions to other people. **ETS2.B: Influence of Engineering, Technology, and Science on Society and the Natural World** People depend on various technologies in their lives; human life would be very different without technology.	**Structure and Function** The shape and stability of structures of natural and designed objects are related to their function(s).

Note: The activities in this lesson will help students move toward the performance expectations listed, which is the goal after multiple activities. However, the activities will not by themselves be sufficient to reach the performance expectations.

Chapter 9: Feel the Heat

Performance Expectations

K-2-ETS1-2: Develop a simple sketch, drawing, or physical model to illustrate how the shape of an object helps it function as needed to solve a given problem.

K-PS3-1: Make observations to determine the effect of sunlight on Earth's surface.

K-PS3-2: Use tools and materials to design and build a structure that will reduce the warming effect of sunlight on an area.

Science and Engineering Practices	Disciplinary Core Ideas	Crosscutting Concepts
Planning and Carrying Out Investigations With guidance, plan and conduct an investigation in collaboration with peers. **Using Mathematics and Computational Thinking** Describe, measure, and/or compare quantitative attributes of different objects and display the data using simple graphs. **Constructing Explanations and Designing Solutions** Use tools and/or materials to design and/or build a device that solves a specific problem or a solution to a specific problem..	**PS3.B: Conservation of Energy and Energy Transfer** Sunlight warms Earth's surface. **ETS1.B: Developing Possible Solutions** Designs can be conveyed through sketches, drawings, or physical models. These representations are useful in communicating ideas for a problem's solutions to other people.	**Cause and Effect** Events have causes that generate observable patterns. **Scale, Proportion, and Quantity** Relative scales allow objects and events to be compared and described (e.g., bigger and smaller, hotter and colder, faster and slower).

Note: The activities in this lesson will help students move toward the performance expectations listed, which is the goal after multiple activities. However, the activities will not by themselves be sufficient to reach the performance expectations.

Chapter 10: Move It!

Performance Expectations

K-PS2-2: Analyze data to determine if a design solution works as intended to change the speed or direction of an object with a push or a pull.

K-2-ETS1-3: Analyze data from tests of two objects designed to solve the same problem to compare the strengths and weakness of how each performs.

Science and Engineering Practices	Disciplinary Core Ideas	Crosscutting Concepts
Analyzing and Interpreting Data Use observations (firsthand or from media) to describe patterns and/or relationships in the natural and designed world(s) in order to answer scientific questions and solve problems. Analyze data from tests of an object or tool to determine if it works as intended. **Constructing Explanations and Designing Solutions** Use tools and/or materials to design and/or build a device that solves a specific problem or a solution to a specific problem.	**PS2.A: Forces and Motion** Pushes and pulls can have different strengths and directions. Pushing or pulling on an object can change the speed or direction of its motion and can start or stop it. **ETS1.C: Optimizing the Design Solution** Because there is always more than one possible solution to a problem, it is useful to compare and test designs.	**Cause and Effect** Simple tests can be designed to gather evidence to support or refute student ideas about causes. **Scale, Proportion, and Quantity** Relative scales allow objects and events to be compared and described (e.g., bigger and smaller, hotter and colder, faster and slower).

Note: The activities in this lesson will help students move toward the performance expectations listed, which is the goal after multiple activities. However, the activities will not by themselves be sufficient to reach the performance expectations.

Chapter 11: Let's Drum!

Performance Expectations

1-PS4-1: Plan and conduct investigations to provide evidence that vibrating materials can make sound and that sound can make materials vibrate.

K-2-ETS1-2: Develop a simple sketch, drawing, or physical model to illustrate how the shape of an object helps it function as needed to solve a given problem.

Science and Engineering Practices	Disciplinary Core Ideas	Crosscutting Concepts
Constructing Explanations and Designing Solutions Use tools and/or materials to design and/or build a device that solves a specific problem or a solution to a specific problem. **Obtaining, Evaluating, and Communicating Information** Read grade-appropriate texts and/or use media to obtain scientific and/or technical information to determine patterns in and/or evidence about the natural and designed world(s).	**PS4.A: Wave Properties** Sound can make matter vibrate, and vibrating matter can make sound. **ETS1.B: Developing Possible Solutions** Designs can be conveyed through sketches, drawings, or physical models. These representations are useful in communicating ideas to a problem's solutions to other people.	**Patterns** Patterns in the natural and human designed world can be observed, used to describe phenomena, and used as evidence. **Scale, Proportion, and Quantity** Relative scales allow objects and events to be compared and described (e.g., bigger and smaller, hotter and colder, faster and slower.)

Note: The activities in this lesson will help students move toward the performance expectations listed, which is the goal after multiple activities. However, the activities will not by themselves be sufficient to reach the performance expectations.

Chapter 12: Get the Message

Performance Expectations

1-PS4-4: Use tools and materials to design and build a device that uses light or sound to solve the problem of communicating over a distance.

K-2-ETS1-3: Analyze data from tests of two objects designed to solve the same problem to compare the strengths and weaknesses of how each performs.

Science and Engineering Practices	Disciplinary Core Ideas	Crosscutting Concept
Constructing Explanations and Designing Solutions Use tools and/or materials to design and/or build a device that solves a specific problem or a solution to a specific problem. **Engaging in Argument From Evidence** Make a claim about the effectiveness of an object, tool, or solution that is supported by relevant evidence.	**PS4.C: Information Technologies and Instrumentation** People also use a variety of devices to communicate (send and receive information) over long distances. **ETS1.C: Optimizing the Design Solution** Because there is always more than one possible solution to a problem, it is useful to compare and test designs. **ETS2.B: Influence of Engineering, Technology, and Science on Society and the Natural World** People depend on various technologies in their lives; human life would be very different without technology.	**Patterns** Patterns in the natural and human designed world can be observed, used to describe phenomena, and used as evidence.

Note: The activities in this lesson will help students move toward the performance expectations listed, which is the goal after multiple activities. However, the activities will not by themselves be sufficient to reach the performance expectations.

Chapter 13: Science Mysteries

Performance Expectation		
2-PS1-1: Plan and conduct an investigation to describe and classify different kinds of materials by their observable properties.		
Science and Engineering Practices	**Disciplinary Core Ideas**	**Crosscutting Concepts**
Asking Questions and Defining Problems Ask and/or identify questions that can be answered by an investigation. **Planning and Carrying Out Investigations** Make observations (firsthand or from media) and/or measurements of a proposed object or tool or solution to determine if it solves a problem or meets a goal. **Constructing Explanations and Designing Solutions** Make observations (firsthand or from media) to construct an evidence-based account for natural phenomena. **Engaging in Argument From Evidence** Construct an argument with evidence to support a claim.	**PS1.A: Structure and Properties of Matter** Different kinds of matter exist and many of them can be either solid or liquid, depending on temperature. Matter can be described and classified by its observable properties. **ETS2.A: Interdependence of Science, Engineering, and Technology** Science and engineering involve the use of tools to observe and measure things.	**Energy and Matter** Objects may break into smaller pieces, be put together into larger pieces, or change shapes. **Patterns** Patterns in the natural and human designed world can be observed, used to describe phenomena, and used as evidence.

Note: The activities in this lesson will help students move toward the performance expectation listed, which is the goal after multiple activities. However, the activities will not by themselves be sufficient to reach the performance expectations.

Chapter 14: Crayons

Performance Expectations

2-PS1-4: Construct an argument with evidence that some changes caused by heating or cooling can be reversed and some cannot.

K-2-ETS1-1: Ask questions, make observations, and gather information about a situation people want to change to define a simple problem that can be solved through the development of a new or improved object or tool.

Science and Engineering Practices	Disciplinary Core Ideas	Crosscutting Concepts
Asking Questions and Defining Problems Ask questions based on observations to find more information about the natural and/or designed world(s). Ask and/or identify questions that can be answered by an investigation. **Planning and Carrying Out Investigations** With guidance, plan and conduct an investigation in collaboration with peers. **Obtaining, Evaluating, and Communicating Information** Read grade-appropriate texts and/or use media to obtain scientific and/or technical information to determine patterns in and/or evidence about the natural and designed world(s).	**PS1.B: Chemical Reactions** Heating or cooling a substance may cause changes that can be observed. Sometimes these changes are reversible, and sometimes they are not. **ETS1.A: Defining and Delimiting Engineering Problems** A situation that people want to change or create can be approached as a problem to be solved through engineering. Such problems may have many acceptable solutions.	**Energy and Matter** Objects may break into smaller pieces, be put together into larger pieces, or change shapes. **Cause and Effect** Events have causes that generate observable patterns.

Note: The activities in this lesson will help students move toward the performance expectations listed, which is the goal after multiple activities. However, the activities will not by themselves be sufficient to reach the performance expectations.

Chapter 15: Design a Habitat

Performance Expectations

K-LS1-1: Use observations to describe patterns of what plants and animals (including humans) need to survive.

K-2-ETS1-2: Develop a simple sketch, drawing, or physical model to illustrate how the shape of an object helps it function as needed to solve a given problem.

Science and Engineering Practices	Disciplinary Core Ideas	Crosscutting Concepts
Engaging in Argument From Evidence Construct an argument with evidence to support a claim. **Developing and Using Models** Develop a simple model based on evidence to represent a proposed object or tool.	**LS1.C: Organization for Matter and Energy Flow in Organisms** All animals need food in order to live and grow. They obtain their food from plants or from other animals. Plants need water and light to live and grow. **ETS1.B: Developing Possible Solutions** Designs can be conveyed through sketches, drawings, or physical models. These representations are useful in communicating ideas for a problem's solutions to other people.	**Patterns** Patterns in the natural and human designed world can be observed, used to describe phenomena, and used as evidence. **Structure and Function** The shape and stability of structures of natural and designed objects are related to their function(s).

Note: The activities in this lesson will help students move toward the performance expectations listed, which is the goal after multiple activities. However, the activities will not by themselves be sufficient to reach the performance expectations.

Chapter 16: Plant a Tree

Performance Expectations

K-ESS3-3: Communicate solutions that will reduce the impact of humans on the land, water, air, and/or other living things in the local environment.

K-2-ETS1-1: Ask questions, make observations, and gather information about a situation people want to change to define a simple problem that can be solved through the development of a new or improved object or tool.

Science and Engineering Practices	Disciplinary Core Ideas	Crosscutting Concept
Asking Questions and Defining Problems Ask questions based on observations to find more information about the natural and/or designed world(s). **Obtaining, Evaluating, and Communicating Information** Read grade-appropriate texts and/or use media to obtain scientific and/or technical information to determine patterns in and/or evidence about the natural and designed world(s).	**ESS3.C: Human Impacts on Earth Systems** Things that people do to live comfortably can affect the world around them. But they can make choices that reduce their impacts on the land, water, air, and other living things. **ETS1.A: Defining and Delimiting Engineering Problems** A situation that people want to change or create can be approached as a problem to be solved through engineering. **ETS2.B: Influence of Engineering, Technology, and Science on Society and the Natural World** People depend on various technologies in their lives; human life would be very different without technology.	**Systems and System Models** Systems in the natural and designed world have parts that work together.

Note: The activities in this lesson will help students move toward the performance expectations listed, which is the goal after multiple activities. However, the activities will not by themselves be sufficient to reach the performance expectations.

Chapter 17: Pillbots

Performance Expectations

1-LS1-1: Use materials to design a solution to a human problem by mimicking how plants and/or animals use their external parts to help them survive, grow, and meet their needs.

K-2-ETS1-2: Develop a simple sketch, drawing, or physical model to illustrate how the shape of an object helps it function as needed to solve a given problem.

Science and Engineering Practices	Disciplinary Core Ideas	Crosscutting Concept
Developing and Using Models Develop a simple model based on evidence to represent a proposed object or tool. **Constructing Explanations and Designing Solutions** Use tools and/or materials to design and/or build a device that solves a specific problem or a solution to a specific problem.	**LS1.A: Structure and Function** All organisms have external parts. Different animals use their body parts in different ways to see, hear, grasp objects, protect themselves, move from place to place, and seek, find, and take in food, water, and air. **ETS1.B: Developing Possible Solutions** Designs can be conveyed through sketches, drawings, or physical models. These representations are useful in communicating ideas for a problem's solutions to other people. **ETS2.B: Influence of Engineering, Technology, and Science on Society and the Natural World** People depend on various technologies in their lives; human life would be very different without technology.	**Structure and Function** The shape and stability of structures of natural and designed objects are related to their function(s).

Note: The activities in this lesson will help students move toward the performance expectations listed, which is the goal after multiple activities. However, the activities will not by themselves be sufficient to reach the performance expectations.

Chapter 18: Flight of the Pollinators

Performance Expectations

K-2-ETS1-2: Develop a simple sketch, drawing, or physical model to illustrate how the shape of an object helps it function as needed to solve a given problem.

2-LS2-2: Develop a simple model that mimics the function of an animal in dispersing seeds or pollinating plants.

Science and Engineering Practices	Disciplinary Core Ideas	Crosscutting Concepts
Developing and Using Models Develop and/or use a model to represent amounts, relationships, relative scales (bigger, smaller), and/or patterns in the natural and designed world(s). **Obtaining, Evaluating, and Communicating Information** Read grade-appropriate texts and/or use media to obtain scientific and/or technical information to determine patterns in and/or evidence about the natural and designed world(s).	**LS2.A: Interdependent Relationships in Ecosystems** Plants depend on animals for pollination or to move their seeds around. **ETS1.B: Developing Possible Solutions** Designs can be conveyed through sketches, drawings, or physical models. These representations are useful in communicating ideas for a problem's solutions to other people.	**Structure and Function** The shape and stability of structures of natural and designed objects are related to their function(s). **Systems and System Models** Systems in the natural and designed world have parts that work together. Objects and organisms can be described in terms of their parts.

Note: The activities in this lesson will help students move toward the performance expectations listed, which is the goal after multiple activities. However, the activities will not by themselves be sufficient to reach the performance expectations.

Chapter 19: A Birthday Is No Ordinary Day

Performance Expectation		
1-ESS1-2: Make observations at different times of year to relate the amount of daylight to the time of year.		

Science and Engineering Practices	Disciplinary Core Idea	Crosscutting Concepts
Analyzing and Interpreting Data Use observations (firsthand or from media) to describe patterns and/or relationships in the natural and designed world(s) in order to answer scientific questions and solve problems. Analyze data from tests of an object or tool to determine if it works as intended. **Using Mathematics and Computational Thinking** Describe, measure, and/or compare quantitative attributes of different objects and display the data using simple graphs.	**ESS1.B: Earth and the Solar System** Seasonal patterns of sunrise and sunset can be observed, described, and predicted.	**Patterns** Patterns in the natural and human-designed world can be observed, used to describe phenomena, and used as evidence. **Cause and Effect** Events have causes that generate observable patterns.

Note: The activities in this lesson will help students move toward the performance expectation listed, which is the goal after multiple activities. However, the activities will not by themselves be sufficient to reach the performance expectations.

Chapter 20: Our Blue Planet

Performance Expectations

2-ESS2-2: Develop a model to represent the shapes and kinds of land and bodies of water in an area.

2-ESS2-3: Obtain information to identify where water is found on Earth and that it can be solid or liquid.

Science and Engineering Practices	Disciplinary Core Ideas	Crosscutting Concept
Developing and Using Models Develop and/or use a model to represent amounts, relationships, relative scales (bigger, smaller), and/or patterns in the natural and designed world(s). **Obtaining, Evaluating, and Communicating Information** Read grade-appropriate texts and/or use media to obtain scientific and/or technical information to determine patterns in and/or evidence about the natural and designed world(s).	**ESS2.B: Plate Tectonics and Large-Scale System Interactions** Maps show where things are located. One can map the shapes and kinds of land and water in any area. **ESS2.C: The Roles of Water in Earth's Surface Processes** Water is found in the oceans, rivers, lakes, and ponds. Water exists as solid ice and in liquid form. **ETS2.A: Interdependence of Science, Engineering, and Technology** Science and engineering involve the use of tools to observe and measure things.	**Scale, Proportion, and Quantity** Relative scales allow objects to be compared and described (e.g., bigger and smaller; hotter and colder; faster and slower)

Note: The activities in this lesson will help students move toward the performance expectations listed, which is the goal after multiple activities. However, the activities will not by themselves be sufficient to reach the performance expectations.

Index

Page numbers printed in **boldface type** indicate tables, figures, or illustrations.